Experimental Psychology and Human Agency

Davood Gozli

Experimental Psychology and Human Agency

 Springer

Davood Gozli
Department of Psychology
University of Macau
Taipa, Macao

ISBN 978-3-030-20421-1   ISBN 978-3-030-20422-8   (eBook)
https://doi.org/10.1007/978-3-030-20422-8

Cover Image © The Print Collector / Alamy Stock Photo

This Springer imprint is published by the registered company Springer Nature Switzerland AG
The registered company address is: Gewerbestrasse 11, 6330 Cham, Switzerland

Preface

Critique of an activity is a form of engagement with the activity, which stimulates new ways of thinking about it. Good critique does not come from a will to dismiss. Neither does it come from pessimism or despair. That is not to say that critics should find no trace of pessimism in their minds but that pessimism does not have to be the only, or the primary, force behind their work. Critique can be grounded in hope and commitment. It can be the expression of one's attachment to one's tradition. Critics might be less certain and less engrossed in the assumptions of their tradition, but they are not necessarily less attached or less engaged. The present book, despite its critical approach, is written in a spirit of hopeful engagement. It reflects my effort to become aware of, and to make explicit, the assumptions and practices of my tradition of research.

To claim that critique of an activity is possible, or useful, is to claim that the activity can be done unreflectively, without regard for its significance within the larger context or its direction in the long run. Such a sentiment applies to experimental psychology, in which most of us begin our careers as research assistants. A research assistant begins contributing to a field of research without fully understanding its aims and scope and without the ability to evaluate its progress. A research assistant, for understandable reasons, begins with trust. This trust is placed not only in research activities, but also in the means of evaluating success and merit (e.g., number of publications). We might presuppose that as we continue our training, and while moving up the chain of command, we transition from unknowing and unreflective participants into reflective and knowing investigators, equipped with better means of evaluation, mindful of the broader context and long-term directions. What does such a transition require? Salesmanship, unconditional defense of one's field and one's career, might succeed in keeping a field alive, but it does not produce reflective investigators. What is required is critique. This book makes a case for the place and value of critique in experimental psychology.

Holding unpopular positions becomes easier with the support of friends and colleagues. I would like to thank Bernhard Hommel and Lilith Dorko for encouraging me to write this book. I would also like to thank Lei Chang, Head of Psychology at University of Macau, for giving me a job and the freedom to break the mould. Roland

Pfister, Matt Hilchey, and Paul Seli were among the first who noticed the change in my writing and their comments encouraged me to continue. Thanks also to Jason Rajsic and Greg Huffman, my former lab mates at the University of Toronto, who have kept our stimulating conversations alive despite geographic distance. The same goes for my friends, Thomas Camus, Peter Limberg, Siavash Kazemian, Daniel Kazandjian, and my doctoral advisor, Jay Pratt. I would also like to express thanks to Raymond Bergner, Bruno Bocanegra, Sophia Deng, Nevia Dolcini, Fiona Hibberd, Bryant Jongkees, Jens Mammen, Hyojin Pak, Fenna Poletiek, Roberta Sellaro, Vivienne Tao, Carol Ting, Sara Yanny-Tillar, and Kathy Worthington. I am thankful to my parents, Mina and Kurosh, and my siblings, Pooya and Saba, for their unwavering love and support. Finally, I am grateful to my beloved wife, Kay Wong, for helping me remain resilient and lighthearted.

Taipa, Macao   Davood Gozli
2019

Contents

Chapter 1
Shifting Focus

"Being lost" has different meanings when applied to subjects and objects. When an object is lost for me, I lose contact with it. That means I neither experience it at the moment nor know how to bring it into view. By contrast, being lost for a subject does not mean having lost contact with oneself. It means having lost contact with a frame of reference. To be lost as a subject is to no longer know "one's way around" (Sellars, 1963, p. 1). It is akin to being in the dark. One would reach out or take a step without knowing the consequence. A lost object has to be found. A lost subject has to find its place. Our concern in this book is with finding the place of experimental psychology.

True or false, the claim "Experimental psychology is lost" is meant to highlight that the discipline comprises not only a set of activities and observations but also viewpoints, ways of thinking and talking. It includes viewpoints that can be in contact, or lose contact, with the broader context of human concerns (Blackman, Cromby, Hook, Papadopoulos, & Walkerdine, 2008; Teo, 2018). What does it mean for research to be in contact with a broader context? When we hear about some research findings, we might ask, "So what? What are the imports of what I just heard in the more familiar domains of life, e.g., study, work, leisure, communication, and relationships?"

One common response is to dismiss the concern: "What we are doing is *basic* science. We are not responsible for interpreting what we find in relation to everyday concerns." Although that seems reasonable, let us assume someone is interested in connecting the two domains. How should they go about it? To answer the "So what?" question, one needs to find certain bridges that can connect the findings of an experiment to a larger context. These bridges are not bridges of translation. They do not involve changing one set of words with another. Rather, they are bridges of relevance. They supply the given research findings with a larger network of interconnected concepts and, in so doing, they find a place for the research. They help distinguish the type of research that speaks to everyday experience from the type that does not.

© Springer Nature Switzerland AG 2019
D. Gozli, *Experimental Psychology and Human Agency*,
https://doi.org/10.1007/978-3-030-20422-8_1

Let us replace "experimental findings" with another example. Consider a stamp collection. The collection, described in one way, could be about the number, designs, colors, and sizes of the stamps. Described in another way, it could be about activities of the collector and the family members who helped the collector gather the stamps. It could focus on the large number of contributions by one family member who enjoyed exchanging letters. It might reflect the travels of the collector and the items from different countries. Described yet in another way, the collection could be seen as the reflection of cultural and political changes, such as stamps before and after a major cultural-political change in a country. Each of the descriptions connects the collection of stamps to one network of concepts, in terms of design features, family relations, personal life history, and the cultural context. Each of the descriptions, moreover, corresponds to a way of sorting the stamps. We could sort them based on their colors, their source of acquisition, their country of origin, or their historical-cultural epoch.

When scientists tell us that they are not interested in the connections between basic science and everyday life, they are not advocating an absolute lack of context. They are, instead, advocating for a particular type of context that emphasizes certain attributes of research, and involves specific ways of sorting the research findings. In experimental-cognitive psychology, this tends to be a context that favors a mechanistic view of reality, including cognitive structures and functions. It is a context that removes people and their activities, in order to give room to describe the underlying sub-personal processes that enable those activities. This context of description is removed from common sense. The scientists might add, "To demand a connection between common sense and scientific psychology is to reveal one's ignorance."

We have arrived at a position that admits the separation between experimental psychology and common sense, and one that regards this separation as acceptable for basic science. This position becomes troublesome, however, once we trace the development of psychological research. On a wider timescale, the original motive for Psychology was a widespread interest—particularly in the Western world—in understanding individuals, their capacities, traits, and drives (e.g., Cohen-Cole, 2014; Danziger, 1997). The original motives for the discipline were grounded in lived experience, including personal and communal ambitions. Psychology was to offer new paths for self-understanding. By claiming that Psychology no longer has to be relevant to those motives is to sever the discipline's connection to its own origin.

On a relatively narrower timescale, psychologists continue to borrow concepts and questions from the domain of common sense (Teo, 2018, p. 88–89). Seeing a research grant proposal or hearing the introductory remarks of a research talk makes this clear. Research projects continue to be justified based on a need to understand our capacities for action, perception, or thought. Can we claim independence from the everyday understanding of those capacities once the research project begins? To keep our relationship with common sense, one-sided in this manner seems hypocritical. How can a research project that receives its concepts and rationale from lived experience then turn its back on it, refusing any responsibility in the name of basic science?

Losing contact with the broader context does not apply only to the relation between a field of research and common sense. It applies equally to the relations among different subfields of research. It shows up in complaints about the fragmentation within Psychology departments (Hibberd & Gozli, 2017). Contrary to common belief, the fragmentation in our discipline does not always result from people not talking to each other. Fragmentation can appear within multiple lines of work by one individual researcher. That is because, in accordance with the dominant methods, each project attempts to "isolate" some cognitive capacity, removing others from view (Gozli & Deng, 2018). Each project involves a different type of theoretical abstraction. We could, later on, force the projects to merge by testing interactions between experimental phenomena (e.g., by seeing how the Stroop effect interacts with the Simon effect), but there is a difference between constructing a third line of work by combining two research projects and finding a framework in which both projects are intelligible.

Thus, connecting experimental psychology to a broader context can be expressed in two ways. First, is the connection with the domain of lived experience, such that the relevance, or lack of relevance, of a line of research could be explored as a dimension of the research. Second, involves connecting various subfields with respect to a common frame of reference, such that they can be intelligible within a shared context.

1.1 Recovering the Connections

The first question we might ask is, "How can an activity (research), or the product of an activity (findings), be isolated from its surrounding context?" I will provide a tentative answer in this chapter, in preparation for a more detailed discussion in the following chapters. My first premise is that there are, in fact, bridges between experimental psychology and our everyday world, and those bridges are activities that sustain experimental research, namely the activities of researchers and research participants. By means of a series of rhetorical devices, these activities are rendered less visible. And their invisibility has the effect of concealing the ties between research and common sense (Billig, 2013).

There is a risk of my arguments becoming too formulaic and, just like the target of my criticism, detached from concrete reality. To reduce that risk, let us review some examples. These examples demonstrate how we tend to bring the researcher's hypothesis to the foreground, presenting it as something in the category of law or law-like regularity, while keeping the particular details of the method—including what participants do in the experiment—in the background. The strategy increases the apparent plausibility of the hypothesis, its law-like status, and conceals plausible alternative interpretations. I do not claim that researchers adopt these strategies consciously. One might tacitly adopt the habits of one's tradition, particularly those which have been repeatedly reinforced (Smaldino & McElreath, 2016). It is, however, possible to become aware of them.

Our first example is a study about the sensitivity of visual attention to predictable events (Zhao, Al-Aidroos, & Turk-Browne, 2013). The hypothesis was that a predictable sequence of events would be more effective in drawing observers' attention, relative to a random sequence. To test this hypothesis, the researchers instructed their participants to view multiple simultaneous streams. One of the streams contained a predictable sequence. Figure 1.1 shows a simplified model with only two streams (left: predictable; right: random). Occasionally, the streams were interrupted by the presentation of a "probe" (the rotated "L" and "T" in Fig. 1.1). Participants were instructed to passively view the streams until they saw the probe, after which they had to find the "T" and then press a button to report the orientation of the "T". If attention is drawn toward the predictable sequence, the authors reasoned, then responses should be faster when the target appears at the predictable stream. Confirming their hypothesis, they found faster responses to targets at the predictable stream, relative to those at the random streams.

Let us set aside the researchers' hypothesis and pay attention to their method. Participants were instructed to passively view the sequence of items and watch out for the probe, which included the target ("T"). The probe, therefore, would come as an *interruption* of the sequences. But why should we assume that the interruption itself is equally salient at the different locations? Is it possible that interrupting a predictable sequence is more salient than interrupting a random sequence? Consider the word "shark" first in the sequence "I opened the drawer and ... shark", and then in the sequence, "drawer opened I a and the... shark". Isn't it reasonable to assume that the word is more of an interruption in the first case (Hasson, Chen, & Honey, 2015)? By the same logic, the interruption at the predictable sequence might have been more salient than the interruption at the random sequence.

Considering this possibility prevents the claim that attention was drawn toward the predictable stream *before* the interruption. An equally reasonable claim would be that attention was drawn more frequently toward the interruption (i.e., the probe)

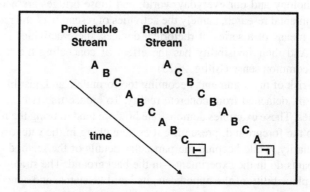

Fig. 1.1 A simplified model of the displays used by Zhao et al. (2013). Participants were shown multiple streams of visual items, which were then interrupted by a probe display (containing the target, a rotated "T"). Target location was equally likely to be at the predictable or the random stream. Participants were instructed to identify the target (its orientation) as rapidly as possible

after it appeared at the predictable stream. There is sufficient ground for assuming that, without the interruption, a predictable sequence is less effective in drawing attention. A predictable event does not produce prediction error, generating an attenuated neural response compared to an unpredictable event (Friston, 2010; Summerfield & Egner, 2009). When multiple sequences are viewed at the same time, the predictability of one sequence enables the observer to attend more to the random sequence in an attempt to decipher its pattern. This should be considered especially when the ongoing sequences themselves were irrelevant to the participants' response, given that the participants were instructed to watch out for the interruption (a relatively rare event in the stream of events).

What was found in the experiment can be taken as supportive for two incompatible hypotheses. In the context of existing literature, the authors' hypothesis is less plausible. Research with non-human animals and human infants typically assumes that familiarity with an event reduces attention toward the event (Kominsky et al., 2017). When a known and predictable contingency is replaced by a new and unpredictable contingency, animals become more intensely engaged (Ferster & Skinner, 1957). There is, moreover, evidence that perception of predictable events is attenuated, compared to the perception of unpredictable events (Cardoso-Leite, Mamassian, Schütz-Bosbach, & Waszak, 2010; Eagleman, 2008), especially when the predictable event is not relevant to the response, as was the case in Zhao et al.'s experiments (Gozli, Aslam, & Pratt, 2016). With a single stream of stimuli, research has shown that participants' thoughts are more likely to wander away from the task if the stream is predictable, compared to when it is unpredictable (Seli, Risko, & Smilek, 2016). Thus, in the context of existing literature, Zhao et al.'s interpretation—that attention is drawn toward the predictable sequence of events—appears less plausible. The apparent plausibility of their interpretation was in part due to presenting the hypothesis at the outset, effectively excluding alternative ways of thinking about the method and the findings.

The second example involves accuracy of visual memory as it relates to the arrangement of objects (Emrich & Ferber, 2012). The hypothesis was that "binding errors" (e.g., remembering a blue pen as yellow, after seeing it next to a yellow cup) result from competition between the representation of objects (the cup and the pen competing for the limited-capacity visual memory). Emrich and Ferber (2012) intended to vary the competition between objects by presenting them in close or distant arrangements, corresponding to high- and low-competition conditions, respectively (Fig. 1.2). Soon after a brief viewing of each display, participants were asked to report the color of one of the objects. Participants were more likely to report the color of another object on the display (binding error) with close arrangements, compared to distant arrangements, which the authors took as confirmation that competition among object representations is a factor in causing binding errors.

Let us pay attention to the close and distant arrangements (Fig. 1.2). Comparing the left and right panels in Fig. 1.2, could we not assume that the close arrangement is more likely to give rise to the perception of a gestalt figure? Is the arrangement in the "high-competition" condition not a better gestalt, compared to the arrangement in the "low-competition" condition? If the items are perceived as a gestalt, then the

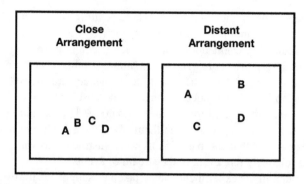

Fig. 1.2 A simplified model of the types of display used by Emrich and Ferber (2012). Participants saw one arrangement per trial, which could include relatively close or relatively distant items. After a brief exposure to the display, they were then asked to report the color of one item from the display

gestalt has precedence over the details of each individual item (Pomerantz & Portillo, 2011). There is ample evidence that the gestalt figure is perceived first (Navon, 1977), and better remembered compared to its elements (Nie, Müller, & Conci, 2017). According to the alternative interpretation, it is not that the color of object A is erroneously bound to object B in a process of relatively more intense competition. Rather, both colors are perceived as belonging to one and the same object—a gestalt figure. The more frequent "binding errors" reflect the presence of an additional perceptual object, the perception of which supersedes the perception of the elements. This interpretation does not require the idea of competition among internal representations.

These two examples illustrate that experimental studies, despite their restrictions, are not necessarily immune to alternative interpretations. What creates the apparent unambiguity of their original interpretation is a rhetorical strategy that brings the researchers' hypothesis into the foreground. If we pay attention to predictable/random sequences, then the occasional probes are likely to be regarded as incidental attributes of the method, and as a convenient way to assess the participants' bias for/against the different types of event. Similarly, if we focus on varying degrees of competition among the representation of an otherwise identical set of perceptual objects, then the varying distances among the objects are regarded as varying degrees of competition. What the participants actually see and do is placed in the background. After these examples, we can discuss more general formulations of experimental research along with methods for their critical evaluation.

1.2   Experimental-Cognitive Psychology and Its Critique

Experimental psychology is an exercise of human rationality. It is an activity that aims to offer defensible statements about how people think and act. The statements ought not to be observer-dependent. The grounds for verifying them should be accessible and repeatable by others. We sharpen and revise our statements such that they can appear reasonable from the standpoint of someone with whom we share minimal common ground. We can think of that minimal common ground, the place where my statements can be treated independently of my particular viewpoint, as the domain of facts, rationality, or objectivity (Davidson, 2001).

I have two related aims in this section. My first aim is to outline the general forms of statements offered by experimental psychology. My second aim is to identify several paths, again in general form, toward critiquing such statements. With regard to the general forms of statements, let us consider the following as a first candidate.

> S1. We compared a sample of participants under several conditions (C_1, C_2, ... C_n), using several dependent measures (M_1, M_2, ..., M_n), and we observed some difference across the conditions.

This statement is incomplete, but it serves well as a starting point. Imagine a simple experiment with only two conditions and one dependent measure. Participants in this experiment are instructed to read aloud a series of words, presented one at a time. Half of the words are presented in red (C1), the other half in green (C2). Our dependent measure is the time it takes to begin saying the word (or more fancifully, the onset of the vocal response). It is clear that word color, which is what we manipulate, is not the only attribute of the experiment. There is another set of attributes, which we might call "controlled variables" (Fig. 1.3). For example, participants all belong to the same population of neurologically intact college students with normal color vision; they all read the same list of words; they all sit at the same viewing distance from the screen, and so forth. The controlled variables do not exhaust the attributes of the experiment. They belong to a larger set that includes "uncontrolled variables", e.g., participants' motivation to complete the experiment, their like or dislike for the color green, their tendency to follow rules, or their tendency to daydream. We generally assume that the uncontrolled variables are either

Fig. 1.3 A schematic view of an experimental design with two conditions. The two conditions correspond to an independent variable. This variable is embedded in a set of controlled variables, which are themselves in a larger set of mostly uncontrolled variables

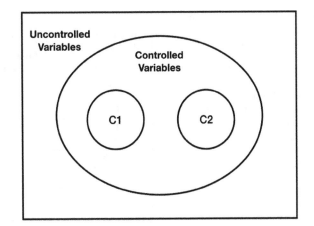

inconsequential or that their presence, being roughly equal across conditions, will not sway the findings in any particular direction.

One common path toward critiquing an experimental study is to show that dividing the experiment into the experimental conditions has an unintended consequence (Fig. 1.4). We might call this the detection of confounds. In our imagined word-reading experiment, we might discover that the green-colored words were also brighter and more visible than the red-colored words. In this case, color difference, which was the intended manipulation, is confounded with brightness, an unintended consequence. We applied this critique to the study by Emrich and Ferber (2012) discussed earlier: I argued that varying between-item distance (regarded as the means of varying between-item memory competition) was confounded with the strength of grouping among items.

Another critical path examines the space of "controlled variables" to identify ways in which researchers failed to control these variables. In our discussion of Zhao et al. (2013), we identified the possibility that presenting the probe at the predictable sequence does not count as the same "controlled" event as presenting the probe at the random sequence, which in turn means that the two types of sequence (predictable vs. random) are not the only objects of comparison. This critique tends to apply more commonly to between-subjects designs, especially when the conditions are determined by differences that already existed prior to the design of the experiment (i.e., quasi-experimental design). To illustrate the critique with examples, it is useful to first modify our general statement to match a quasi-experimental design.

S2. We compared samples of several populations (P_1, P_2, P_3, ... P_n) under the same condition, with regard to some dependent measures (M_1, M_2, ..., M_n), and we observed a difference between the populations.

For example, a series of studies compared Calvinists and atheists on a series of perceptual-motor tasks. One study used a task in which participants had to sustain attention to either the elemental or global features of a display and ignore the other

Fig. 1.4 A schematic view of an experimental design with two conditions, including a confound. The two conditions differ not only with regard to the intended attribute (independent variable) but also with regard to an unintended attribute

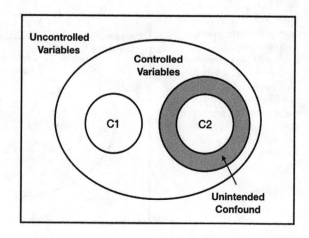

feature (Colzato, Hommel, & Shapiro, 2010). The aim was to measure participants' general bias in favor of the local or global features of a display. The researchers reported a stronger global bias in atheists compared to Calvinists. Another study used a task in which participants had to sustain attention to the color of a circle and ignore the location of the circle (Hommel, Colzato, Scorolli, Borghi, & van den Wildenberg, 2011). The aim was to measure participants' control over the selection of task-relevant features. In this case, the researchers found less influence of distracting features in Calvinists than atheists. These studies are taken to suggest that long-term religious affiliation results in different tuning of attentional mechanisms, such that members of one religious group, on average, have a perceptual bias in favor of the local features of the perceptual world or a narrower bias in favor of what is relevant to their task (for similar studies, see Colzato et al., 2010; Paglieri, Borghi, Colzato, Hommel, & Scorolli, 2013).

Implicit in such statements is the assumption that the groups were comparable with respect to the "controlled variables", including their experience with the experimental setup, their interactions with the researcher, their understanding of the task (all of which must include, similar to the experimental stimuli, local and global features, as well as task-relevant and -irrelevant features). Accepting the researchers' interpretation involves accepting the following two claims: (1) Perceptual biases in tasks involving simple shapes and button-press responses were different among the groups, and (2) the groups had otherwise the same perceptions and thoughts regarding the events in the experiment, including their interaction with the researcher and their understanding of the instructions and the tasks. Put differently, we are required to accept that the two groups differed in terms of a relatively simple process (e.g., responding to circles), but they somehow did not differ with respect to other, more complex processes, involved in the experimental method (e.g., interacting with a researcher and understanding their role in the task). These two claims cannot be held simultaneously. After accepting differences with respect to relatively simple perceptual-motor tasks, the assumption about "controlled variables" is undermined. Consequently, the claim about having isolated between-group differences in the form of simple perceptual-motor functions is undermined. In so far as these quasi-experimental studies fail to isolate differences among groups, they are not particularly informative beyond trivial statements (e.g., there is *some* difference between atheists and Calvinists), which do not require experimental study for their confirmation.

Illustrated in Fig. 1.5 is the idea that, once two groups of participants have been found to differ in their performance in a simple perceptual-motor task, we have reason to doubt that the rest of the experimental procedure was controlled across the groups. Given that researchers relied on those very perceptual-motor capacities to recruit the participants, obtain their consent, and instruct them in the tasks, we should be at least willing to consider that the groups were subjected to not one but two different sets of "controlled conditions". The fact that the samples from the two populations differed in terms of their performance in a simple experiment provides grounds for doubting the adequacy of the controlled conditions in the experiments. Once again, we do not doubt the claim that some difference existed between the

Fig. 1.5 A schematic view of experimental design with two conditions. This diagram shows an unequal application of "controlled variables" across the two conditions. The statements about the differences in C1 and C2 have to be attributed to the experimental procedure as a whole, and not just to the intended manipulations

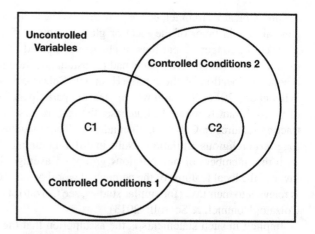

groups (Calvinists vs. atheists), but we can certainly doubt that the difference was isolated by the experiments and can be described with reference to a particular low-level mechanism, such as visuospatial mechanisms.

This issue cannot be avoided in randomized between-subject or within-subject designs. Leaving behind the quasi-experimental designs, let us now imagine that we are interested in, say, the effect of music on ethical decision making. We ask participants to read about ethical dilemmas and make decisions, while we play happy or sad music in the background. Let us imagine that people listening to sad music made more ethical decisions compared to the people who listened to happy music. Can we now conclude that sad music makes people more ethical? Or is it more defensible to say: Participants, when instructed to think about and respond to the ethical dilemmas, more frequently made an ethical decision when listening to sad music, compared to when listening to happy music.

The difference between the two statements is captured in Fig. 1.5. Because of the first hypothesis, regarding the effect of music on moral decisions, we are ready to see an effect of music on decisions, and we do not notice the potential effect of the decision-making task on how people listen to music. If we are willing to accept that music makes people ethical, why should we not consider that thinking about an ethical dilemma changes the way we listen to music? The ethical dilemma, which is initially regarded as a part of the "controlled conditions", must now be considered as differently experienced across the two groups. This criticism applies to a wide range of research questions, e.g., that cleaning ourselves makes us feel less guilty (Zhong & Liljenquist, 2006), or that bitter taste makes us morally restrictive (Eskine, Kacinik, & Prinz, 2011), and so on. To say that the treatment (e.g., music) came before the test (e.g., response to the dilemma) does not solve the problem, because objectively separating the two events in time does not ensure that they are subjectively separated (Dennett, 1991; Gallagher & Zahavi, 2007). The experience of music might change in retrospect, once the person begins considering the ethical dilemma. The two constitute an experiential whole in which the effect of music cannot be neatly separated from the effect of thinking about the ethical dilemma.

A class of problems related to interpreting experimental findings are formulated as the problem of inverse inference. Namely, a low conditional probability of the data given the null hypothesis, $P(D|H_0)$, does not give license to the claim that the probability of the null hypothesis given the data, $P(H_0|D)$, is equally low (Falk & Greenbaum, 1995). This problem is formulated in very general terms, as it highlights the possibility that, for any number of unknown reasons, the data might not be representative of the states of affairs intended to be represented in the study. In this book, I offer specific forms of the inverse-inference problem by pointing out how certain concepts or experimental procedures are not representative of the concepts or states of affairs they purport to represent. In addition, and more importantly, in some cases the problem begins, not when we infer and generalize based on the data, but earlier, in the way we ascribe meaning to the data. For example, we "see" direct evidence for attentional bias toward a predictable stream of events (Zhao et al., 2013), direct evidence for competition causing binding errors (Emrich & Ferber, 2012), or evidence for perceptual-motor differences among members of different religious groups (Colzato et al., 2010, 2011). This type of problem arises from looking at data through the selective lens of a hypothesis and ignoring the role of our methods in data production.

As our examples might have already revealed, something important was missing from the statements, S1 and S2. Experimental researchers have specific interests, which relate to specific psychological capacities. This could be the capacity to perceive, act, think, judge, daydream, or violate a rule. To establish the necessary conditions for the study, we must observe our participants as they engage in the kinds of tasks that express those capacities. An experimental psychologist interested in perception develops a task in which participants perceive a series of objects. We must, accordingly, modify the statement (S1).

S3. We observed a sample of participants *as they were performing a task* under several conditions (C_1, C_2, ..., C_n), and we observed a difference in performance across the conditions using a dependent measure (M).

And, here, we encounter the core engine of experimental psychology—*tasks*. What experimental research generally finds is the sensitivity of task performance to variations in certain features of the situation, and the dependent measures tend to be features of performance (Gozli, 2017).

In the experimental research community, the word "task" is often used interchangeably with the word "paradigm". Drawing from Kuhn's (1970) concept of paradigm enables us to consider a task as involving a set of interconnected attributes. A task is organized around a goal; it involves a pre-specified set of actions, ways of achieving the goals; it involves a set of relevant perceptual objects and events, knowing which distinctions are unimportant and which are important; and, it involves the relationship between those distinctions and task performance. Making coffee, taking a shower, editing a manuscript can all be regarded as tasks. In a task, the relationship between an action and what elicits the action ("the production rule"; Anderson, 1996) can be arbitrary. Once a participant learns how to perform the task, then certain features of the task can be manipulated, with the purpose of identifying corresponding variations in performance.

Other ways of describing a task involve sensorimotor schemes (Piaget, 1954), perception-action cycles (Neisser, 1976), decision cycles (Newell, 1992), or event files (Hommel, Müsseler, Aschersleben, & Prinz, 2001; Memelink & Hommel, 2013). In Chaps. 3, 4, and 5, I will consider the idea that a task is associated with a goal hierarchy, a view that is consistent with several other proposals and highlights the similarities between them. According to all characterizations, a task includes a selective and finite manner of thinking about the present state, in terms of task-relevant features, an understanding of some goal states, and the way to map the two states onto each other. Accordingly, a task involves both a descriptive and a normative dimension—understanding a task means understanding what constitutes good performance in the task (Searle, 1995; Thomson, 2008). By assigning participants to tasks, which the experimenters themselves already understand, they can easily interpret participants' performance in terms of intentions and meaning. Without such an understanding, the intentions behind simple movements would not be transparent (Willett, Marken, Parker, & Mansell, 2017).

The aim of experimental-cognitive research is not to understand particular tasks, but to construct general theories of cognitive structure and function (De Houwer, 2011). It is not desirable to have different theories corresponding to different tasks. It is desirable to have general theories that account for performance in multiple tasks and, as such, enable removing the tasks from the formulation of the theory. Such theories would enable us to predict performance in a new task because they provide an understanding of psychological functions that is task-independent. For this reason, when presenting the findings and interpretation of experiments, researchers tends to de-emphasize the role of tasks.

It is important that we distinguish between the removal of task characteristics from psychological theories, as a *scientific ambition*, and the removal of task characteristics from description, as a *rhetorical strategy*. De-emphasizing the role of tasks in the production of research findings has rhetorical advantages. It allows us to make overly-general claims about human capacities. It leaves the social and normative dimension of the experiment out of consideration, treating participants, or models of the average participant, as isolated entities (Billig, 2013). By de-emphasizing the tasks, experimenters also de-emphasize the mutual understanding of the tasks, achieved through language, which then allows experimenters to maintain their focus to attributes of performance. By neglecting the social-normative dimension of the experiment, we ignore the fact that scientific activity is conducted within a social and cultural context.

Another rhetorical advantage of keeping the task in the background is that it facilitates a type of bait-and-switch trick performed on the audience of the research, including funding agencies and incoming members of the discipline. This trick involves borrowing a concept from its everyday domain to justify the research project. The concept may have rich and varied meanings in its original contexts of use, but after it is operationalized as an attribute of an experimental task, its meaning changes (Smedslund, 1997; Teo, 2018). This creates a gap between the everyday meaning of the concept and the meaning within the experiment. If we de-emphasize the task, we can de-emphasize this gap, talking about the findings as if they apply equally to the experiment and to everyday contexts. We will see examples of this strategy applied to rule-governed behavior (Chap. 4), free choice (Chap. 6), sense of agency (Chap. 7), and mind wandering (Chap. 8).

What is involved in performing a given experimental task? The presence of the rules that constitute the task, such as "press key X every time you see Y", is relatively clear. But what about factors like maintaining a congenial relationship with the experimenter? Are such factors not included in the reasons that keep participants on a task? We often implement automated feedback in the experimental session, in case participants deviate from the rules of the task (e.g., "mistake", "too quick", "too slow"). We expect participants to adjust their performance based on the feedback. Are these automated reactions not part of an ongoing exchange between the participant and the researcher (Fitzgerald & Callard, 2015; Marken & Carey, 2015)?

A critique of experimental psychology, therefore, involves a shifting of focus. By paying close attention to the details of a task, we can trace the link between what happens in the experiment and the meaning of the findings. We can also examine the relation between the use of a given concept in the context of the experiment and its use in everyday language. We can recognize the role of people (researchers and participants) in producing the results. We bring into view participants' capacity to have different motives and ascribe different meanings to the task. As we have seen in the few examples thus far, and as we shall see in the following chapters, this critique can open research findings to multiple interpretations.

1.3   Questions of Interpretation

Scientific training might encourage us to think that philosophical work comes before scientific work, and that philosophers prepare the basis for science. Once scientific work begins, there is no further need for philosophical examination. This attitude is widespread in experimental psychology (Hibberd & Gozli, 2017). However, the proper exchange between philosophical work and scientific work is cyclical. New philosophical problems arise because of scientific progress, and vice versa (Kukla, 2001; Teo, 2018). The same holds for the relation between scientific psychology and common sense and, for that matter, scientific psychology and other neighboring disciplines. Some activities within a discipline lead to isolation, and some lead to connection. What would facilitate the latter is awareness of what surrounds psychological research, including motives and biases that are not themselves scientific.

In response to the enduring problems in our discipline, the currently prevailing response is to emphasize the necessity for robust and reliable findings (Open Science Collaboration, 2015). This strategy leaves unquestioned matters regarding interpretation (Hibberd, 2014). One gets the impression that massive number of replications and meta-analyses, and accurate estimates of experimental effects would eventually address the problem of relevance. However, robustness and replicability are not the only ways to assess research. Other criteria pertain to relevance, meaning, and claims about the representativeness of concepts and states of affairs. While I do not disagree with the need to examine replicability and proper estimation of effects, I believe another, more fundamental, type of ongoing critique is necessary: An ongoing reflection on the questions that motivate research projects, activities that enable and guide research projects, and the meaning of research within broader contexts of human concerns.

In this first chapter, I introduced the outline of the critical approach carried out throughout the book. In Chaps. 3, 4, 5, 6, 7, and 8, I will focus on specific topics of research. But before moving to those topics, I need to draw a sketch of the context of discussion. This sketch is akin to a set of coordinates of experience. It is not meant to restrict our interpretation of research. On the contrary, it is meant to open the possibilities of interpretation, to heighten our sensitivity to enduring features of experience, including ambiguity and openness to re-interpretation.

References

Anderson, J. R. (1996). ACT: A simple theory of complex cognition. *American Psychologist, 51*(4), 355–365.

Billig, M. (2013). *Learn to write badly: How to succeed in the social sciences*. Cambridge, UK: Cambridge University Press.

Blackman, L., Cromby, J., Hook, D., Papadopoulos, D., & Walkerdine, V. (2008). Creating subjectivities. *Subjectivity, 22*(1), 1–27.

Cardoso-Leite, P., Mamassian, P., Schütz-Bosbach, S., & Waszak, F. (2010). A new look at sensory attenuation: Action-effect anticipation affects sensitivity, not response bias. *Psychological Science, 21*(12), 1740–1745.

Cohen-Cole, J. (2014). *The open mind: Cold War politics and the sciences of human nature*. Chicago, IL: University of Chicago Press.

Colzato, L. S., Hommel, B., & Shapiro, K. (2010). Religion and the attentional blink: Depth of faith predicts depth of the blink. *Frontiers in Psychology, 1*, 147.

Colzato, L. S., van Beest, I., van den Wildenberg, W. P. M., Scorolli, C., Dorchin, S., Meiran, N., ... Hommel, B. (2010). God: Do I have your attention? *Cognition, 117*, 87–94.

Danziger, K. (1997). *Naming the mind*. London, UK: Sage Publications.

Davidson, D. (2001). The second person. In *Subjective, intersubjective, objective: Collected essays by Donald Davidson* (Vol. 3). Oxford, UK: Oxford University Press.

De Houwer, J. (2011). Why the cognitive approach in psychology would profit from a functional approach and vice versa. *Perspectives on Psychological Science, 6*(2), 202–209.

Dennett, D. C. (1991). *Consciousness explained*. New York, NY: Little Brown & Co.

Eagleman, D. M. (2008). Human time perception and its illusions. *Current Opinion in Neurobiology, 18*(2), 131–136.

Emrich, S. M., & Ferber, S. (2012). Competition increases binding errors in visual working memory. *Journal of Vision, 12*(4), 1–16.

Eskine, K. J., Kacinik, N. A., & Prinz, J. J. (2011). A bad taste in the mouth: Gustatory disgust influences moral judgment. *Psychological Science, 22*, 295–299.

Falk, R., & Greenbaum, C. W. (1995). Significance tests die hard: The amazing persistence of a probabilistic misconception. *Theory & Psychology, 5*, 75–98.

Ferster, C. B., & Skinner, B. F. (1957). *Schedules of reinforcement*. East Norwalk, CT: Appleton-Century-Crofts.

Fitzgerald, D., & Callard, F. (2015). Social science and neuroscience beyond interdisciplinarity: Experimental entanglements. *Theory, Culture & Society, 32*(1), 3–32.

Friston, K. (2010). The free-energy principle: A unified brain theory? *Nature Reviews Neuroscience, 11*(2), 127–138.

Gallagher, S., & Zahavi, D. (2007). *The phenomenological mind: An introduction to philosophy of mind and cognitive science.* New York, NY: Routledge.

Gozli, D. G. (2017). Behaviour versus performance: The veiled commitment of experimental psychology. *Theory & Psychology, 27*, 741–758.

Gozli, D. G., Aslam, H., & Pratt, J. (2016). Visuospatial cueing by self-caused features: Orienting of attention and action-outcome associative learning. *Psychonomic Bulletin & Review, 23*, 459–467.

Gozli, D. G., & Deng, W. (2018). Building blocks of psychology: On remaking the unkept promises of early schools. *Integrative Psychological and Behavioral Science, 52*, 1–24.

Hasson, U., Chen, J., & Honey, C. J. (2015). Hierarchical process memory: Memory as an integral component of information processing. *Trends in Cognitive Sciences, 19*, 304–313.

Hibberd, F. (2014). The metaphysical basis of a process psychology. *Journal of Theoretical and Philosophical Psychology, 34*(3), 161–186.

Hibberd, F. J., & Gozli, D. G. (2017). Psychology's fragmentation and neglect of foundational assumptions: An interview with Fiona J. Hibberd. *Europe's Journal of Psychology, 13*, 366–374.

Hommel, B., Colzato, L. S., Scorolli, C., Borghi, A. M., & van den Wildenberg, W. P. M. (2011). Religion and action control: Faith-specific modulation of the Simon effect but not stop-signal performance. *Cognition, 120*, 177–185.

Hommel, B., Müsseler, J., Aschersleben, G., & Prinz, W. (2001). The theory of event coding (TEC): A framework for perception and action planning. *Behavioral and Brain Sciences, 24*, 849–878.

Kominsky, J. F., Strickland, B., Wertz, A. E., Elsner, C., Wynn, K., & Keil, F. C. (2017). Categories and constraints in causal perception. *Psychological Science, 28*, 1649–1662.

Kuhn, T. S. (1970). *The structure of scientific revolutions* (2nd ed.). Chicago, IL: University of Chicago Press.

Kukla, A. (2001). *Methods of theoretical psychology.* Cambridge, MA: MIT Press.

Marken, R. S., & Carey, T. A. (2015). *Controlling people: The paradoxical nature of being human.* Samford Valley, Australia: Australian Academic Press.

Memelink, J., & Hommel, B. (2013). Intentional weighting: A basic principle in cognitive control. *Psychological Research, 77*, 249–259.

Navon, D. (1977). Forest before trees: The precedence of global features in visual perception. *Cognitive Psychology, 9*(3), 353–383.

Neisser, U. (1976). *Cognition and reality: Principles and implication of cognitive psychology.* San Francisco, CA: W. H. Freeman and Company.

Newell, A. (1992). *Précis* of unified theories of cognition. *Behavioral and Brain Sciences, 15*, 425–492.

Nie, Q. Y., Müller, H. J., & Conci, M. (2017). Hierarchical organization in visual working memory: From global ensemble to individual object structure. *Cognition, 159*, 85–96.

Open Science Collaboration. (2015). Estimating the reproducibility of psychological science. *Science, 349*(6251), aac4716.

Paglieri, F., Borghi, A. M., Colzato, L. S., Hommel, B., & Scorolli, C. (2013). Heaven can wait: How religion modulates temporal discounting. *Psychological Research, 77*, 738–747.

Piaget, J. (1954). *The construction of reality in the child* (M. Cook, Trans.). New York, NY: Basic Books.

Pomerantz, J. R., & Portillo, M. C. (2011). Grouping and emergent features in vision: Toward a theory of basic Gestalts. *Journal of Experimental Psychology: Human Perception and Performance, 37*, 1331–1349.

Searle, J. R. (1995). *The construction of social reality.* New York, NY: Simon and Schuster.

Seli, P., Risko, E. F., & Smilek, D. (2016). On the necessity of distinguishing between unintentional and intentional mind wandering. *Psychological Science, 27*(5), 685–691.

Sellars, W. (1963). *Science, perception, and reality*. Austin, TX: Ridgeview Publishing.

Smaldino, P. E., & McElreath, R. (2016). The natural selection of bad science. *Royal Society Open Science, 3*(9), 160384.

Smedslund, J. (1997). *The structure of psychological common sense*. Mahwah, NJ: Lawrence Erlbaum.

Summerfield, C., & Egner, T. (2009). Expectation (and attention) in visual cognition. *Trends in Cognitive Sciences, 13*, 403–409.

Teo, T. (2018). *Outline of theoretical psychology: Critical investigations*. London, UK: Palgrave Macmillan.

Thomson, J. J. (2008). *Normativity*. Chicago, IL: Open Court.

Willett, A. B., Marken, R. S., Parker, M. G., & Mansell, W. (2017). Control blindness: Why people can make incorrect inferences about the intentions of others. *Attention, Perception, & Psychophysics, 79*, 841–849.

Zhao, J., Al-Aidroos, N., & Turk-Browne, N. B. (2013). Attention is spontaneously biased toward regularities. *Psychological Science, 24*(5), 667–677.

Zhong, C. B., & Liljenquist, K. (2006). Washing away your sins: Threatened morality and physical cleansing. *Science, 313*, 1451–1452.

Chapter 2
Experience and Reality

If we pick two experiences that are identical in every possible way except for one, we can refer to the one difference as a difference along a single dimension. This chapter discusses three such dimensions: self-reference, value, and presence. My approach to dimensions does not involve breaking down the domain of experience into separable planes, for example, separating self-related and world-related domains, or separating the domain of values from the domain of facts (Lundh, 2018; Pérez-Álvarez, 2018). Experience can vary continuously along each dimension between opposite endpoints. For instance, values and facts represent two endpoints that constitute a single dimension. Together, the three dimensions are a coordinate system for thinking about experience. These dimensions are not exhaustive, as there are probably an infinite number of dimensions to describe human experience, but these three serve a purpose in our upcoming discussions.

Talking about dimensions of experience means we have access to various parts of a given experience, and we can navigate through dimensions and switch our emphasis (Mammen, 2017; Noë, 2012; Sokolowski, 1978). Being mindful of a dimension enables us to notice it as a part of experience, and to see the possibility of moving along the dimension, for example, moving from a subject-centered focus to a world-centered focus.

2.1 Self, Others, and the World

Objects, people, events, and states of affairs can be sorted based on their relation to oneself. A soccer game can be one I am watching as a neutral observer, one I am watching as a fanatic supporter of my team, or one in which I am a participant. A coffee cup can be one I am seeing for the first time at a store, or one I have had for several years that is attached to a lot of memories (Krøjgaard, 2016; Mammen, 2016; Neumann, 2016). A train can be one I notice during a leisurely walk, or one for which I am anxiously waiting.

© Springer Nature Switzerland AG 2019
D. Gozli, *Experimental Psychology and Human Agency*,
https://doi.org/10.1007/978-3-030-20422-8_2

In addition to activities and objects varying in their inherent level of self-reference, we may think about the same object or state of affairs in either a self-referential or a detached manner. I might think about the soccer game I am playing from a detached viewpoint if my team is losing. On the other hand, I can strongly identify with a game I am watching, imagining myself as a player who just scored a goal or a player who just got injured. I can think of my coffee cup and all its associated sentiments from the perspective of someone who is indifferent to it. As I am waiting for a train to arrive, I can acknowledge that the train is running precisely on schedule, even though I perceive its arrival as too late for my appointment.

The self is not a place in the map of reality, but a frame of reference against which other objects acquire meaning. A person does not relate to all objects and people in the same way. We have attachments, cooperative relations, people we admire, and so forth. Each person faces an uneven distribution of significance. We will miss the point of the distinction between self-centered and world-centered viewpoints if we treat a person as only an entity among other entities in the world (Gallagher & Zahavi, 2007; Zahavi, 2014). We can recognize that the world exists in a certain way *for* a person, which means we understand that the self is associated with an uneven field of significance (Dennett, 1991).

Experimental psychologists have found differences in how people respond to something that is associated with them, compared with something that is not (Sui & Humphreys, 2015). Even when we assign an object or an idea to someone within the short timeframe of an experiment, they might treat it more favorably than alternative objects or ideas (Constable, Welsh, Huffman, & Pratt, 2019; Gregg, Mahadevan, & Sedikides, 2017). Let us consider some examples.

Imagine seeing two pictures appearing on a screen and having to report which one came first. This is called the *temporal order judgment* task. Constable et al. (2019) used this task to examine responses to pictures that vary in self-reference. Prior to performing this task, each participant was given a coffee mug as a gift. An image of their newly owned coffee mug was one of the images used in the experiment, together with the image of another mug. In their first experiment, participants reported temporal order with reference to ownership (i.e., "my mug appeared first" vs. "the other mug appeared first") and showed a slight tendency to judge their own mug as appearing first.

The authors next considered whether the advantage for one's own mug was a perceptual bias or a post-perceptual bias in judgment (Constable et al., 2019, Experiment 3). The former type of bias would be more remarkable, because it indicates a bias in early (or "low-level") perception, whereas the latter type of bias arises after the initial perception. To discriminate between the two possibilities, instead of reporting temporal order with reference to ownership ("my mug" vs. "the other mug"), the researchers instructed participants to report the location of the image that appeared first ("left" vs. "right"). In this experiment, no advantage was found for one's own mug over the other mug. The researchers argued that the advantage in their first experiment could not have been perceptual. In summary, Constable et al. (2019) showed that we have a bias in favor of a self-related object, compared with another object, when the two are simultaneously presented. They further argued that this advantage arises in later stages of judgment, rather than arising in early perception, because the self-reference bias appeared when participants judged temporal order based on ownership (e.g., "my mug appeared first") and disappeared when they judged temporal order based on location (e.g., "left image appeared first").

The authors' interpretation presupposes that the perception of the objects did not vary under the two tasks. It presupposes that we have the same (early) perception when we are asked to report temporal order based on ownership and when we are asked to report based on location. Given that we are able to perform the two tasks, however, we must at least accept that thinking about the owned object is flexible enough to emphasize either its location or its self-reference. If we accept differences in thought, which enable the two tasks in the first place, while at the same time presupposing similar perception in the two tasks, then we are already accepting the independence of perception and thought. If we do not presuppose the independence of thought and perception, then we must consider it possible that ownership or self-reference was *perceptually* more salient when participants used ownership as the basis of their judgment. And, if we accept this possibility, then we can no longer assume that the "controlled conditions" served their intended purpose across the two experiments. Our experience of an object can vary along the dimension of self-reference, because our activities always and inevitably abstract a subset of what is available in the object. Depending on the activity, we could think of, and perceive, a coffee mug in terms of its location, such as when reaching to take a sip, or in terms of ownership, for example, when reminiscing about its history (Mammen, 2017).

Constable et al.'s (2019) first task emphasized ownership, whereas their follow-up task emphasized location. What is emphasized in the task might have influenced perception; therefore, absence of an effect in the latter experiment does not limit the interpretation of the first experiment. It could, instead, point to the capacity to perceive the same objects with different degrees of self-reference. Nevertheless, the study provides evidence for a self-reference bias, particularly when ownership has been recently assigned (Krøjgaard, 2016).

The self-reference bias is not confined to objects. It also extends to ideas. Our next example is an experiment that tested the effect of self-reference in judgment of theories (Gregg et al., 2017). Participants were presented with a theory about two imagined species living on another planet. Half of the participants were asked to imagine the theory as proposed by themselves, an arbitrary assignment, not based on the participant's own decision. The other half of the participants were asked to imagine the theory as proposed by someone else. Next, they were provided with a series of "facts" (seven in total), the last three of which were inconsistent with the theory. After the presentation of each fact, participants estimated the truth likelihood of the theory. As expected, confidence in the theory decreased as a result of inconsistent facts, but there was a sustained advantage for the theory in the group that regarded the theory as their own, compared with the group that were evaluating another person's theory. A simplified version of this pattern is shown in the middle graph of Fig. 2.1.

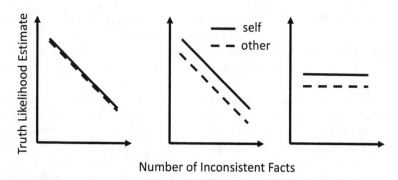

Fig. 2.1 The middle graph represents a simplified model of the findings reported by Gregg et al. (2017, responses 4–8, which corresponded to the facts that contradicted the theory). This pattern could result from combining two models, one that disregards self-reference and responds based on the facts (left panel), and one that disregards facts and responds based on self-reference (right panel)

It is possible that the pattern of the aggregate data represents participants' uniform tendency to be responsive to facts while maintaining a self-reference bias. It is also possible that the magnitude of the two effects on decisions was roughly the same for all the participants. On the other hand, it is possible that some participants were more responsive to facts (left panel in Fig. 2.1), while others were more influenced by self-reference (right panel). Because individual differences were not examined by Gregg et al., we do not know if participants could be grouped based on what predominantly influenced their responses (self-reference vs. facts). It is, furthermore, possible that at least a subset of participants changed their mode of responding during the experiment, sometimes responding based on facts and sometimes based on a self-reference bias.

Finding individual differences in the self-reference bias will not necessarily support differences in character trait. It might, instead, support differences in participants' understanding of the instructions or some kind of transient state (e.g., alertness or fatigue). We can assume most participants had the capacity to respond based on facts, as well as having the capacity to form a self-reference bias. What determined the dominant basis of their response might have resulted from their understanding of the task, their level of alertness, their mood, or other factors.

Common sense tells us that we want to believe what is true (Smedslund, 1997, p. 40). By implication, we prefer to be able to verify our existing beliefs. This is not to deny the presence of other desires that might counteract the preference to hold true beliefs. For instance, we also want to "minimize exertion" (Smedslund, 1997, p. 25). Careful consideration of evidence in relation to theory is generally more demanding and time-consuming than responding based on some pre-existing bias. If the desire to minimize exertion is stronger at the moment of decision, then the response will follow the pattern shown on the right side of Fig. 2.1. If, on the other hand, the desire to match judgment to evidence is stronger, then the response will follow the pattern on the left side of the figure. The crucial point here is to consider the possibility that one can *vary* one's emphasis between self-reference and veracity.

We should note that as part of their instructions, participants in Gregg et al.'s (2017) study were told that "there were no right or wrong answers" (p. 999). The observed magnitude of the self-reference bias, therefore, might have been partly due to the "controlled conditions" of the experiments. Had they been encouraged to find "the right answer", the self-reference bias might have been weaker. Regardless of the precise magnitude, flexibility, or generality of the effect, the study provides evidence of self-reference bias in judgment of ideas.

In both of the reviewed studies, self-reference bias appeared against a background of generally correct judgments. Participants were responsive to facts that disconfirmed a theory (Gregg et al., 2017). Similarly, the ownership bias in temporal order judgment disappeared when participants were asked to respond based on object location (Constable et al., 2019). Even when the self-reference bias affected temporal order judgment, it had a small effect on an otherwise accurate performance. Indeed, we understand such biases—including self-reference bias—as deviation from accurate judgment. Without the capacity to be responsive to states of affairs, that is, without understanding the wish to believe the facts of the matter, the concept of self-reference bias would not be intelligible.

The idea we ought to consider is that self-referential bias is not a constant feature of all judgments. It is a factor whose effect might be intensified or diminished, depending on the presence of other factors. This is not a controversial claim. In a given situation, we can point to what is easily shared, agreed upon, or verifiable by others, as much as we can point to what is relatively more difficult to be understood, agreed upon, or verifiable by others. We can distinguish between perspectives that seem to be anchored to a shared experience of reality and those that seem to be anchored to the experience of a particular person. Recall that we are not discussing two different planes of existence, but different ways of attending to the same state of affairs. When we switch between the subject-dependent and the subject-independent perspectives, we switch between different modes of engagement or different sets of skills (Noë, 2012; Searle, 1995). I can say, for instance, that the person in front of me is wearing a blue shirt or that he seems to have lost weight. These statements can be understood and verified by others. I can also say, about the same person, that it is the first time I am seeing him after his divorce, or that I worry about how much weight he has lost.

If we insist that a subject-independent viewpoint yields the correct way to describe any state of affairs, we would neglect the dependence of those descriptions on subjective experience (Davidson, 2001). If we forget that the description of an objective world is an achievement of subjects, if we equate reality with what we describe from a world-centered perspective, we produce an unbridgeable divide between experience and reality. Why would I say that my observation of my friend's weight loss (a fact about the world) and my worry about his weight loss (a fact about my experience) are statements about two different worlds, rather than arising from different modes of engagement? Subjective perspectives already include a consideration of a shared world, of the perspective of others, and of potential disagreements and conflict (Ossorio, 2006; Smedslund, 1997). A world-centered perspective, by contrast, removes reference to particular subjects and, in so doing, might present the impression of a world that is not accessible from a subjective perspective (Mammen, 2017).

An understanding of the shared world is present, not only in the form of reflective judgment but even in our unreflective perception. Normal perception of objects includes, as an intrinsic feature, a sense of certainty that the objects are truly there (Merleau-Ponty, 1945). To see a coffee cup on the desk is to recognize its persistence as a part of a stable world. Such a recognition rests on an understanding of how to navigate through the perceived world, such that most changes in the sensory flow, especially those that are self-caused (by eye movements, head movements, or walking around), do not disturb the stability with which the environment is perceived (Gibson, 1979). This perceived stability allows us to "untie" the objects of perception from our subjective perspectives. The ties are not, in fact, removed but simply pushed into the background. To be aware of the hidden ties between the cup and my perspective requires focusing on the tacit understanding, inherent in our acts of perception, that make the stability of our perceived objects possible (Noë, 2004, 2012). What is stable is not the sensory impression of the cup, but the way that sensory impressions change as a result of my actions.

The capacity to perceive and describe states of affairs is, for us, embedded within the social environment, in the sense that, for example, I know how to talk about the coffee cup in a way with which others could agree (Searle, 1995). Objectivity is one of the ways of engaging with reality, which means that claims about the objective world are grounded in subjectivity (Davidson, 2001; Husserl, 1970).

We do not all share the same world-centered viewpoint. My world-centered viewpoint might differ from yours. Nonetheless, we both have beliefs that we recognize as belonging to the world-centered category of beliefs. Imagine that someone you know is about to give a public speech, and he is concerned about the possibility of a negative reaction from the audience. You tell him not to worry. You are not telling your friend that he should disregard the world-centered viewpoint and remain self-centered during his speech, but that if he adopts the proper world-centered viewpoint, the negative reaction of the audience would not matter. We can argue about better world-centered viewpoints and change each other's beliefs about aspects of our respective world-centered views (Bergner, 2005; Billig, 1996).

Does this mean that we can arbitrarily construct world-centered views? Could you, for example, tell your friend, who is anxious about public speaking, that gently tapping on the microphone twice with his left index finger will cast a magical spell that guarantees a successful speech? In general, even though we work together to construct our beliefs about reality, there are ways of constructing that image that prevent or limit successful activity. In other words, there are standards and limits for a successful world-centered perspective, and those standards and limits are not themselves socially constructed (Hibberd, 2005). A successful perspective of our shared world is a collective achievement against the constraints of reality.

We should not neglect the social nature of world-centered viewpoints, the sense in which the world-centered viewpoint is other-centered. We adopt a world-centered perspective, not only to engage with the inanimate world but also to interact with others. It is a viewpoint we adopt, collectively, when we argue over matters in our shared world, when we attempt to find common ground (Searle, 1995; Zahavi, 2014). It is a viewpoint that achieves its strongest expressions in our philosophical, scientific, and legal objectives.

So far, I have discussed the self-centered and the world-centered perspectives, as perspectives we can adopt for the same objects, events, or states of affairs. Our world-centered perspective is achieved by carefully cutting out or reformulating the parts of a subject-centered perspective that are too personal or biased to be acceptable in the transition into world-centered conversations. To recognize this is to recognize that subject-centered experiences contain the bridges that connect us to our world-centered perspective, and that the latter emerges out of our history of interaction with the social and physical world (Fig. 2.2). This characterization sees one type of perspective as the outcome of overcoming the other, or at least overcoming certain tendencies in the other perspective, ignoring interactions between the two perspectives.

Going beyond Fig. 2.2, we can observe how the different perspectives enrich each other by pointing out blind spots in one another. World-centered perspectives offer categories, with which we describe states of affairs in a manner that is collectively intelligible (Mammen, 2017). Those categories are then used by us, individually, as we understand our subjective experiences. Subject-centered perspectives, on the other hand, contain the remainders of such descriptions, what is left out, what defies the application of world-centered categories. These include, for instance, what is left out of a description of my wife after I enumerate all the collectively intelligible facts about her (Krøjgaard, 2016; Neumann, 2016).

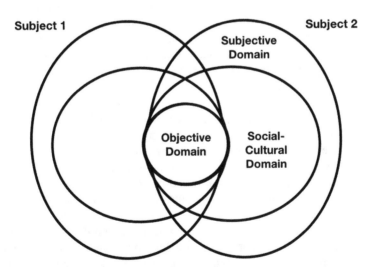

Fig. 2.2 An illustration of the idea that the objective domain is a subset of the social-cultural domain, which is itself a subset of the subjective domain. The objective domain is characterized in terms of the potential agreement of other subjects or in terms of the removal of attributes that are tied to particular subject-centered perspectives

One example of the exchange between the world-centered and subject-center perspectives is demonstrated by Raymond Bergner's (2017) analysis of the concept *self*. He began his analysis with a general description of the concept of *personhood*, connecting it to a set of collectively intelligible categories (e.g., disposition, attitude, ability, and knowledge). After listing the categories related to personhood, Bergner derives an account of self—the referent of the word "I."

> 'I' means simply and essentially '*this person*'; that is, the holistically considered, flesh and blood individual I intend when I use the term 'I' [...] as opposed to '*that person*' ... (Bergner, 2017, p. 85)

The word "this" in reference to self is serving an extraordinary function. It points to the speaker from a world-centered perspective, which equates him or her with other people. The difference between oneself (*this* person) and another (*that* person) becomes a matter of the direction at which I am pointing. Not only does this open the way of describing oneself from a world-centered perspective, that is, categories known within the shared world, it also opens the way to regard others as carriers of subject-centered perspectives, whose world of experience will never be exhaustively described in terms of collectively intelligible categories.

2.2   Value

My description of the subject-centered viewpoint already included hints of the dimension of value. Recall the example of the train station. I am waiting for a train that is delayed and I will be late for my meeting. Viewed from a world-centered perspective, the delay of the train, or my delay for the meeting, is a matter of fact. When I say something is a mere matter of fact from a given perspective, I am suggesting that it is a matter of indifference. However, from my perspective, running late for a meeting and the train's delay are charged with value. Implied in my statement, "The train is late", are statements such as, "I wish the train were not late" and "It is bad that I am running late for the meeting."

We are sometimes forced, as part of a quest to understand value, to combine the two types of perspective. Someone who is studying the neurophysiology of emotion would be interested in my anxiety about being late for the meeting or my anger about the delay of the train. She would want to describe my emotion in terms of neurophysiological events, events that would be open to observation and verification by others. The description of those events, however, would unavoidably involve references to my experience. The neurophysiological events would be understandable because the neurophysiologist is already familiar with the domain of experience. Her starting point is not neurophysiology but common sense (Robinson, 2016). There are statements of fact, such as those about the neurophysiological correlates of anger, that cannot be understood unless we have prior familiarity with statements of value.

Following David Hume, questions regarding facts and values are often posed in terms of an impossibility to move from a statement of fact ("is") to a statement of value ("ought"). Based on our analysis of subject- and world-centered perspectives, it should be easy to see that this apparent impossibility results from ignoring how much work it takes to arrive at a fact. Statements of fact are achievements of subjects—they are formulated such that they are intelligible, communicable, and acceptable to others with whom we share minimal common ground. Among other requirements, this process involves removing references to the concerns of particular subjects. After having removed all references to subject-centered evaluations, we might then "discover" that a world-centered perspective does not include evaluation at all (Wittgenstein, 1965). Our demand to go from facts to values, therefore, involves a pair of inconsistent assumptions that (1) the proper world-centered perspective is one that excludes all statements of value, and (2) from a set of factual statements, it is not possible to recover statements of value.

Not everyone agrees that values exist only from a subject-centered perspective. Our world-centered perspective includes concepts that bring their own standards of goodness (Brinkmann, 2004; Thomson, 2008). A coffee cup with a hole in the bottom is not a good coffee cup. A train that does not move is not a good train. A policeman who cooperates with criminals is not a good policeman. Thomson (2008) called such categories *goodness-fixing* categories, which, when understood properly, equip us with knowledge of what it means to be a good member of the category. These categories differ from, for instance, clouds or electrons. It is not possible to understand what a coffee cup is without also understanding what it means to be a good coffee cup, but the same cannot be said about understanding clouds. Goodness-fixing categories could involve function (Searle, 1995), but they could also include perceptual categories. It is sensible, for example, to speak of a shape as a *good square* or a *good blue* (Rosch, 1973). Part of what I mean when I call something a "good square", or a good representative of the category of *squares*, is the high likelihood that other observers would agree with me calling it a square.

You might note that the goodness of the cup takes a different meaning when the cup contains my morning coffee, compared with when I am evaluating it from a neutral, world-centered perspective. Perhaps the additional attitude in my self-centered perspective is essential to the concept of value. When people deny the presence of value in a world-centered viewpoint, they do not deny standards of goodness, but the presence of care. I care that I cannot drink my coffee from this cup. But my coffee cup, after exclusion of my viewpoint and aims, is simply an object. It is true that it is no longer a good member of the category of coffee cups, but we could revoke its membership in that category and stop thinking about it with respect to the function it was once supposed to serve. In short, the meaning we assign to the concept of value determines whether we have a place for it in our world-centered perspective.

We could certainly define value in such a way to make it impossible to go from a statement of fact to a statement of value, but handling the two concepts in this way does not do justice to how they are related in experience. In experience, we often do the reverse. We go from values to facts. That is, our values sensitize us to the identification of relevant facts (Mammen, 2017). A lawyer seeks and uses facts in the justification of a legal argument; a scientist seeks and uses facts in response to a scientific question. We would not say the lawyer and the scientist do not care about their respective facts. We would, instead, say that they formulate the facts in a way that would appeal even to an apathetic or an antagonistic audience. A properly formulated fact is one that does not contain any trace of a subject-centered bias. In such contexts, *fact* itself can be regarded as a goodness-fixing category (Thomson, 2008).

Which facts we attend to reveal our values. This becomes apparent if we consider stating a fact under inappropriate circumstances. Imagine an uncontrollable fire starts in a building. I run downstairs and meet a group of people on the ground floor. I can shout, "It is 3 PM!" or "I never noticed the blue couch in this room!" or "The building is on fire!" All three are statements of facts and, although we might not be able to construct values based on them, we can infer values. One fact might imply, "It is good if you know that the building is on fire". The other two statements also carry implications, such as it is good to keep track of time or to notice details in the environment, which is part of what makes them inappropriate under the circumstances.

Values are tied to subject-centered perspectives (I care about the train's delay) or collective perspectives (we care about the meeting starting on-time). Facts can be conceived as the outcome of setting aside attributes that might be tied to particular perspectives, but invisible from other perspectives. Yet, we do not have to assign priority to values and downgrade facts. The two are interdependent. I cannot make a statement of value without implying some statement of fact. If I say, "It is better if the building is not on fire", I am implying, "A building can be on fire". It is, therefore, not necessary to give priority to either facts or values. We can consider them as endpoints along a dimension of experience. We can attend to one and ignore the other, but ignoring values, or leaving them out of description, does not mean they are eliminated from reality or experience.

2.3 Presence

What I experience at a train station includes, among other things, railways, vending machines, signs, maps, other people, queues, the late arrival of the train, and the possibility of my late arrival for the meeting. These are attributes of experience, matters I could communicate to others, even though parts of my experience are about what is not perceptually present (Sokolowski, 1978). The late train is part of my experience, but it is not part of the perceptual environment. Yet, I experience the absence of the train. The longer I wait, the more intensely I focus on the absent train. In *Being and Nothingness*, Jean-Paul Sartre (1956) described the experience of waiting at a café for his friend, Pierre. He described how the focus of his experience was the absence of Pierre, not the presence of the other objects or people in the café. The perceptual parts of the café organized themselves into a background against which Pierre was, in his absence, the focus of Sartre's experience. When Pierre finally arrived, he remained the focus, but now in a perceptually present form. Similarly, when anxiously awaiting the arrival of a delayed train, parts of the perceptually accessible train station are organized into a background against which the late train, in its absence, is the focus of my experience.

Perceptual objects, even when directly present to us, retain parts that are absent in the immediate experience (Noë, 2012; Sokolowski, 1978, 2000). Absent features include, for example, the back of an apple that is on the kitchen table, or the rectangular shape of the tabletop. To see the back of the apple, I would have to go to the other side of the table. To see the rectangular shape of the table, I would have to look at it directly from above or below. The absent features are not incidental limitations of some perceptual experiences; they are intrinsic to perception. We do not usually reflect on these absences, for example, the back of an apple, because the particular perspective of the apple is not usually a relevant feature of our experience. We might say that, in its unreflective form, our perception of the apple is already inclined toward the facts about the apple, that is, "untying" it from our particular viewpoint. In reflective perception, I can become aware of the visible and the invisible sides of the apple, and their dependence on my point of view. I can shift my focus to the fact that it is *I*, not someone else, who is seeing and thinking about the apple.

Presence and absence are not determined only by physical properties. They are also determined by our capacities for perception, action, and thought. An imperfect circle can bring to mind the idea of a perfect circle. An incomplete arithmetic equation, such as "5 + 1 =", can bring to mind what is absent in it. Our capacities become apparent in the way we perceive the presence of value. The craving for an extra piece of cake or another cigarette can be more present to me than the negative effects of over-eating and smoking, perhaps because I am relatively more efficient at learning to enjoy smoking than at learning about its harm. Nonetheless, both are accessible to me.

Niels Engelsted (2017), following Aristotle and Aleksei N. Leontiev, proposed a taxonomy that is useful in understanding the interplay of presence and absence. He described the domain of awareness (ways of knowing) in terms of four categories. The first, *sentience*, is the capacity to be responsive to what is present at this moment. Sentience enables me to be aware of qualities, such as my sense of hunger and the immediately visible features of the apple on the kitchen table. The second category, *intentionality*, is the capacity for future- and object-directed movement, such as moving toward and reaching for the apple. The third category, *mind*, is the capacity to regard ("stage") objects in a variety of ways, to remember past strategies for identifying and pursuing future goals. I can experience the apple as a snack, an object of beauty, or an object of philosophical reflection. The fourth category, *human consciousness*, is the capacity to participate in collectively constructed world-centered perspectives. It enables my awareness of the nutritious value of the apple, or the harms of smoking. (It is easy to distort Engelsted's taxonomy in such a brief summary. The main point here is to show that the interplay between presence and absence features in different categories of knowing.) Although the different categories of knowing shape each other, they can also overshadow each other in any given instance. Knowing of a fashionable brand (or a prestigous publication outlet) can overshadow an object's (or an article's) lack of intrinsic value, just as knowing the harm of over-eating can overshadow the pleasure of eating an extra piece of cake.

I rarely reflect on my perception of an apple in terms of sentience, focusing on the visible and the invisible sides or the particular shades of color, or in relation to, for example, farming and transportation of apples, although those reflections are accessible to me. There are ways of seeing the apple that are relatively effortless, which is to say some attributes of the apple are more readily present. We can generalize this insight. Certain ways of approaching the observable reality come effortlessly, as some features of reality appear to us more readily. Signs of this are evident in our descriptions. We do not usually point to an animal and say, "Mammal!" or "West African lion!" but rather "Lion!". *Mammal* is usually too abstract for our purpose, whereas *West African lion* is often too specific. Eleanor Rosch (1978) described the concept *lion* as the optimal point in the trade-off between being informative and minimizing cognitive effort. She called such concepts *basic-level categories*.

Rosch (1978) contrasted basic-level categories with superordinate and subordinate categories. While *chair* is a basic-level category, *furniture* is a superordinate category, and *executive office chair* is a subordinate category. When I see a lion, it tends to be more present to me *as lion* than as *mammal* or as *animal* or as *West African lion*. The way we think about it tends to gravitate toward a particular category, which in turn renders other categories absent from experience. Rosch described basic-level categories as those that we most readily imagine and identify.

How are basic-level categories formed? We encounter a wide range of objects, belonging to different subordinate categories, but the features of these subordinate categories, on average, usually comprise a set of common features that have the most relevance to us. These common features form basic-level categories (Rosch, 1973). This process applies even in the case of perceptual features. There are many ways to be an imperfect square, and those imperfections are not all the same. This is why, on average, the impression of a thousand imperfect squares brings us close to the basic-level category *square*.

In addition to averaging the instances of perception, correlations among features enable the formation of basic categories. There are correlations among typical bird features (beak, feather, flying) and typical mammalian features (mouth, fur, walking). Basic categories are optimally informative because they reflect regularities in the world (bundles of sensorimotor features). The world contains regularities and these regularities, partly through our categories, shape our experience of presence and absence (Rosch, 1978).

Basic-level categories also apply to human action. *Opening the door* is a basic-level category of action relative to *pushing the door open forcefully with the right hand*. Similar to basic-level perceptual categories, the categories of human action need to be optimally informative and contain bundles of correlated features. Among these correlations are those between movements and intentions. We can identify gestures that are commonly used to request silence, gestures that can substitute for "hello!" and "goodbye!" and those that express frustration. Being familiar with these associations makes intentions transparent (present) to us. It is when we do not know someone's intention that we must attend to the details or the subordinate features of their activity (Willett, Marken, Parker, & Mansell, 2017). I leave a more extensive discussion of human actions for Chap. 3. At this point, I turn to the issue of "false presence" or illusion, and how we can understand it in terms of the dynamic interplay between presence and absence.

2.4 Illusions

Our perception is typically charged with a sense of confidence and objectivity, for example, the cup of coffee is really there on the desk and is not just in my experience, or the red color of the apple is a real feature of the apple (Merleau-Ponty, 1945). We may challenge this sense of confidence by pointing to illusions. Illusions show that it is possible to see an object as something other than what it is. We might regard illusions as perceptual anomalies, as signs that something has gone wrong in the process of perception (Palacios, Escobar, & Céspedes, 2017). A more useful characterization is to say illusions are seen within a limited range of experience (Kennedy, Green, Nicholls, & Liu, 1992; Kennedy & Portal, 1990). If anything is anomalous about illusions, it is that the observer is deprived of engaging in the kinds of activity that remove the illusion and reveal the true objects of perception. That is, in fact, the typical situation in which most empirical work on visual perception is conducted, often with brief presentations of static images, which are insensitive to the observer's movement. The same applies to the famous cases of disagreement among observers, for example, the color of "The Dress". When observing these images, we are deprived of many actions that could eliminate individual differences, such as gauging the brightness of the room in which The Dress was photographed.

Consider the illusions in Fig. 2.3. I look at these figures the same way I would look at their non-illusory counterparts. My activity of observing the Kanizsa triangle, which sustains the illusory features, is not different from the activity of observing a modified, non-illusory variant of the same figure. The differences between the illusory and non-illusory images begin to emerge when I interact with the figures. I can see that the contours of the Kanizsa triangle are illusory, or that lines in the

Fig. 2.3 The illusory Kanizsa triangle (left) and the Müller-Lyer illusion (right)

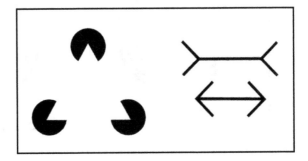

Müller-Lyer figure are of equal length, by covering or moving parts of the figures. When I cover parts of the figure, I am placing the figure within a different stream of activity. Illusory attributes are revealed as those that do not survive transition from one activity to another (Kennedy & Portal, 1990; see also, Dennett, 1991; Gozli, 2017b).

What we perceive is embedded within activities, within actual and potential streams of perception and action. My perception of a hot teapot is shaped by my understanding that, if I hold it, it will burn my hand. My perception of an angry man is shaped by my understanding that if I talk to him, he might burst out with rage. My perception of a cheesecake is shaped by my understanding that a bite of it will taste delicious. My perception of a good friend is shaped by my understanding that I can confide in him without fear of betrayal (Parks & Floyd, 1996). An instance of perception cannot be separated from the temporal stream within which it is embedded, and the temporal stream is itself shaped by the observer's embodied-sensorimotor understanding (Merleau-Ponty, 1945; Noë, 2004, 2012). An object of perception, at a given moment, is caught within a stream that extends into both the past and the anticipated future.

A magician who sustains the sense of magic in his audience is systematically depriving the audience from observing a subset of his actions. A man who is cheating on his spouse maintains the illusion of loyalty by systematically cutting his spouse's access to parts of reality. The same applies to experimenters who sustain perceptual illusions in their participants by cutting out the possibility of certain interactions with the displays (Kennedy et al., 1992; Kennedy & Portal, 1990). Illusory features demonstrate how the perception of a part, an instance of experience, is shaped by the perception of the whole, the ongoing stream of perception and action. What enables the ongoing stream of perception is not only the environment but also the perceiver's implicit understanding of sensorimotor contingencies (Noë, 2004, 2012).

Figure 2.4 (left side) shows the Orbison illusion (Ehrenstein, 1925, cited by Kennedy & Portal, 1990). Imagine this illusion in three dimensions, with the

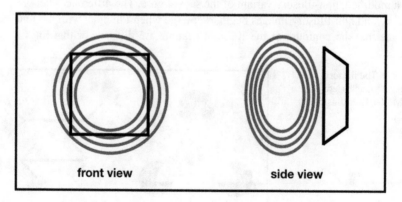

Fig. 2.4 The Orbison illusion (Ehrenstein, 1925) imagined in 3D space

concentric circles on one plane and the square in front of them on a separate plane. With these separate planes, if we walk around the objects and look at them from the side, the illusion disappears (Fig. 2.4 right side). If we then return to the front view, the illusion re-appears. This process gives us access to the transitions between the two perceptual states, which makes it easier to judge the real shape of the square (Gibson, 1979). Notice in this example that neither of the perspectives gives us access to the appearance of a square. The front view shows the illusion, with the sides bent toward the center, while the side view gives us a trapezoid. We do, however, *see* a square, because of the way the appearance of the shape changes with our movement and the angle of view (Gibson, 1979; Noë, 2012). Being a true square is not just about a certain way of appearing through a fixed perspective. It is about a certain way of changing as a result of the observer's movements.

Kennedy and Portal (1990, Experiment 3) used the two-dimensional version of the Orbison illusion, and rotated the figure for the participants multiple times. Participants had to distinguish figures with a square from figures in which the sides were truly bent. Since the transitions appear differently for a square, compared to the illusory figure, over 85% of the participants correctly judged the shape after seeing the rotations. By contrast, when viewing the figure in a single orientation, performance was at chance level (50%).

Knowing about an illusion does not necessarily eliminate it. Even after knowing about the unmarked spaces in the Kanizsa figure or the straight lines of the Orbison square, we continue to see the illusions. This observation has been taken as support for the claim that our perception is separate from our knowledge (Firestone & Scholl, 2016; Rubin, 1950), although the claim neglects an important point. Namely, the conflict between the illusory perception (presence of the triangle) and the veridical belief (absence of the triangle) is not between a belief and a percept. It is between two beliefs and, correspondingly, between two percepts. Observers for whom the conflict remains unresolved are deprived of the activities that would resolve the conflict (e.g., erasing, covering, and moving). The illusory perceptual attributes, thus, continue to support an incorrect belief. In some cases, the incorrect belief/ perception is supported by memory, such as when we see a slight shade of yellow on a gray banana (Hansen, Olkkonen, Walter, & Gegenfurtner, 2006). Memory-driven illusions show that the illusion-reality dichotomy does not map onto the perception-knowledge dichotomy because in those cases the illusion depends on knowledge.

In contrast to illusions, which compel non-veridical belief/perception, when a perceptual state is ambiguous, when it does not provide strong grounds for one particular belief, then thoughts can more easily guide perception. Consider the case of intentionally switching between two states of a bi-stable image, for example, the Necker cube. In the case of perceptual ambiguity, we can entertain multiple beliefs that could be associated with the image, but each belief is manifest in a way of seeing. Once again, belief and perception are not separate.

After noting that perception is embedded within an ongoing stream of activity, I proposed that we should describe illusory attributes as attributes that do not persist transition from one activity to another (Dennett, 1991; Gibson, 1979; Kennedy et al., 1992; Kennedy & Portal, 1990). This proposal will face the following objection: we can always find an activity that removes a veridical percept from experience. The red color of an apple will not persist when I take it into a completely dark room or if I close my eyes. If persistence is our standard of veridical perception, then all experience will count as illusory. To avoid this, we should rephrase the proposal: An illusory percept does not survive a transition from one activity to another, presuming that such a transition would not remove a veridical perception. Knowing how an attribute persists, changes, or disappears across transitions is itself part of our implicit sensorimotor understanding.

What is the connection between illusions and the coordinates of experience I have outlined? The connection to presence and absence is in the fact that the activities themselves, including those that sustain and those that can remove an illusion, are often absent from view (though present, in fact). The activities remain in the background, and this results in a mischaracterization of illusions. Rather than pointing to the limited range of activity in which an illusion survives, we might hastily conclude that our perception is subjective, private, and unreliably reflective of reality. A better use of illusions, therefore, is in bringing into view our activities that contextualize our perceptual experience.

Neglecting the fact that observers are deprived of testing the illusions cuts the link between the subject- and world-centered perspectives. Figure 2.4 illustrates two possible experiences, among an infinite number, of a three-dimensional model of the Orbison figure. Both views are subject-centered, but by virtue of their difference, they can support a veridical world-centered judgment about the square. Emphasizing the observer's activity brings to light the connection between the self- and world-centered perspectives and prevents overstating the significance of illusions (Gozli, 2017b).

Let me make an additional point about illusions and their relevance to subject-centered perspectives and values. It is possible to over-extend the application of the category of *illusions* in areas of experience that should not be treated as illusory. My analysis is intended to sensitize us to instances in which the concept of illusion is misapplied. Our values, affections, sentiments, and commitments may not survive the transition into a discussion of natural phenomena, but that does not make them illusory. Recall that an illusory experience does not survive a transition from one activity to another, *presuming that such a transition would not remove a veridical experience.* In the construction of a world-centered perspective, such as those used for the discussion of scientific and legal matters, certain subject-centered attributes are excluded as a matter of definition. We expect that transition from one perspective to another would render them absent, but that does not make them illusory (Mammen, 1993).

2.5   Description

Perspective, value, and presence change through description. Descriptions can guide attention within the available coordinates of experience, emphasize parts that were previously neglected. Through description, we can point out the abstractions involved in an activity, opening the way for seeing alternative abstractions. When we describe an activity, we are staging it for possible reflection and critique (Noë, 2015). As such, description opens the path for re-organizing our activities. When we stage a conversation between two lovers in a screenplay, it becomes possible to reflect on the conversation or on romantic relationships in general. Similarly, we stage thinking in works of philosophy in order to clarify, understand, and express the activity of thinking (Noë, 2015; Sokolowski, 1978).

Some have argued that the task of psychology is to stage the human reality for the purpose of understanding and change (Bergner, 2010; Ossorio, 2006; Smedslund, 1997). The aim is to avoid the risk of focusing too narrowly on parts of the psychological domain and creating the illusion that what we leave out in our descriptions is absent or irrelevant. To avoid this risk, some have proposed systems of description, establishing coordinates that are necessarily involved in the human experience (Engelsted, 2017; Hibberd, 2014; Mammen, 2017; Ossorio, 2006; Smedslund, 1997). In this chapter, I have attempted something similar with my analysis of the three dimensions. One of my aims has been to show the general style of description and its function in psychology.

The task of description can begin like this. We ask, if we call something X, what else must be true about X? For instance, if we call someone a *person*, what else must be true about this person? Being a person is something with which we are already familiar. But this familiarity has more to do with acting as a person among other persons than as a description (Ossorio, 2006). Description forces us to go beyond our sense of familiarity. We have participated in activities and roles in which being a person is essential (e.g., as a family member, student, friend, and citizen), but the concept *person* might not have been staged with words in your view. Acts of description take us from the first, implicit form of familiarity to an explicit and articulated form of familiarity.

To illustrate the corrective aim of description, imagine a neuroscientist who is interested in understanding friendship. She might scan your brain while asking you to think about your close friends. Through careful measurement and appropriate control conditions, she finds out that every time you think about your friends, activity increases in a particular neural network in your brain. The neuroscientist might then conclude that friendship can be defined as activity in this neural network. What is missing in this interpretation, and can be corrected with a descriptive approach, is that a friendship necessarily involves two people and a shared history. Your friendship, and its history, cannot be described in the language of brain function. Understanding them requires attention to the world outside the brain (Hibberd, 2014; Mammen, 1993).

Description is a type of action (Melser, 2004). First, like other types of action, description is selective. From the moment we begin describing something, we select some parts and ignore others. Second, description relies on skill and understanding. It relies on the ability to control the process of thinking and talking, which is itself learned. Third, like other types of action, description results in outcomes. Some of those outcomes are intended and others are unintended. An intended outcome might be a detail I wish to recall. I might wish to remember my reasons for making a difficult decision (e.g., "Why did I lend money to my friend?"). An unintended outcome might be an emotional response associated with the object of description (e.g., getting upset when I remember lending the money).

Similar to the objects of motor action, the objects of description are not themselves completely under our control. This can be true even when dealing with abstract ideas and concepts—objects of thought. As John Conway said, when we are describing numbers, we discover how the objects of our thoughts resist certain ways of manipulation. The resistance to manipulation, or "stubbornness", in the case of numbers, gives the impression that numbers have a reality akin to the reality of physical objects.

> [Numbers are] very real things. I still don't know the sense in which mathematical objects exist, but they do. Of course, it's hard to say in what sense a cat is out there, too, but we know it is, very definitely. Cats have a stubborn reality but maybe numbers are stubborner still. You can't push a cat in a direction it doesn't want to go. You can't push a number either. (Cook, 2009, p. 18)

The stubbornness of the objects of thought put constraints around what outcomes we can accomplish while thinking and talking about them. We rely on this property when we use thought experiments, which are usually designed to help us notice such constraints (Brown, 1991). Galileo Galilei used a thought experiment—a light stone attached to a heavy stone, both falling from a height—to illustrate that the speed of the fall cannot depend on the objects' mass. Philosophical zombies have been used both to reinforce and to challenge the divide between experience and behavior (Dennett, 1991). We might be asked to imagine zombies who, despite having no conscious experience, follow rules, pursue goals, use language, tell jokes, apologize for mistakes, and verbally reflect on their own states. As we attempt to think of such creatures, as we move them through various scenarios, we are forced into seeing how they are really inconceivable. Through this "stubbornness", philosophical zombies bring to light the inevitable association between characteristic human behavior, on one hand, and conscious experience, on the other hand.

Another thought experiment, by Dan Zahavi (2014, p. 23), was designed to emphasize the ideas of selfhood and subjectivity. We are asked to imagine a pair of identical twin brothers, Mick and Mack. They are standing side by side and looking at the same white wall. What is the "stubbornness" in this scenario that we are invited to notice? As we imagine the same-ness of the brothers, in their genetics, neurophysiology, life history, and their current object of perception, we notice that the two experiences are not completely identical. The difference between the two experiences is that they belong to two different subjects; they are two distinct subject-centered perspectives. Mick's experience is Mick's. It has a *for-me-ness* quality that is not shared by his twin brother.

Descriptions guide us through the available coordinates of experience. They can move us from a subjective-centered perspective to a world-centered perspective, and vice versa. They can, on one hand, help us notice values and, on the other hand, they can help us notice how those values can be matters of indifference. To describe a state of affairs is to participate in the interplay of presence and absence (Sokolowski, 1978). It is useful to recognize the types of description to which objects and states of affairs most readily lend themselves (at least for members of a given cultural community), which was the point made in our review of Rosch's basic-level categories. At the same time, recognizing stable and common patterns of description does not negate our role in reinforcing, challenging, or changing those patterns.

2.6 Implications

I outlined three dimensions along which our experiences can vary: perspective (self- vs. world-centered), value, and presence. I extended the analysis to two other topics, illusions and description. I argued against the use of illusion to depict an unbridgeable gap between subjective and objective perspectives. Doing so neglects the constraints imposed on the observers' activity, an important requirement for producing illusions. The illusion–veridicality gap can be closed when observers extend the range of their activities in relation to the perceptual objects. Similarly, descriptions ought not be viewed as neutral or passive, but as ways of moving through the available coordinates of experience, shifting focus, emphasis, or perspective. Descriptions, including thought experiments, help us notice the constraints ("stubbornness") in the objects of our thoughts.

Experimental psychology is concerned with constructing world-centered perspectives of human experience and behavior. Central features of experience and behavior, however, end up systematically excluded from these world-centered perspectives. The participants of an experiment may have individual differences in perspective and interpretation of the task. We collect data from groups and discuss the findings in terms of the aggregate data (Billig, 2013; Lamiell, 2000). An average value can serve as a representative of the values obtained from each participant. This, unfortunately, is a self-defeating exercise, because what is lost in the aggregate data is precisely the subject matter of psychology—people's perspectives, their values, and how their experience and behavior deviates from the average values that represent them (Giorgi, 2013).

Variations in participants' perspectives were not considered in our sample of studies that examined ownership effects (Constable et al., 2019) or self-reference bias (Gregg et al., 2017), maintaining the impression that what is being studied is (a) uniform across people and (b) unchanging in each person. Because we describe the experimental setup and the findings from a particular "world-centered" perspective (i.e., a perspective that is intelligible and acceptable to other researchers), we bypass participants' perspectives and interpretations. Even the motivation to participate or disengage from experiments is rarely addressed, because it does not easily fit within the experimenters' perspective (Gozli, 2017a; Seli, Schacter, Risko, & Smilek, 2017).

The distribution of focus (presence and absence) is managed through formulating hypotheses. I noted several examples of this tendency in Chap. 1. Let us review one more example here. A group of researchers asked how we communicate to computers, compared to how we communicate to other people (Tenbrink, Ross,

Thomas, Dethlefs, & Andonova, 2010). Participants gave route instructions either to a computer program or to a person. Tenbrink et al. (2010) found a narrower range of language use and a more sequential (step-by-step) manner of communication in the human–computer condition, compared with the human–human condition. Based on the researchers' emphasis, we might readily conclude that these observed differences reflect essential differences between human–human and human–computer communication. It is, however, possible that people regarded the computer program as a relatively less competent user of their language. If this is the case, then we should observe a similar pattern when comparing communication directed at fluent and non-fluent speakers of a language.

We will rely on the groundwork laid in this chapter. In Chap. 3, I will return to basic-level categories and their application in the domain of human action. With their salience in our thoughts and descriptions, basic-level intentions can mask superordinate and subordinate intentions. Bringing attention to various levels of action and intention highlights the contingent relationship between different levels of the control hierarchy. The discussion of hierarchies will continue in Chap. 4, where I will distinguish subject- and world-centered perspectives of rules and rule-violation.

Chapter 5 focuses on the general notion of an experimental task as part of a descriptive process. A task not only gives the participants something to do but also helps construct a normative-descriptive context and a world-centered perspective. Unsurprisingly, we do not find much trace of the participants' own perspectives or values in these descriptions. In experimental psychology, tasks are engines of data production. To obtain or replicate a given set of results, it is necessary to enact the series of steps that yield the results. Neglecting the role of our actions in producing the results, and neglecting the possibility that a different series of actions (i.e., different methods) might yield different results, is akin to sustaining an illusion. Following Chap. 5, I will extend the analysis of tasks to the more specific topics of free choice, felt agency, and mind wandering.

Chapter 6 focuses on the topic of free choice. I will argue that the absence of subject-centered perspectives and value-based descriptions is closely tied to the particular meaning of the word "free" in this area of research. Chapter 7 is concerned with research on the sense of agency. The study of this topic involves limiting the participants' access to the relevant facts, which—as we discussed in this chapter—constitutes an effective way of producing illusions related to agency. In Chap. 8, which is primarily about mind wandering, I will argue that the uniform description of participants' performance with reference to a task helps build the impression that their disengagement from the task is also uniform.

The point of introducing the three dimensions was not to provide a definitive and exhaustive set of descriptive tools. We could add other dimensions: implicit–explicit, conscious–unconscious, simple–complex, and so forth. My aim was to show the consequence of being mindful of such coordinates, regardless of their number or complexity. By remaining mindful of what is necessarily and inevitably involved in an instance of experience, we can more easily detect its openness to alternative interpretation. With respect to experimental psychology, such mindfulness enables us to see our findings in a new light, discover their ambiguities, their openness to interpretation, and their relation to the domain of everyday experience.

References

Bergner, R. M. (2005). World reconstruction in psychotherapy. *American Journal of Psychotherapy, 59*, 333–349.

Bergner, R. M. (2010). What is descriptive psychology? An introduction. In K. Davis, F. Lubuguin, & W. Schwartz (Eds.), *Advances in descriptive psychology, vol. 9* (pp. 325–360). Ann Arbor, MI: Descriptive Psychology Press.

Bergner, R. M. (2017). What is a person? What is the self? Formulations for a science of psychology. *Journal of Theoretical and Philosophical Psychology, 37*(2), 77–90.

Billig, M. (1996). *Arguing and thinking: A rhetorical approach to social psychology.* Cambridge, UK: Cambridge University Press.

Billig, M. (2013). *Learn to write badly: How to succeed in the social sciences.* Cambridge, UK: Cambridge University Press.

Brinkmann, S. (2004). The topography of moral ecology. *Theory & Psychology, 14*, 57–80.

Brown, J. R. (1991). *The laboratory of the mind: Thought experiments in the natural sciences.* Abingdon, UK: Routledge.

Constable, M. D., Welsh, T. N., Huffman, G., & Pratt, J. (2019). I before U: Temporal order judgements reveal bias for self-owned objects. *The Quarterly Journal of Experimental Psychology, 72*(3), 589–598.

Cook, M. (2009). *Mathematicians: An outer view of the inner world.* Princeton, NJ: Princeton University Press.

Davidson, D. (2001). The second person. In *Subjective, Intersubjective, objective: Collected essays by Donald Davidson* (Vol. 3). Oxford, UK: Oxford University Press.

Dennett, D. C. (1991). *Consciousness explained.* New York, NY: Little Brown & Co.

Ehrenstein, W. (1925). Versuch uber die beziehugen zwischen bewegungs und gestaltwarhrnehmung [Research on the relationship between motion and form perception]. *Zeitschrift für Psychologie, 95*, 305–352.

Engelsted, N. (2017). *Catching up with Aristotle: A journey in quest of general psychology.* New York, NY: Springer.

Firestone, C., & Scholl, B. J. (2016). Cognition does not affect perception: Evaluating the evidence for 'top-down' effects. *Behavioral & Brain Sciences, e229*, 1–19.

Gallagher, S., & Zahavi, D. (2007). *The phenomenological mind: An introduction to philosophy of mind and cognitive science.* New York, NY: Routledge.

Gibson, J. J. (1979). *The ecological approach to visual perception.* Boston, MA: Houghton Mifflin.

Giorgi, A. (2013). Reflections on the status and direction of psychology: An external historical perspective. *Journal of Phenomenological Psychology, 44*(2), 244–261.

Gozli, D. G. (2017a). Behaviour versus performance: The veiled commitment of experimental psychology. *Theory & Psychology, 27*, 741–758.

Gozli, D. G. (2017b). The lackluster role of misperceptions in an enactivist paradigm. *Constructivist Foundations, 13*, 133–135.

Gregg, A. P., Mahadevan, N., & Sedikides, C. (2017). The SPOT effect: People spontaneously prefer their own theories. *Quarterly Journal of Experimental Psychology, 70*, 996–1010.

Hansen, T., Olkkonen, M., Walter, S., & Gegenfurtner, K. R. (2006). Memory modulates color appearance. *Nature Neuroscience, 9*, 1367–1368.

Hibberd, F. (2005). *Unfolding social constructionism.* New York, NY: Springer.

Hibberd, F. (2014). The metaphysical basis of a process psychology. *Journal of Theoretical and Philosophical Psychology, 34*, 161–186.

Husserl, E. (1970). *The crisis of European sciences and transcendental phenomenology*. Evanston, IL: Northwestern University Press.

Kennedy, J. M., Green, C. D., Nicholls, A., & Liu, C. H. (1992). Illusions and knowing what is real. *Ecological Psychology, 4*(3), 153–172.

Kennedy, J. M., & Portal, A. (1990). Illusions: Can change of vantage point and invariant impressions remove deception? *Ecological Psychology, 2*(1), 37–53.

Krøjgaard, P. (2016). Keeping track of individuals: Insights from developmental psychology. *Integrative Psychological & Behavioral Science., 50*(2), 264–276.

Lamiell, J. T. (2000). A periodic table of personality elements? The "Big Five" and trait "psychology" in critical perspective. *Journal of Theoretical and Philosophical Psychology, 20*, 1–24.

Lundh, L. G. (2018). Psychological science within a three-dimensional ontology. *Integrative Psychological and Behavioral Science, 52*, 52–66.

Mammen, J. (1993). The elements of psychology. In N. Engelsted, M. Hedegaard, B. Karpatschof, & A. Mortensen (Eds.), *The societal subject* (pp. 29–44). Aarhus, Denmark: Aarhus University Press.

Mammen, J. (2016). Using a topological model in psychology: Developing sense and choice categories. *Integrative Psychological and Behavioral Science, 50*(2), 196–233.

Mammen, J. (2017). *A new logical foundation for psychology*. New York, NY: Springer.

Melser, D. (2004). *The act of thinking*. Cambridge, MA: MIT Press.

Merleau-Ponty, M. (1945, 2012). *Phenomenology of Perception* (D. Landes, Trans.). London, UK: Routledge.

Neumann, A. (2016). Looking for a symphony. *Integrative Psychological & Behavioral Science, 50*(2), 257–263.

Noë, A. (2004). *Action in perception*. Cambridge, MA: MIT press.

Noë, A. (2012). *Varieties of presence*. Cambridge, MA: Harvard University Press.

Noë, A. (2015). *Strange tools: Art and human nature*. New York, NY: Hill and Wang.

Ossorio, P. G. (2006). *The behavior of persons*. Ann Arbor, MI: Descriptive Psychology Press.

Palacios, A. G., Escobar, M. J., & Céspedes, E. (2017). Missing colors: The enactivist approach to perception. *Constructivist Foundations, 13*(1), 117–125.

Parks, M. R., & Floyd, K. (1996). Meanings for closeness and intimacy in friendship. *Journal of Social and Personal Relationships, 13*(1), 85–107.

Pérez-Álvarez, M. (2018). Psychology as a science of subject and comportment, beyond the mind and behavior. *Integrative Psychological and Behavioral Science, 52*(1), 25–51.

Robinson, D. N. (2016). Explanation and the "brain sciences". *Theory & Psychology, 26*(3), 324–332.

Rosch, E. (1973). Natural categories. *Cognitive Psychology, 4*, 328–350.

Rosch, E. (1978). Principles of categorization. In E. Margolis & S. Laurence (Eds.), *Concepts: Core readings* (pp. 189–206). Cambridge, MA: MIT Press.

Rosch, E., Mervis, C. B., Gray, W. D., Johnson, D. M., & Boyes-Braem, P. (1976). Basic objects in natural categories. *Cognitive Psychology, 8*(3), 382–439.

Rubin, E. (1950). Visual figures apparently incompatible with geometry. *Acta Psychologica, 7*, 365–387.

Sartre, J. P. (1956). *Being and nothingness*. New York, NY: Philosophical Library.

Searle, J. R. (1995). *The construction of social reality*. New York, NY: Simon & Schuster.

Seli, P., Schacter, D. L., Risko, E. F., & Smilek, D. (2017). Increasing participant motivation reduces rates of intentional and unintentional mind wandering. *Psychological Research* (Online first).

Smedslund, J. (1997). *The structure of psychological common sense*. Mahwah, NJ: Lawrence Erlbaum.

Sokolowski, R. (1978). *Presence and absence: A philosophical investigation of language and being*. Bloomington, IN: Indiana University Press.

Sokolowski, R. (2000). *Introduction to phenomenology*. New York, NY: Cambridge University Press.

Sui, J., & Humphreys, G. W. (2015). The integrative self: How self-reference integrates perception and memory. *Trends in Cognitive Sciences, 19*, 719–728.

Tenbrink, T., Ross, R. J., Thomas, K. E., Dethlefs, N., & Andonova, E. (2010). Route instructions in map-based human–human and human–computer dialogue: A comparative analysis. *Journal of Visual Languages & Computing, 21*(5), 292–309.

Thomson, J. J. (2008). *Normativity*. Chicago, IL: Open Court.

Willett, A. B., Marken, R. S., Parker, M. G., & Mansell, W. (2017). Control blindness: Why people can make incorrect inferences about the intentions of others. *Attention, Perception, & Psychophysics, 79*, 841–849.

Wittgenstein, L. (1965). I: A lecture on ethics. *The Philosophical Review, 74*(1), 3–12.

Zahavi, D. (2014). *Self and other: Exploring subjectivity, empathy, and shame*. Oxford, UK: Oxford University Press.

Chapter 3
Hierarchies of Purpose

This chapter is about goals and actions. Our intuitive image of the relation between goals and actions is straightforward: Our actions are directed toward goals, and goals motivate action. The plan of this chapter is to elaborate on this intuitive image. First, the relation between a given goal and a given action is contingent, rather than necessary, which is to say knowing one does not give us definite knowledge of the other. Second, a goal belongs to a hierarchy of goals, which means a goal can be analyzed in terms of a set of subordinate goals, while being nested within a super-ordinate goal (Powers, 1998). Third, often one level within a hierarchy of goals is visible to us, and that is the level that serves as the object of description. Goals at this level are basic-level categories (Rosch, 1978). Fourth, there is a type of action—explorative action or improvisation—that forces us to suspend our simple image of the relation between goals and actions. Attention to this type of action makes it easier to become aware of the hierarchical nature of goals, the varying strength of the relation between actions and goals, and the possible reorganization of goal hierarchies.

3.1 Actions and Goals

Our actions imply goals, and goals motivate actions. Jim tells a joke to make his friends laugh. Amy asks for directions to find the place of her appointment. Rick walks into his superior's office to ask for a raise. It is possible, of course, for Jim to tell the same joke with a different goal. He could use the joke to evade an uncomfortable topic of conversation; Amy might ask for directions to practice speaking in her second language; and, Rick might walk into his superior's office to test the effectiveness of his new blood-pressure treatment. Observing behavior does not provide infallible access to goals. This has to be clarified further when we talk about goal hierarchies.

© Springer Nature Switzerland AG 2019
D. Gozli, *Experimental Psychology and Human Agency*,
https://doi.org/10.1007/978-3-030-20422-8_3

On the other hand, knowing a goal does not give us certainty in predicting a person's action. To make his friends laugh, Jim might show them a video clip. To find the restaurant, Amy might look at a map. To receive a raise, Rick might organize a conspiracy with sympathetic coworkers. The contingent associations between actions and goals have been a problem for any research that relies exclusively on studying the observable behavior, an approach we often refer to as behaviorism (Kukla & Walmsley, 2006). Given the way we are approaching the topic of goals and actions, behaviorism might seem obviously and trivially false. It would be a mistake to dismiss the behaviorist approach without acknowledging its merits.

We are not going to deal with the silly behaviorist who defines hunger as nothing but "the duration of time passed with no access to food" (stimulus) or as "the amount of food eaten after having access to food" (response). This silly behaviorist takes a look at our examples and says, Jim's goal for making his friends laugh is nothing but the number of jokes he tells at a gathering; Amy's need for finding an unknown destination is nothing but her direction-seeking behavior; Rick's desire for a raise is nothing but the requests made to his superior.

We are going to consider a reasonable behaviorist who recognizes the distinction between wanting to make your friends laugh and the expression of that goal, for instance, telling jokes. This behaviorist might define the strength of the goal in terms of the number of jokes. What the silly (ontological) and the reasonable (methodological) behaviorist share in common is an understanding of the relation between the performed set of actions and the goal expressed by the actions. The latter side of the relation, i.e., goal, according to the silly behaviorist, is a folk-psychological fiction that has no explanatory value. According to the reasonable behaviorist, a goal is a genuine psychological category, but it cannot be a target of rigorous scientific observation.

A reasonable behaviorist might rely on the correlations between some actions and goals. Let us consider the three actions, telling a joke, asking for direction, walking into the boss's office, and the three goals, wanting to make friends laugh, wanting to find a place, and wanting a higher salary. From a logical point of view, all nine (3 × 3) action-goal combinations are possible, but they are not all equally probable (Rosch, 1978). Wanting to make your friends laugh is difficult to associate with either asking for direction or walking into the boss's office, unless under unusual circumstances. It is similarly difficult to imagine how wanting a raise can be expressed by asking for directions. By contrast, asking for direction is highly correlated with wanting to know one's way to a destination. These correlations—grounded in everyday experience—give rise to the impression that, when we observe actions, we are observing goals. The correlations make other people's goals *present* to us, despite the fact that we, strictly speaking, only observe their overt actions. We observe goals, in the sense that we observe anger in a frown, or joy in a laughter, flirtation in a lingering eye contact, or the command "stop!" in a policeman's hand gesture. Describing our observations as "inferences" does not do them justice. We see through the surface features of an action, with an implicit sense of assurance, and observe the goal (Merleau-Ponty, 1945). The reasonable behaviorist, on the basis of these regularities, might feel justified in treating goals as synonymous with their associated actions.

The reasonable behaviorist, furthermore, detects the mistaken position of wishing to *point to* someone's goal when we are observing their action. We can point to and describe something as an action, but we cannot do the same pointing-and-naming of the goal that is motivating the action. The goal of an action can be distinguished from the action itself, but the distinction does not correspond to two different objects to which we can point. The action is the expression of the goal. If I ask a student, "Where is your desire to succeed in the course?" I am not complaining about the fact that I cannot see his/her goal directly. I am complaining that there is no evidence of that desire, such as studying, attending lectures, and completing assignments. If I see a student who is completing all those requirements, I will not ask him/her, "where is your goal?" (Ryle, 1949; Wittgenstein, 1953).

So far, I have agreed with the behaviorist claims that goals (a) do not exist separately from actions and (b) are often visible in actions. Why do we not drop goals and talk only about actions? Why distinguish between the two? One reason is that action-goal associations can diverge from the prototypical instances, in which case the "visible" goal is akin to an illusion (pretending to enjoy a meal prepared by a friend; asking for directions to practice a language; telling a joke to repress a topic of conversation).

Dissociating actions and goals justifies adopting a modest approach regarding our knowledge of goals. Imagine Amy and Matt, each approaching a stranger in a Chinese city. Both ask for directions. Amy is practicing Chinese. Matt wants to find a place. Amy will be happy even when the stranger does not know the address; Matt will not. On the other hand, Matt will be happy if the stranger helps him find his way in English; Amy will not. If the stranger changes the subject and begins talking about the weather, Amy will be happy, but Matt will not. We observe them at the time they ask for directions and we cannot tell that they are driven by different goals.

The behaviorist objects: "These are not the same actions. They only appear to be the same actions within that short slice of time." That is correct, but when a behaviorist makes this objection, it could be overruled because the behaviorist began by denying himself the distinction between two apparently identical actions. From a behaviorist perspective, it is difficult to explain why we need to extend our scope of observation and to determine when and why we should stop extending the scope. The behaviorist task of distinguishing between the actions of Amy and Matt, without talking about their goal, is akin to the task of distinguishing between an illusion and a veridical perception without reference to beliefs.

The behaviorist responds: "Our analysis is not based on an action in isolation. It is about a series of actions, what triggers each action in the sequence, and what is brought about by each action." Amy's expression of joy after having a conversation distinguishes her from Matt, who is unhappy with not obtaining directions. Can the behaviorist description of overt actions, along a larger timescale, replace talk of goals with talk of action sequences? No. The problem is that we need to be able to highlight important differences between actors and action sequences and ignore unimportant differences. That is, while we would want to distinguish Amy and Matt, we would not want to distinguish two sequences of action that differ in many respects but are pursuing the same goal (practicing Chinese). To express the difference between actors, we would need to refer to actions at a higher level of abstraction. Referring to goals equips us to think about an action, and sequences of actions, at relatively larger timescales, picking out important differences between actions and ignoring unimportant differences.

The similarity between my analysis of goals and my analysis of perceptual illusions (Chap. 2) is not accidental. In discussing perceptual illusions, I noted that what distinguishes an illusion from a veridical perception is not perception in that instance, but how the percept changes upon further exploration. The same applies to goals. The difference between being right and being wrong about someone's goal can be distinguished with further interaction (Marken, 2014). If I am wrong about a person's goal, there are certain places that I cannot take the interactions, although I might falsely believe that I can.

Are Amy and Matt performing the same action? The answer could be "yes" and "no" depending on our level of description. This is, again, similar to the comparison between illusory and veridical perception. The two lines of the Müller-Lyer figure are the same if we measure them in isolation, and they appear different because of the surrounding elements. Similarly, the actions of Amy and Matt are the same if we observe them in isolation, and they are different because they belong to different streams of activity (language-learning vs. navigation).

There is another good reason to maintain the distinction between goal and action. Goals emphasize the outward nature of actions. Goals are desired states that an agent wishes to maintain or bring about (Marken, 2014; Powers, 1998). Two different goals giving rise to similar actions are concerned with different aspects of self and environment. Amy is learning to establish control over her command of a new language. Matt is navigating within an unfamiliar environment. We can express the difference between the two in terms of what can and cannot interrupt them. An event that interrupts one of them might not affect the other.

The basic point in this section was that the relation between action and goal is contingent—knowing one does not give us definite knowledge about the other. This recognition enables us to appreciate better the distinction between a goal and an expression of that goal in activity. Given the nature of our discussion, we had a brief encounter with behaviorism. In contrast to behaviorism, I argued that goals must be considered as distinct from actions. But should we maintain a duality between actions and goals? Should we assume the two as existing along separate planes? That is the perspective we must abandon in the next section.

3.2 Subordinate and Superordinate Goals

Within any conceptual hierarchy, relatively subordinate categories (fig tree) are nested within relatively superordinate categories (tree). The former are instantiations of the latter. When you point to a fig tree, you are pointing at an instantiation of tree—the relatively more superordinate concept. The same applies to a hierarchy of goals. When you are telling a joke, you are at the same time enacting something that belongs to a relatively more superordinate category of *things you do to entertain friends.* When you ask for direction, the superordinate category could be *seeking help* or *practicing a language.* When you storm into your superior's office, you are enacting the superordinate category of *confrontation.*

When I consider separating an action from its associated goal, I am not referring to two separable processes. To say, "Telling a joke can be associated with different goals" is a form of saying "We can imagine different instances of telling the same joke that differ in their goal." That is similar to imagining the same tone with higher volume or imagining the same melody in a different key. When considering a particular action, we cannot separate it from its goal, just as we cannot separate the volume of a particular tone from its pitch. Thus, when we distinguish, for one particular action, its overt features and its goal, we are distinguishing different attributes of one and the same process.

Subordinate goals could also be described as "proximal" and "concrete", such as making a manual movement or pushing a button, whereas superordinate goals can be described as "distal" and "abstract", such as changing the brightness or the temperature of a room. The descriptions, "uttering a series of words" and "asking for direction," refer to the same activity, although they select different attributes. They both refer to an expression of goals. Their differences include (a) the timescale of their referent and (b) the degree to which they include the context and meaning of the activity (Gozli & Dolcini, 2018; Pacherie, 2008; Powers, 1998).

Wanting to make his friends laugh might be embedded within Jim's more general goal of enjoying his time with friends. Amy's attempt to find the way might be embedded within the goal of wanting to attend a meeting. Rick's request for a raise might be embedded within the goal of leading a financially secure life. The notion of a goal being embedded within another goal is metaphorical. Another way to describe the relation is in terms of levels of abstraction (Rosch, 1978). An abstract goal is embodied and expressed in terms of a more concrete goal. According to this taxonomy, the word "action" is synonymous with "subordinate goal"

The degree to which we are aware of our own superordinate goals can vary (Billig, 1999). Rick might say he wants to make his friends laugh, while his real motive might be to affirm his belief that he is the life and soul of the party. Superordinate goals might not be within the scope of the person who is enacting them. Goals can be assigned to us by other people (Caspar, Cleeremans, & Haggard, 2018; Milgram, 1963). A research participant might be enacting the goal of an experimenter, without really understanding it (Hommel, 2017), for example, in response to, "just follow my instructions and I will explain later."

In his book, *Making Sense of Behavior,* William Powers (1998) uses the example of a military march and identifies three distinct levels in the goal hierarchy. At the middle level, the soldiers are marching. At the subordinate level, the soldiers are taking step after step, keeping their balance and tempo. At the superordinate level, the soldiers are following their commander. At the superordinate level, the soldiers and their commander share a goal in common. Their coordination implies this shared goal, although it is the soldiers who are giving expression to this shared goal (the commander would spring into action if he notices any insubordination). In general, coordination requires shared goals. If you coerce someone into doing something, you are coercing them into enacting your goal.

Our implicit understanding of goal hierarchies appears in everyday talk. The idea that goals are hierarchically organized does not seem controversial. If you ask me, "Are you in control of your finger movements?" when I am typing on a keyboard, my answer will be, "Yes." If you ask me the same question, when I am trying to play a difficult piece of music on the classical guitar, my answer will be "No." Assuming that my ability to control my fingers, in general, does not change across the two scenarios, I adjust my answer with respect to the relatively superordinate goal of my activity. Moreover, we talk about *the right reasons* for doing something, which is a way of saying a subordinate goal can be embedded within better or worse superordinate goals. A student can study to achieve a good grade, to compete with his or her classmates, to avoid disappointing the teacher, or to fulfill a long-term career plan. A researcher can be driven by curiosity, fame, competition, or by a desire to address a need in her community. We criticize people whose subordinate goals are not embedded within appropriate superordinate goals. Sometimes, no superordinate goal seems to be present. Such activities might be described as explorative (Gozli & Dolcini, 2018) or intrinsically motivated (Di Domenico & Ryan, 2017). We will address the topic of exploration later in this chapter.

Another way to become aware of the hierarchical nature of goals is by showing how an action would cease to be intelligible if its superordinate goals are unknown. Think about participating in a lab experiment. Usually, experimental participation is embedded within a series of interactions between the participant and the experimenter. The experimenter provides the participants with instructions (what to do when they see a certain event) and expectations ("the experiment will take about 30 min"). Looking at a participant who is engaged in the experiment is intelligible, but not because of where the participant is sitting, or the actions she is performing. If I walk into the lab one morning and find a stranger sitting at a lab desk, completing one of my experiments, I will be puzzled. The interactions within which the experimental participation is embedded serve multiple functions. They provide participants with the necessary knowledge for completing the experiment, including what is relevant and what is irrelevant to their task. In addition, they enable the experimenter to make sense of the participants' behavior. Instructions ensure that experimental participation is embedded within the experimenters' superordinate goals.

Related to the notion of goal hierarchies, I should also introduce two additional concepts: sense of agency and sense of control. Sense of agency is the awareness that an event has resulted from one's own action (Haggard & Chambon, 2012). By contrast, sense of control refers to the awareness that one can use available actions to bring about desired events (Gozli & Brown, 2011; Wolpert, 1997). A person pushes a button without knowing the consequence, and observes a light turning on. Here, the action involves agency ("I turned on the light!") but not control ("I did not know the button was linked to the light!"). Applying the concept of control to goal hierarchies reveals the possibility of having control at one level (subordinate goals), yet not having control at another level (superordinate goal). It is possible to have full control over a sequence of navigations while lacking control over one's final destination; it is possible to have full control over one's utterances and gestures without knowing the listener's response (when a comedian is trying a new joke; or, when one tries speaking in a new language). These distinctions are crucial in understanding the nature of goal-directed action.

Researchers might sometimes neglect the hierarchical nature of goals. We might regard the goal of an action as a single attribute, which is to say we might identify only one level of the goal hierarchy (Gozli & Dolcini, 2018). Borhani, Beck, and Haggard (2017) used a simple task with two buttons. Both buttons resulted in participants receiving an aversive stimulus, although they differed in the intensity of the stimulus. They used this task to examine the role of two variables in determining the sense of agency: Having choice over which button to press (variable 1) and having control over pressing the selected button (variable 2). That is, participants sometimes pressed the button themselves, regardless of how the button was chosen, and sometimes the experimenter pressed their finger on the button.

It may seem that only the first variable has something to do with the goal of the action. Accordingly, after a participant selects a goal/outcome, i.e., a to-be-pressed button or the intensity of the aversive stimulus, the goal can be fulfilled either by the participants' own action or by the action of the experimenter. Sense of agency was found to be highest when the button was chosen voluntarily *and* was performed by the participants. Moreover, the combined effect of the two variables was more than the sum of the individual effects (Borhani et al., 2017).

In reference to the concept of goal hierarchy, Borhani et al.'s two variables correspond to superordinate and subordinate goals. We cannot identify goals (or outcomes) of action in their task only in terms of the button being pushed down. The sensorimotor process that brings about the button-press is also an outcome (Pfister, 2019). Whereas the tactile sensation of one's own movement is a subordinate goal, this sensation is not a goal when it results from the experimenter pushing one's finger against the key. Thus, the finger movement is a subordinate goal in one condition, but not in the other condition. Given that both superordinate and subordinate goals are attributes of an action, we cannot vary one of the attributes without changing the entire action.

One might say that I am not taking the critique far enough. What the researchers described as "voluntary choice" is embedded within a relatively more superordinate goal, which is itself not chosen by the participants. Therefore, calling it "voluntary choice" is misleading. Compare, for instance, performing a voluntarily chosen key, which results in the delivery of an aversive stimulus, with performing the same key-press following instruction (Borhani et al., 2017). How should we compare the two actions?

When two actions seem identical because of their similar subordinate goals (both involve pressing a button and receiving an aversive stimulus), viewing them with respect to their superordinate goals might reveal differences. Similarly, when two actions seem different in terms of their subordinate goals (one being a voluntary choice and the other being a rule-based choice), viewing the two actions with respect to their superordinate goals might reveal similarities.

Two actions can be described as follows:

1. Pressing a key that results in an aversive outcome, *based on one's voluntary choice, in a task that requires variations in one's voluntary choice over a block of trials*, which is embedded in a temporary experimenter–participant social contract
2. Pressing a key that results in an aversive outcome, *based on the experimenters' request, in a task that requires key-presses in accordance with the instructions*, which is embedded in a temporary experimenter–participant social contract

The descriptions above highlight the similarity between "voluntary" and "instructed" choice, while at the same time highlighting the difference between the seemingly identical finger movements in the two cases. I will return in Chap. 6 to the discussion of voluntary choice and its characterization within experimental psychology. At this point, we shall return to the concept of goal hierarchy and its possible neglect in experimental research.

Our next example is a series of studies by Wen, Yamashita, and Asama (2015, 2016). The researchers were interested in understanding the role of goals in the sense of agency. In their tasks, participants had different levels of sensorimotor control over the movements of a dot on a computer screen. In subset of conditions, a static frame on the screen was identified as the "goal," and participants were instructed to try to move the dot into the goal location as many times as possible. Another subset of conditions had no goal location and participants simply tried to move the dot in any direction they wished. Wen et al. found a relatively higher sense of agency when participants performed without a target location, which was the basis for their claim that having a goal can reduce one's sense of agency.

The tasks used by Wen et al. (2015, 2016) involved both a superordinate goal (hitting the target) and subordinate goals (exerting control over the moving dot). The condition that had no ostensible goal still required participants to try controlling the moving dot and report, at the end of each trial, the degree to which they felt in control of its movements. When describing a task, we might overlook that fulfilling the ostensive goal is not possible without fulfilling a series of subordinate goals. Therefore, when we ask participants to perform the task without pursuing the ostensive goal, we might regard it as goal-free. The goals we readily identify usually belong to a particular level of the goal hierarchy that is neither too abstract ("be a good person") nor too specific ("apply downward force against the button with the right index finger"), which means other necessarily present superordinate/subordinate goals tend to be neglected.

Figure 3.1 illustrates the relation between superordinate and subordinate goals. Note, first, that the relation between superordinate and subordinate goals is not sequential. It is not necessary to satisfy subordinate goals before their superordinate associates. One action can express goals at multiple levels of the hierarchy. Second, what is expressed at any given time is not the entirety of the hierarchy but a "strand" of it. This is because the expressions become increasingly specific at the subordinate

Fig. 3.1 The relation between goals in a goal hierarchy in a simple model. Within a superordinate goal, we have multiple mutually inconsistent subordinate goals. An active goal will inhibit its neighbors. For instance, "opening the door" can be satisfied (at different times) by the mutually inconsistent subordinate goals of "pushing" or "pulling" the door

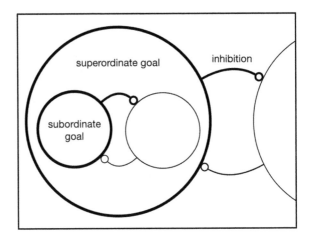

level. Choices have to be made because multiple subordinate goals, although mutually incongruent, can satisfy the same superordinate goal.

As we move toward superordinate goals, we are moving toward goals that represent stability and equilibrium, such as maintaining the temperature of one's home within a desired range, being the life of a party, or being a truthful person (Piaget, 1954). By contrast, as we move toward subordinate goals, we move toward goals that have to do with pursuit and change, such as opening the window or turning on the air conditioner. Thus, subordinate goals are relatively transient compared with their superordinate associated. In an attempt to satisfy the superordinate goal of winning a soccer match, the players must satisfy a series of relatively subordinate goals, such as coordinated movements, successful passing, and scoring goals. Each of these latter goals can also serve as a superordinate goal for relatively more subordinate goals, such as passing the ball successfully in one particular moment in the game. Stated differently, as we move from superordinate goals toward subordinate goals, we are moving from a wide range of possible states (the infinite number of ways to win a soccer match), toward an increasingly narrow range of possible states (the few ways in which a player can pass the ball successfully in one given instance of the game).

Because superordinate and subordinate goals are associated with different ranges of observation, when we observe another person, our existing knowledge about their subordinate and superordinate goals can guide our judgment. If we expect someone to pursue a subordinate goal (rotating one of the match sticks in Fig. 3.2), then confirming our expectation requires specific evidence. By contrast, if we have an expectation about someone pursuing a superordinate goal (building a gestalt figure with the match sticks), then confirming our expectation does not require the same kind of specificity in observation. This idea was demonstrated in studies by Chambon et al. (2011, 2017).

Participants in the studies by Chambon et al. (2011, 2017) observed video clips of actions with subordinate goals of, say, rotating or transporting an object, and superordinate goals of, say, moving an object to build/break a gestalt figure. The

Fig. 3.2 An example of
the relation between
subordinate goals (rotating
vs. transporting a match
stick) and a superordinate
goal (moving the match
stick in order to build a
gestalt figure)

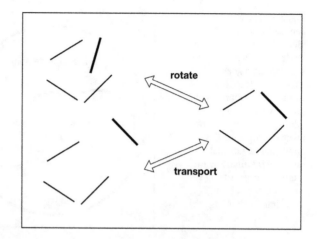

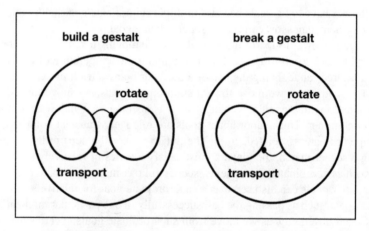

Fig. 3.3 The relation between goals within a hierarchical model of a simple movement task. A subordinate goal (e.g., rotate) can fulfill different superordinate goals, depending on the context, which makes the superordinate goal less tied to specific perceptual states

task was to categorize the action with respect to one of the levels of goal hierarchy. Two variables were manipulated. First, the strength of perceptual evidence was varied by changing the length of the video clip. Second, the expectation to observe a goal was selectively varied at one of the levels (superordinate or subordinate). That is, alternative goals were equiprobable at one level, say, rotating versus transporting, but they had unequal probability at the other level (actor being more likely to build/ break the gestalt figure). With this manipulation, participants were given prior expectation regarding the goal at one of the two levels. Participants' responses were sensitive to both the strength of perceptual evidence and to prior expectation. However, prior expectation had a stronger influence in the judgment of superordinate goals. This finding demonstrates that subordinate goals are characterized in terms of more specific perceptions, compared to superordinate goals (Fig. 3.3).

What if Chambon et al. (2011, 2017) had found equal effects of prior expectation on judgment of superordinate and subordinate goals? Could we then claim that the two categories of goals are dependent on perceptual input to the same degree? The problem is that superordinate goals are, by definition, those that are perceptually less specific. They are, by definition, more abstract than subordinate goals, which means they can be expressed by a wider range of perceptible states (Hasson, Chen, & Honey, 2015; Powers, 1998). Therefore, if we conduct an experiment and find that judgments of subordinate and superordinate goals are equally sensitive to perceptual evidence, that would only indicate a procedural failure in distinguishing the two categories (Smedslund, 2002). Chambon et al.'s success consisted primarily in developing a procedure in which participants can effectively distinguish the two levels of goals, rather than discovering that the judgment of the two types of goals differ in their sensitivity to perceptual evidence. The latter is implicit in our understanding of conceptual hierarchies. Although their claim about testing an empirical hypothesis would be overstated (Smedslund, 2002), Chambon et al.'s studies are interesting and effective in highlighting the hierarchical organization of goals.

An agent who is aware of a hierarchy of goals can focus his/her attention on a specific level within the hierarchy. When Jim tells a joke to his friends, he can consider fulfilling the goal of making his friends laugh (superordinate goal), or he can focus on enacting the sequence of utterances and gestures that constitute telling the joke. The same awareness enables us to recognize that the skills required to fulfill a subordinate goal also could be used to fulfill different superordinate goals. You could employ the same conversational skills to share bad news; you could employ the same skills that enabled one sequence of navigations in order to arrive at a different destination. Nonetheless, in a specific instance, subordinate goals and superordinate goals are integral parts of an action, which means the action would change if either of the goals change. Compare, for instance, when Jim tells the joke himself with when he instructs one of his friends to tell the joke. The goal of making others laugh remains the same, but it is now shared by Jim and his friend, who is the agent who fulfills the goal of telling the joke. When participants in Borhani et al.'s (2017) study pressed a button and received an aversive stimulus, they were similarly fulfilling a goal that was given to them by other agents. Paying attention to the agents involved in enacting a hierarchy of goals is useful in determining whether different agents correspond to different levels of the goal hierarchy (Caspar et al., 2018; Gozli, 2017; Powers, 1998).

Here is another example from my teaching experience. Some of my students are uncomfortable asking questions during or after lectures. In some cases, I receive someone's question indirectly, "My friend is wondering…" or "My friend would like to know…". The students who deliver a classmate's question tend to emphasize the fact that it is not their own question. You might think, "Well, it doesn't matter who is asking the question, as long as the question is asked." Yes, but my concern here goes beyond that point. If the person behind the question does not matter, why would we ever wish to emphasize that we are not asking our own question? Why does the student emphasize that he or she is, to use our terminology, enacting the subordinate goal (uttering a set of words) in order to serve someone else's subordinate goal (asking a question)?

When thinking about a person, we regard the highest level of his or her goal hierarchy as a relatively stable feature, which we might describe as a character trait (DeYoung, 2015). We are tacitly aware of this and express our awareness when we distance ourselves from our actions. We might say, "I am just following the cultural norm", or "this is what people are supposed to do in this situation", or "I would like to do otherwise, but I would be judged harshly". When academics say, "I will pursue my own interests after I get tenure", they imply that their current activities are expressing a set of superordinate goals that mismatch their own. They are similar to the student who is asking someone else's question.

In this section, my primary aim was to highlight the presence of goal hierarchies. Recognizing the presence of goal hierarchies eliminates the strict distinction between actions and goals. Attaching fixed labels ("action" vs. "goal") to different levels is beside the point. As far as I am concerned, any level in the hierarchy is open to description as a goal or as an action. What is important is remaining mindful of goal hierarchies and multiple levels of control. Goal hierarchies tend to be absent from view because of our strong tendency to identify goals with only one level. We now turn to a discussion of these readily visible goals.

3.3   Basic-Level Goals

The world around us includes objects and events. Basic-level (or mid-level) categories are those that come to mind most readily (Rosch, 1978). Our world also includes actions. And the idea of basic-level categories can be extended to actions and goals. If you ask, "Why did Rick ask for a raise?" it would be unusual to hear, "Because he wants to maximize the probability of his survival and reproduction." When we talk about goals, we are typically talking about more immediate reasons for action. The goals we talk about in everyday language are, by definition, basic-level goals. It takes more effort to point out subordinate and superordinate goals because the basic-level categories are most relevant for identifying actions (striking the balance between requiring cognitive effort and being informative). Basic-level goals are also more relevant in our interactions with other people, including when we wish to help or interfere with someone's action. Helping friends move a dining table is a straight-forward matter, compared to helping them enhance the interior design of their home.

Following Rosch (1978), we could describe basic-level goals (*asking for directions*) as those that (a) come to mind most readily when we understand an activity, (b) evoke rather specific images when we think about them, and (c) can be identified by a set of optimally informative features common to all members of the category. By comparison, members of a superordinate category (*communicating*) share fewer features in common with each other, while members of a subordinate category (saying, "excuse me") share many features with members of other subordinate categories.

The visibility of basic-level goals does not guarantee that we judge them accurately. Our discussion of illusions (Chap. 2) can apply to basic-level goals. We are more likely to form an accurate judgment of someone's goal if we change our own activity in relation to him. More specifically, we find out about someone's goals when we find out what counts as an interruption for him. Marken (2013) uses the example of a fugitive, who thinks he is being chased by a driver behind him. What the fugitive identifies as chasing is an accidental similarity of the path taken by the other driver. To test his judgment, the fugitive needs to change his path and see whether the apparent chase is responsive to his change. If the path of the other driver is independent of the path taken by the fugitive, then it cannot be disturbed by the sudden changes in the path of the fugitive. If, on the other hand, the other driver is responsive to changes in the fugitive's path, then the fugitive can be more certain about the chase. In general, to test whether an apparent intention is genuine, we can test whether the agent responds to disturbances of the apparent intention (Marken, 2013).

What we regard as basic-level changes with experience. A novice guitar player does not differentiate between different ways of playing a string, but an experienced player can differentiate between, for instance, the resting stroke (*apoyando*) and a free stroke (*tirando*). An experienced player makes the distinctions based not only on her finger movements but also on the sound qualities that are associated with the strokes and knowledge about when to use each one. Similarly, a novice chess player might think that the King's pawn opening, which is identified by a single move, reflects a basic-level category of games. For an experienced chess player, by contrast, the King's pawn opening is very general. For the experienced player, a basic-level category of games might be characterized at five to ten moves into the game (e.g., the Najdorf variation of the Sicilian defense). We could think of similar examples in dance or martial arts, where experience can change what is visible to us, where we can differentiate one move/intention from another move/intention. The point here is that basic-level categories, including basic-level goals, are not constant or universal. "Basic-level", just like "subordinate" and "superordinate", is a relative term. A goal can be relatively more basic-level, compared to another goal. And, given a particular perspective and a particular set of prior experiences, a goal can become more basic-level.

In addition to experience and expertise, context can change what we regard as basic-level goals. Two surgeons discussing an operation would talk with different degrees of specificity during surgery (when they need to maintain detailed and accurate coordination), a day after the surgery (when they are reviewing the procedure), and a year after the surgery (when they are discussing a group of similar operations). We also describe our actions differently, pointing to different basic-level goals, depending on our conversation partners. Consider a teacher asking her students a question. She might describe her goal to the students as, "discussing the course content", while she might describe her goal to a colleague as, "trying to stimulate the students' curiosity". What is a basic-level goal in a conversation among teachers might not be basic-level in a student–teacher conversation.

We could consider the hierarchy of goals in relation to habits and goals. We are often advised not to focus on goals and, instead, to focus on habits (Silvia, 2007). The popular distinction between goal-based strategy and habit-based strategy can be reformulated either in terms of what one *does* (distinguishing between basic-level and subordinate goals) or in terms of what one *pays attention* to (what is identified as the basic-level goal?). We might hear the advice, "Do not aim to finish writing a book project within a certain time period (goal). Instead, aim to write a certain amount every day (habit)." Similarly, we might hear "Do not aim to lose a certain amount of weight within a time period (goal). Instead, aim to eat healthy and be active every day (habit)." The habit-based strategy involves—in the short term—a shift of focus from basic-level goals, which come to mind rather effortlessly, to subordinate goals, which might come to mind with extra effort. In the long term, however, this strategy aims to shift the basic-level (visible) goals toward a smaller and more manageable timescale.

To summarize, there is a level of abstraction that comes to mind rather effortlessly when we perceive and describe goals. Attention to the basic-level goals can cause us to neglect the hierarchical organization of goals, and the presence of superordinate and subordinate goals. Moreover, despite their relative visibility, perception of basic-level goals is not always accurate. Our perception becomes accurate as we find out what kinds of activities count as interruption for the actor who is pursuing the goal. Finally, what is regarded as a basic-level goal can change with experience and context.

3.4 Explorative Action

Jeff Pressing (1984) wrote, "To the extent that we are unpredictable, we improvise. Everything else is repeating ourselves or following orders" (p. 345). In this section, I draw your attention to the distinction between *exploitation* and *exploration* (Hills et al., 2015). Exploitation refers to activities directed at specific goals and relying on existing strategies. Exploration, on the other hand, refers to activities that are either not directed at a specific goal or deviate from the existing strategies. I will be using "exploration" and "improvisation" interchangeably. Pressing (1984) said that we are unpredictable when we improvise, but that tells only part of the story. We also improvise in unpredictable situations. We explore and improvise in order to extend the domain of predictability (Anselme & Güntürkün, 2019; Gozli & Dolcini, 2018; Gozli & Gao, 2019; Hills et al., 2015).

We can think about exploration as a superordinate category of goals (Gozli & Dolcini, 2018; Hills et al., 2015). The distinction between exploitation and exploration has also been framed in terms of the opposition between *narrow search* and *wide search*, as well as the distinction between *persistence* and *flexibility* (Hommel, 2015). The narrow/wide distinction refers to the trade-off between searching within a known area for a predictable outcome and searching within an unknown area for an unpredictable—but possibly more rewarding—outcome (Hills et al., 2015). The persistence–flexibility distinction refers to the trade-off between maintaining known strategies and being open to new—potentially more effective—strategies (Goschke, 2013; Hommel, 2015).

There is a bias in action research, based on a neglect of goal hierarchies, which regards explorations as activities without a goal. This way of thinking faces serious difficulty outside of the context of human laboratory experiments. Animals in environments with scarce and unpredictable food sources tend to explore (Anselme & Güntürkün, 2019). Is an animal exploring a resource-scarce environment acting without a goal?

Let us return our three examples. Jim is telling a joke to make his friends laugh, Amy is asking for directions to find a restaurant, and Rick is storming into his boss's office to ask for a raise. What would be the explorative version of these actions? What if Jim doesn't know whether his friends would laugh at his joke? Maybe he has never told a joke in public. Maybe he is not sure whether this particular joke is funny. What if Amy lives in a city where most people are unfriendly to strangers and ignore her request for help. What if Amy knows this and asks for help, anyway? What if Rick knows that his boss will most likely decline his request? With these modifications in our actors' beliefs, we give their actions an explorative dimension. They are now reaching into the unknown, doing something without knowing the consequences. We removed the actors' certainty about their relatively basic-level goals, while leaving their ability fully intact to perform the relatively subordinate goals (uttering words, performing gestures, asking questions, walking into an office). Therefore, the difference between exploitative and explorative activity is not in a total presence/absence of goals, but in a selective presence/absence of goal at one level of a goal hierarchy.

Running in a marathon is clearly a goal-driven activity, whereas taking a leisurely walk in the park does not seem goal-driven in the same way. The marathon runner's path is easy to see. Someone who is on a leisurely walk might change her course on a whim, without changing the nature of her activity. A person on a leisurely walk does not have a fixed path. She cannot be interrupted in the same way that a marathon runner can be interrupted. She might stop to play with a friend's dog or take a look at some flowers. At the same time, if she does not encounter the dog or the flowers, she will not think that her walk was a failure. In comparison, a marathon runner stopping mid-way to look at flowers or play with a dog would be an odd event. We might explain this by saying that the marathon runner has a goal and, therefore, he can be interrupted. The leisurely walk, however, can also be interrupted if the person encounters an unpleasant event, such as a terrible traffic accident. Such an event would reveal that the leisurely walk had an implicit goal (to relax, to enjoy, etc.), though this goal is more loosely connected to the subordinate actions and, thus, more immune to interruptions.

By identifying only a single level of the goal hierarchy, Wen et al. (2015, 2016) claimed that their participants did not have a goal when moving a cursor without an explicit target area. As discussed above, participants in the "no-goal" condition still had the superordinate goal of completing the experiment, which required exploring with the cursor and evaluating their sense of control over it. This goal is interrupted if we completely remove the connection between participants' actions and the movements of the cursor. By noticing how explorative actions are also susceptible to interruption, we recognize that they are goal-directed (Marken, 2013).

In general, exploration implies control over subordinate goals, although those goals are not tightly attached to particular superordinate goals. Jim will find out whether he can make his friends laugh after he tells the joke. Amy will find out whether asking for directions can help her navigate the city after she asks for help. Rick will know whether he can persuade his boss or, at least, whether he has the courage to confront him, after he makes the attempt. As such, exploration is a process that can create ties between subordinate and superordinate goals. By exercising the capacity for explorative action, we open the possibility for the reorganization of goal hierarchies.

The openness and interest in unpredictable superordinate goals is perhaps what distinguishes exploration from addictive or impulsive behavior (Chen & Chang, 2016; Young, 1998). Addictive behavior is similar to exploration in its persistence on subordinate goals and control over events that occur on a relatively short timescale. However, it differs from exploration because it disregards and discounts superordinate/long-term goals, whereas exploration is open to finding and learning about superordinate goals. Whereas addictive or impulsive behavior might imply a kind of hopelessness with regard to the future, explorative activity implies hope despite uncertainty (Anselme & Güntürkün, 2019; Engelsted, 2017).

The present approach should be compared with the model of action control proposed by Hommel (Hommel, 2015; Hommel & Colzato, 2017). The model's essential parameters are shown in Fig. 3.4 (left panel). We are imagining one trial of a two-choice task, whereby the sensorimotor states that correspond to action 1 (pushing button #1) and action 2 (pushing button #2) are set up in a mutually inhibiting relation. The correct action is determined by the "goal". I have modified Hommel's model in the right panel of Fig. 3.4, in order to demonstrate the hierarchical relation between goals and actions (Gozli & Dolcini, 2018; Powers, 1998). The relation between a goal and other (competing) goals resembles the relation between an action and other (competing) actions. What we call goal can be called action, and vice versa, depending on our scope of analysis.

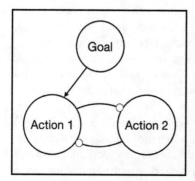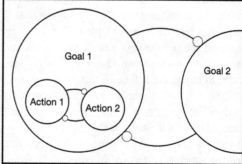

Fig. 3.4 Comparing two models of goal-directed action. The left panel is based on a relatively clear distinction between goals and actions (Hommel, 2015). The right panel shows the present model, in which there is no clear distinction between goals and actions. What we call a goal can be referred to as an action, and vice versa, depending on the scope of analysis

Hommel's (2015) model is primarily a model of exploitation—it regards exploitation as the default mode of action. Consequently, it regards exploration as a deviation from the default mode of action. Specifically, switching from exploitation to exploration is described in terms of two changes. First, the link between the goal and the action is weakened. Second, the inhibitory connections between alternative actions are weakened. The advantage of this model is that it treats exploration and exploitation modes as endpoints of a continuum, thus offering a unifying model of action control. Its disadvantages are that (1) it encourages a goal-free view of exploration and (2) it neglects the phylogenetic and ontogenetic primacy of pre-reflective activity, driven by goals unknown to the organism (Engelsted, 1989, 2017; Mammen, 2017, p. 31–33). Modifying this model, based on the hierarchical organization of goals/actions, recognizes the goal-driven nature of exploration.

As shown in the right panel of Fig. 3.4, a superordinate goal is constituted partly as the inhibitory relation between subordinate goals. The same logic applies to goals at different levels of the hierarchy, illustrated by the inhibitory relation between (superordinate) "goal 1" and "goal 2". We can think about the competing goals and the competing actions as possible discoveries of exploration. Jim might find out, after several attempts to entertain his friends, that he can either remain in his comfort zone or continue to improve his joke-telling skills. Rick might find out, after several confrontations, that he can pursue either the goal of maintaining peace at work or the goal of defending his rights. Understanding the mutually exclusive relation among these goal states can later be used in exploitative action.

Alternatively, exploration can lead to the discovery that certain goal states are not inconsistent with each other, and that one does not have to choose only one among seemingly conflicting goals. For example, Amy might believe that she has to choose either to avoid unfriendly strangers or to ask for directions. After asking for directions, she discovers that the two goal states can overlap, which means the avoidance of unfriendly strangers will be less likely to stop her from asking for help in the future. Just as exploitation corresponds to the possibility of goal fulfillment, exploration corresponds to the possibility of goal discovery and the reorganization of goal hierarchies. This idea is neglected if we regard exploration as a detachment from goals.

I contrasted superordinate goals, such as exploration and exploitation, with basic-level goals, such as telling a joke. You might ask whether it is possible for exploration to become a basic-level goal. Are there instances when we point to someone and say, "She is improvising"? Recall how Pressing (1984) associated improvisation with unpredictability. Perhaps our failure to predict someone's behavior, under certain circumstances, can bring to mind the idea that they are improvising. Perhaps, under such circumstances, exploration—at least for a time—becomes a basic-level goal. But we cannot continue, ad infinitum, to describe an activity merely as "improvisation" unless we maintain a degree of distance from it. I will explain this point with reference to performance arts, and I will point out its relevance to experimental research.

In theater and music, improvisation is a recognized form of performance. Artists and audiences can share an understanding that what is being performed is improvised. In theatrical improvisation, the audience expects to be surprised by humorous twists, divergent ideas that might quickly transform one narrative into another. In musical improvisation, the audience expects to hear variations and deviations from certain musical reference points or themes (Pressing, 1984). Before being immersed in performance, we might treat improvisation as a basic-level goal, as a label for describing performance. When immersed in improvisation, however, as a performer or an audience, improvisation tends to become a superordinate goal, receding into the background of our experience. Instead of thinking, "I am improvising", performers will think of rather specific moves and techniques involved in the craft of improvising. During the performance, the specific moves would serve as basic-level goals. The way in which improvisation, initially a basic-level goal, recedes into the background and becomes a superordinate goal resembles the way in which participation in experimental research (by becoming a superordinate goal) recedes into the background of our descriptions. We stop paying attention to the fact of research participation and focus on specific steps that, within the established set of constraints, complete the experiment.

To summarize, recognizing the hierarchical organization of goals is helpful in understanding exploration as a superordinate goal. Exploration does not mean an absence of goals, but the presence of goals at relatively subordinate levels, and the agents' openness to encounter unpredictable outcomes. As such, exploration implies the possibility of a new organization among goals at different levels, or new ways in which subordinate goals and superordinate goals can correspond to each other. Therefore, exploitation is not necessarily the default mode of goal-directed activity. A history of exploratory activity, through which an agent learns associations between actions and goals, is a prerequisite for exploitative action (Hommel, 2013). While exploitation corresponds to pursuing known goals, exploration corresponds to the possibility of discovering new goals and the reorganization of goal hierarchies.

3.5 Implications

We considered a scenario in which Jim instructed a friend to tell a joke at a party. Later on, Jim can tell the story of his friend telling the joke, not mentioning himself. By keeping himself out of the story, Jim can repress the possibility that his friend did not really want to tell the joke. This is similar to what experimental psychologists do with their participants. To successfully complete an experiment, the experimenters and the participants must share a superordinate goal (completing the experiment, collection of data, following the instructions specific to the experiment). Doing so requires participant to adopt and enact a set of basic-level goals (those goals which the experimenters discuss later among themselves, "our participants performed accurately in this experimental condition"), keeping themselves out of the discussion.

To the extent that experimental participants enable testing particular hypotheses, their behavior must remain within a pre-specified range. This includes the goal(s) they pursue during the experiment. Focusing on participants' ostensible goals during the experiment, their basic-level goals from the standpoint of the experimenters, sustains the impression that research participants are pursuing their own superordinate goals and that their activity in the experiment can be discussed without an explicit reference to the experimental condition and its associated goal hierarchy (Gozli, 2017; Gozli & Dolcini, 2018). We ignore the fact that participants could refuse to participate, or could stop in the middle of an experiment, or that they might participate begrudgingly and with very little motivation.

Let us consider, for example, the study by Van Steenbergen, Langeslag, Band, and Hommel (2014), who claimed that people who are passionately in love might have lower cognitive control. The researchers recruited participants who had fallen in love within the 6 months prior to the study. At the beginning of the experiment, participants completed a questionnaire that quantified their romantic feelings (Passionate Love Scale; Hatfield & Sprecher, 1986). Next, the experimenters attempted to evoke thoughts and feelings related to romantic love, through imagination, writing, and listening to self-selected music. Participants then performed tasks that required selective attention to targets and ignoring distractors. Researchers found a positive correlation between distractibility and the measure of passionate love, which they took as evidence for reduced cognitive control in passionate lovers.

A superficial critique of this study can point out that the researchers did not try to evoke other types of potentially distracting thoughts at the beginning of their experiment, including thoughts of natural disasters, participants' worries about the future, unpleasant memories, hobbies, work, family, and friends. The researchers also did not test cognitive control before (without) priming romantic thoughts to see how much of the participants' distractibility could be attributed to their method of evoking romantic feelings.

A deeper critique of the study can begin by pointing out that passionate love is not merely a domain of feelings and thoughts. It is also a domain of actions and goals. By asking participants to think about their love, we are evoking a goal hierarchy. The goals related to passionate love have nothing to do with the experimental tasks designed to measure cognitive control. What would happen if we were to ask participants, in a similar study, to perform a task related to their beloved (memorizing new facts about them, classifying photographs of them, etc.)? What if we were to ask them to plan a romantic activity? Would the participants be equally distractible during these tasks? Would their distractibility similarly correlate with their scores on the passionate love measure? Can we confidently predict, based on van Steenbergen's results, that the passionate lovers will perform poorly in tasks that are related to their romantic love? It is highly unlikely. Instead of claiming, "cognitive control is reduced in passionate lovers", it is more reasonable to claim, "people perform poorly when asked to pursue goals about which they care little, especially after we remind them of something else about which they care very much." Of course, the latter claim is not very surprising.

Our discussion can be extended to the well-known phenomenon of priming. We instruct participants to repeatedly choose between two options ("up" vs. "down"). Occasionally, we present them with a very brief image of a flying bird. We find that immediately after the presentation of the image, participants are more likely to choose "up" than "down". We even find that most participants are unaware of the image of the bird. What shall we conclude from such a finding? A conclusion that is not mindful of goal hierarchies and their presence in the experimental context might be, "seeing a brief image of a flying bird automatically, and unconsciously, biases us in an upward direction". A more cautious conclusion would be, "when someone is required to choose one, and only one, of two options, their choice might be influenced by imperceptible situational factors that are associated with one of the options" (Newell & Shanks, 2014). The goal of having to choose between two options, and the particular characteristics of the options ("up" vs. "down"), can sensitize us to related information in the environment, making us susceptible to influence by situational factors (Hommel, 2000; Mammen, 2017, p. 81). We cannot conclude that the influences are independent of the goals given to the participants and, consequently, we cannot claim that the findings generalize to situations outside of the experiment.

When playing the role of a research participant, one's actions are expressions of a goal hierarchy maintained by the experimenters. Enacting the role of a research participant is an expression of a superordinate goal. These superordinate goals, once adopted by the participants, recede into the background of our discussions, sustaining the impression that participants are expressing their own superordinate goals.

If we keep the participant–researcher relationship in the background, we might pay attention only to the immediately observable features of the experiment and performance, such as accuracy and reaction time. If we keep the participant–researcher relationship in mind, however, we can notice the normative dimensions of the experiment, including whether participants understood and followed the instructions of the task, whether they should be included as participants, whether they were motivated, and so forth. In the next chapter, we will turn to the normative dimension of human behavior, identifying possible biases of researchers in their treatment of the concepts of rule and rule-based activity.

References

Anselme, P., & Güntürkün, O. (2019). How foraging works: Uncertainty magnifies food-seeking motivation. *Behavioral and Brain Sciences, 42*, e35.

Billig, M. (1999). *Freudian repression: Conversation creating the unconscious*. New York, NY: Cambridge University Press.

Borhani, K., Beck, B., & Haggard, P. (2017). Choosing, doing, and controlling: Implicit sense of agency over somatosensory events. *Psychological Science, 28*, 882–893.

Caspar, E. A., Cleeremans, A., & Haggard, P. (2018). Only giving orders? An experimental study of the sense of agency when giving or receiving commands. *PLoS One, 13*(9), e0204027.

Chambon, V., Domenech, P., Jacquet, P. O., Barbalat, G., Bouton, S., Pacherie, E., ... Farrer, C. (2017). Neural coding of prior expectations in hierarchical intention inference. *Scientific Reports, 7*(1), 1278.

Chambon, V., Domenech, P., Pacherie, E., Koechlin, E., Baraduc, P., & Farrer, C. (2011). What are they up to? The role of sensory evidence and prior knowledge in action understanding. *PLoS One, 6*(2), e17133.

Chen, B.-B., & Chang, L. (2016). Procrastination as a fast life history strategy. *Evolutionary Psychology, 14*(1), 1–5.

DeYoung, C. G. (2015). Cybernetic big five theory. *Journal of Research in Personality, 56*, 33–58.

Di Domenico, S. I., & Ryan, R. M. (2017). The emerging neuroscience of intrinsic motivation: A new frontier in self-determination research. *Frontiers in Human Neuroscience, 11*, 145.

Engelsted, N. (1989). What is the psyche and how did it get into the world? In N. Engelsted, L. Hem, & J. Mammen (Eds.), *Essays in general psychology: Seven Danish contributions presented to Henrik Poulsen*. Aarhus, Denmark: Aarhus University Press.

Engelsted, N. (2017). *Catching up with Aristotle: A journey in quest of general psychology*. New York, NY: Springer.

Goschke, T. (2013). Volition in action: Intentions, control dilemmas and the dynamic regulation of intentional control. In W. Prinz, A. Beisert, & A. Herwig (Eds.), *Action science: Foundations of an emerging discipline* (pp. 409–434). Cambridge, MA: MIT Press.

Gozli, D. G. (2017). Behaviour versus performance: The veiled commitment of experimental psychology. *Theory & Psychology, 27*, 741–758.

Gozli, D. G., & Brown, L. E. (2011). Agency and control for the integration of a virtual tool into the peripersonal space. *Perception, 40*, 1309–1319.

Gozli, D. G., & Dolcini, N. (2018). Reaching into the unknown: Actions, goal hierarchies, and explorative agency. *Frontiers in Psychology, 9*, 266.

Gozli, D. G., & Gao, C. J. (2019). Hope, exploration, and equilibrated action schemes. *Behavioral and Brain Sciences, 42*, E41.

Haggard, P., & Chambon, V. (2012). Sense of agency. *Current Biology, 22*(10), R390–R392.

Hasson, U., Chen, J., & Honey, C. J. (2015). Hierarchical process memory: Memory as an integral component of information processing. *Trends in Cognitive Sciences, 19*(6), 304–313.

Hatfield, E., & Sprecher, S. (1986). Measuring passionate love in intimate relationships. *Journal of Adolescence, 9*(4), 383–410.

Hills, T. T., Todd, P. M., Lazer, D., Redish, A. D., Couzin, I. D., & Cognitive Search Research Group. (2015). Exploration versus exploitation in space, mind, and society. *Trends in Cognitive Sciences, 19*, 46–54.

Hommel, B. (2000). The prepared reflex: Automaticity and control in stimulus-response translation. In S. Monsell & J. Driver (Eds.), *Control of cognitive processes: Attention and performance* (Vol. XVIII, pp. 247–273). Cambridge, MA: MIT Press.

Hommel, B. (2013). Ideomotor action control: On the perceptual grounding of voluntary actions and agents. In W. Prinz, M. Beisert, & A. Herwig (Eds.), *Action science: Foundations of an emerging discipline* (pp. 113–136). Cambridge, MA: MIT Press.

Hommel, B. (2015). Between persistence and flexibility: The yin and Yang of action control. In A. J. Elliot (Ed.), *Advances in motivation science* (Vol. 2, pp. 33–67). New York, NY: Elsevier.

Hommel, B. (2017). Consciousness and action control. In T. Egner (Ed.), *Handbook of cognitive control* (pp. 111–123). Chichester, UK: Wiley.

Hommel, B., & Colzato, L. S. (2017). The social transmission of metacontrol policies: Mechanisms underlying the interpersonal transfer of persistence and flexibility. *Neuroscience and Biobehavioral Reviews, 81*, 43–58.

Kukla, A., & Walmsley, J. (2006). *Mind: A historical and philosophical introduction to the major theories*. Indianapolis, IN: Hackett Publishing.

Mammen, J. (2017). *A new logical foundation for psychology*. New York, NY: Springer.

Marken, R. S. (2013). Taking purpose into account in experimental psychology: Testing for controlled variables. *Psychological Reports, 112*(1), 184–201.

Marken, R. S. (2014). *Doing research on purpose: A control theory approach to experimental psychology*. Chapel Hill, NC: New View.

Merleau-Ponty, M. (1945, 2012). *Phenomenology of perception* (D. Landes, Trans.). London, UK: Routledge.

Milgram, S. (1963). Behavioral study of obedience. *The Journal of Abnormal and Social Psychology, 67*(4), 371–378.

Newell, B. R., & Shanks, D. R. (2014). Unconscious influences on decision making: A critical review. *Behavioral and Brain Sciences, 37*(1), 1–19.

Pacherie, E. (2008). The phenomenology of action: A conceptual framework. *Cognition, 107*, 179–217.

Pfister, R. (2019). Effect-based action control with body-related effects: Implications for empirical approaches to ideomotor action control. *Psychological Review, 126*(1), 153–161.

Piaget, J. (1954). *The construction of reality in the child* (M. Cook, Trans.). New York, NY: Basic Books.

Powers, W. T. (1998). *Making sense of behavior*. Montclair, NJ: Benchmark Publications.

Pressing, J. (1984). Cognitive processes in improvisation. *Advances in Psychology, 19*, 345–363.

Rosch, E. (1978). Principles of categorization. In E. Margolis & S. Laurence (Eds.), *Concepts: Core readings* (pp. 189–206). Cambridge, MA: MIT Press.

Ryle, G. (1949). *The concept of mind*. London, UK: Hutchinson.

Silvia, P. J. (2007). *How to write a lot: A practical guide to productive academic writing*. Washington, DC: American Psychological Association.

Smedslund, J. (2002). From hypothesis-testing psychology to procedure-testing psychologic. *Review of General Psychology, 6*(1), 51–72.

Van Steenbergen, H., Langeslag, S. J., Band, G. P., & Hommel, B. (2014). Reduced cognitive control in passionate lovers. *Motivation and Emotion, 38*, 444–450.

Wen, W., Yamashita, A., & Asama, H. (2015). The influence of goals on sense of control. *Consciousness and Cognition, 37*, 83–90.

Wen, W., Yamashita, A., & Asama, H. (2016). Divided attention and processes underlying sense of agency. *Frontiers in Psychology, 7*, 35.

Wittgenstein, L. (1953). *Philosophical investigations*. New York, NY: Macmillan.

Wolpert, D. M. (1997). Computational approaches to motor control. *Trends in Cognitive Sciences, 1*, 209–216.

Young, K. S. (1998). Internet addiction: The emergence of a new clinical disorder. *Cyberpsychology & Behavior, 1*, 237–244.

Chapter 4
Rules of a Task

In Chap. 3, our focus was on actions and goals. In this chapter, we shift our focus to the social context of action, including expectations, rules, and norms. I will highlight the importance of rules in conducting an experiment. The topic of rule-violation is interesting, in part, because it helps shed light on the nature of rule-governed activity. A rule can be regarded as a solution to a problem that involves multiple agents (Lewis, 1969). Intersections have traffic lights, or stop signs, because multiple drivers with conflicting goals may arrive at an intersection at the same time. Rules for intersections enable multiple drivers to coordinate their movements. In general, therefore, rules enable multiple actors to coordinate their actions in a shared situation.

A rule implies the openness of a shared situation to multiple, potentially conflicting, perspectives/goals. Two drivers wish to continue moving along their respective paths. If all they have is their own subject-centered perspective, then they might rely on chance ("I will drive fast and hope to cross the intersection before the other car") or coercion ("I will shoot the other driver") or some other ad hoc strategy. Rules are constructed from a shared, world-centered perspective, in which a situation, such as the one involving multiple drivers at an intersection, can be assessed according to a shared set of standards. A rule implies the possibility of good (rule-following) and bad (rule-breaking) decisions, and it indicates the underlying wish to determine good and bad within a shared perspective.

4.1 Honest Participants

Imagine that you are playing a game with a group of friends. Participating in the game means having a shared understanding of the rules of the game; it means acting, in coordination with your friends, according to those rules (Lewis, 1969); it also means your friends have beliefs and expectations about your behavior in the game.

© Springer Nature Switzerland AG 2019
D. Gozli, *Experimental Psychology and Human Agency*,
https://doi.org/10.1007/978-3-030-20422-8_4

In addition to the particular rules and expectations attached to any specific game, the players bring a set of concepts into games. These concepts include turn-taking, competition, winning, losing, and the concept of a rule. Many such concepts are not discussed explicitly by the players. Rather, they are enacted, expressed through play. We now turn to one such concept, to which I refer as the *honest participant* concept.

The honest participant concept refers to a role, a mode of participation; there are many ways to describe this role. For one, an honest participant intends to follow the rules of the game. If she fails to follow a rule, the failure is assumed to be an unintended mistake. An honest participant can be relied on to correct others' mistakes when she detects them. As such, an honest participant might be relied on to instruct beginners of the game (Piaget, 1965). She will not take advantage of a beginner who does not have mastery of the rules. The actions of an honest participant are independent of the transparency of the game. As such, an honest participant is immune to a close scrutiny by other players, which is to say a close scrutiny would not violate the assumption of honesty. Typically, players of a game implicitly assume that everyone else occupies the role of an honest participant. This enables us to focus on other relevant features of the play, make predictions, such as "He will not deceive the novices," make inferences, and explain each other's behavior, such as "His rule-violation was an honest mistake."

Recall from our discussion in Chaps. 2 and 3, the correlations between basic-level goals (what is most *visible* in an action, and how the action tends to be described), and subordinate goals (movements, gestures, words, and whatever else embodies the basic-level goal), which are precisely why basic-level intentions seem transparent to us when we observe others. We could say, with regard to an honest participant, that she does not intentionally rely on the correlations to deceive her fellow participants.

The honest participant concept has a wide application beyond games. At a restaurant, we usually do not check whether or not our food is poisoned. At a hospital, we usually do not ask whether the doctor is financially tied to a particular drug company. At a movie theater, we usually do not consider whether or not the staff are trying to sell us tickets to unpopular movies. We implicitly rely on the assumption that the restaurant staff, the doctor, and the box office staff are honest participants in their respective activities. Of course, surprises occur, and some people take advantage of the honest participant concept to mislead us. Nonetheless, the concept is useful in narrowing down our attention and facilitating our interactions with others.

4.2 Cheaters

We return to our imagined game. Imagine that it is your turn now to play a move in the game. For whatever reason, you have decided to do something that deviates from the beliefs and expectations of the other players. Our concern is now with such deviations, their varieties, their significance, and ultimately their possible treatment in experimental psychology.

There are several ways you can deviate from your friends' expectations. Let us start with covert rule-violation or cheating. Our understanding of cheating is usually in terms of the combination of two motives: the motive to win and the motive to maintain the appearance of an honest participant. Someone who cheats wishes other players to continue to apply the concept of the honest participant when making sense of her behavior in the game. If successful, the cheater's behavior would be fully intelligible using the honest participant concept. Assuming that the cheater is knowingly cheating, the concept of honest participant is insufficient in the cheater's understanding of her own behavior in the game. A cheater's description of her own play, if truthful, must deviate from a description offered by the other players.

What is being pursued in cheating? Although a cheater may wish to win the game, winning is not the only possible goal. For example, someone might be more concerned with ending the game than with winning. Imagine a mother who is playing a game with her children. It is past the children's bedtime and she is tired. Their game can end if, and only if, someone wins. She decides to cheat not because she desires a crushing victory against the children, but because she wants to send the children to bed and have some rest. If she ends the game prematurely, announcing the end before they have a winner, she would be overtly violating the rules. The children might protest and refuse to end the game. Thus, she continues to follow a subset of rules, including the rule that says there must be a winner before a game can end, but she violates the rules that dictate how a player can win.

This example illustrates two points. First, cheating can be driven by superordinate goals outside the domain of the game, as in the case of a mother who wishes to send her children to bed and get some rest. This possibility prevents the cheater's behavior from being fully transparent to other players. Second, cheating complies with part of the rules and the goal of the game, for the sake of maintaining the appearance of an honest participant. A cheater aims to preserve his or her status as an honest participant.

What does a cheater sacrifice? The discrepancy between the cheater's self-understanding and how other players view his play is akin to the discrepancy between an illusionist and his audience. A successful illusionist maintains a discrepancy between the perceived state and the actual state of affairs. He has the audience believe they are seeing one set of objects (e.g., empty cups), while in fact they are presented with another set of objects (e.g., a ball hidden under each cup). To succeed in maintaining the illusion, the illusionist counts on a certain predictability in the behavior of the audience (Dennett, 1991, pp. 9–10; Gozli, 2017b). That is, maintaining the illusion requires the illusionist and the audience to stay within a finite range of activity. Cheating does not survive an exhaustive scrutiny; similarly, an illusion does not survive an exhaustive scrutiny. Upon sufficient scrutiny, a cheater will be deprived of the status of an honest participant. Thus, one outcome of cheating is becoming vulnerable to scrutiny, which limits the possible activities of the cheater.

If you read the memoir of Diederik Stapel (2016), in which he recounts how he forged scientific data, you might find a striking aspect of his story, namely his increasing isolation. The deeper he went into fabricating data, the more he deprived himself of social interaction. "I became more and more isolated," he wrote, "more and more detached from reality, because I couldn't be myself. I was accumulating secrets and had more and more to hide" (p. 128). He offers an example of the sacrifice involved in cheating.

When the true status of a cheater is revealed, as someone who has intentionally deviated from the rules, as someone who has misused his honest participant status, others might wish to exclude him from the game. Whatever the cheater has accomplished in the game must be discounted or, at least, re-examined. It is also possible that the cheater hurts the very stability of the game. He brings attention to the failure of trust among the participants, and to the fact that the game in its present form, including its rules, can be misused.

Before returning to our imagined game, I should note the association between cheating and two other factors. First, the decision to cheat might change based on whether the decision implicates one's character trait or identity. Second, the decision to cheat might change as a result of the similarity between cheating (lie) and non-cheating (truth). Let us turn to an empirical study for each point.

We noted, in Chap. 2, that an experience can vary with respect to self-reference. This applies to cheating, too. Someone who cheats can think about her activity with a relatively weak or relatively strong self-reference ("I cheated on this round" vs. "I am a cheater"), and this can influence the probability of cheating. In a study by Bryan, Adams, and Monin (2013), people were asked to think of a number between 1 and 10. They were then told that if their number is even, they would receive $5, and otherwise they would receive nothing. For half the participants, the researchers emphasized the participants' self/identity in the instruction (e.g., "we want to estimate the number of cheaters in this game" and "we cannot know if you are a cheater"). For the other half of the participants, emphasis was placed on the behavior of cheating (e.g., "we want to estimate the rate of cheating" and "we cannot know if you cheat"). The rate of reporting an even number suggested that some participants lied in the latter condition, but there was no sign of cheating in the former condition. The study suggests that we are less likely to cheat when our self/identity is implicated in the act of cheating.

One's identity might be regarded in terms of relatively superordinate goals (Chap. 3), which raises a question regarding the interpretation of Bryan et al.'s findings. Does self-reference per se reduce the likelihood of cheating, or is it framing of cheating behavior in terms of a relatively superordinate goal (an abstract guiding principle that exerts influence over many decisions over a large timescale)? We could investigate this line of thought by comparing the effect of "Don't be a cheater!" and "Don't be a cheater in this task!" Moreover, regardless of self-reference, we could compare cheating frequency in decisions that have short-term effects with decisions that have long-lasting effects on a given task. We could also change the status of participants within the same multi-player task (Caspar, Cleeremans, &

Haggard, 2018). If we raise the status of a participant within a goal hierarchy, will the participant be less likely to cheat?

The idea that people prefer not to cheat when cheating has long-term or superordinate consequences fits with the observation that, even when people decide to cheat, they tend to stay close to the truth. Put simply, it is preferable to tell a lie that is closer to the truth than a lie that is further from the truth. Hilbig and Hessler (2013) asked people to play a simple game that involved an opportunity to cheat. Each participant was given a target number (e.g., "4") and was asked to roll a die and report whether the outcome matched the target number. Since the die was inside a cup, it was visible only to the participant. Out of the 765 participants, 36% reported a match, which is 19% above what is expected with fair dice. We could, therefore, infer that about 19% of the participants lied about the outcome of their die roll. Interestingly, the probability of lying was not equal for all target numbers—it was lowest for target numbers "1" and "6" and highest for target numbers "3" and "4". Note that the average distance between the observed outcomes and the target outcome is highest for "1" and "6" (2.5) and lowest for "3" and "4" (1.5). Hilbig and Hessler reasoned that the probability of telling a lie decreases with the distance between the lie and the truth.

Other studies have suggested a possible association between reward and cheating frequency and individual differences in the tendency to cheat (Fischbacher & Föllmi-Heusi, 2013; Hilbig & Thielmann, 2017; Verschuere, Prati, & Houwer, 2009). I will discuss some of these later in this chapter. At this point, let us turn to another way of deviating from the rules of a game.

4.3 Rebels

Instead of cheating, you might overtly violate a rule. What can we say about someone who openly and blatantly violates a rule? We may call her a *rebel*. Whereas cheaters pretend to follow rules, rebels openly refuse to follow rules. A variety of goals might be pursued by a rebel. A rebel might wish to question the merit of a rule; she might be unhappy with the progress of the game; she might be trying to force other participants to improve the game in a way that requires changing the rules; she might have discovered a conflict between the rules and some other value. A child might find out she has no chance at winning against her older siblings. She refuses to play her turn. The rest of the family then discuss the matter and, assuming that they all wish to continue the game, they agree to give the child certain advantages so that she has a chance at winning. This would be an example of rebellion changing the game.

Other possible outcomes of rebellion include interrupting the game, surprising or upsetting other participants, and triggering inquiry or negotiation. Similar to cheating, rebellion is not a total abandonment of the game and its rules. Unlike cheating, rebelling is not only immune to scrutiny, it might even invite it. Rebellion does not produce a gap between the private and the public understanding of one's participation, it does not violate the assumption of an honest participant, it makes rules explicit, and it makes the agency of the rebel visible.

Aside from the domain of games, we can consider rebellion more generally. A rebel might wish to improve a domain of human activity, or communicate to others that important values are being ignored or violated because of some existing rule. Rebellion can involve personal risk. When Henry David Thoreau refused to pay taxes, as a way of objecting to slavery and the Mexican-American war, he was rebelling. When Rosa Parks refused to give up her bus seat, as a way of objecting to racial discrimination, she was rebelling. When women in Iran, the Girls of Enghelab Street, refused to wear the hijab in public, they were rebelling (Fig. 4.1).

The well-known experiments by Milgram (1963) brought the concept of rebellion into the lab. Participants had to choose between, on one hand, following the rules of the experiment and hurting someone, and on the other hand, refusing to follow the rules and not causing harm. The option to rebel was not offered to participants at the outset of the study, although it was anticipated by the experimenters as an option. Rebellion was held to express the values and agency of the participants. It was anticipated as a spontaneous act, not based on previous plans or agreement, but in response to the participants' evaluation of the situation. These features of Milgram's studies should be contrasted with studies in which participants violate rules based on experimenters' instructions (e.g., Pfister et al., 2016; Pfister, Wirth, Schwarz, Steinhauser, & Kunde, 2016).

At the same time, it is worth noting that Milgram did not report all of his experimental findings (Perry, 2013). There was, in particular, one condition in which the subjects of the experiment knew the person who would receive the electric shocks (a friend or a family member). This so-called "relationship" condition was not reported, possibly because of its ethical implication and also possibly because it did not fit with Milgram's overall conclusions about obedience to authority (Perry, 2013). In the relationship condition, 85% of the subjects rebelled against the instructions, which is higher than the rate in the reported conditions (usually <40%;

Fig. 4.1 A woman's objection to forced hijab in Iran. Source: *Daily Mail* (goo.gl/TnWTFQ)

Blass, 1999). As I argued above, controlling the discrepancy between the perceived state and the actual state of affairs, including when we selectively report experimental findings, is a feature of cheating.

4.4 Innovators

Cheaters and rebels are not the only ones who surprise us. People also deviate from expectation, without abandoning the rules. When someone innovates, we cannot usually accuse them of breaking a rule. Some people might find a particular instance of innovation objectionable, perhaps as a matter of taste, but the grounds for their objection are not the existing rules. An innovation could be a way to succeed that is more effective or efficient than common practice. When Richard Fosbury and Debbie Brill developed their style of high-jumping, which involved turning their back to the bar, they innovated.

We do not usually consider innovation as a type of rule-violation. We should consider innovation as a type of *norm*-violation (needless to say, not all norm-violations are innovative). Unlike rebels, innovators do not bring the collective activity to a halt. They tend to rejuvenate the activity by introducing some previously unrecognized potential. Innovation could occur through the introduction of a new set of conceptual tools. It could be through a new way to deal with old concepts. A philosopher is innovative when he or she discusses the compatibility between voluntary action and determinism (Dennett, 2004). When gestalt psychologists claimed that holistic structures were more fundamental and basic than their elementary building blocks, they were innovating (Köhler, 1947). When early psychoanalysts were exploring the seemingly mundane activity of talking freely, they were innovating (Freud & Breuer, 1895). Innovators reveal the value of paying attention to something that was previously ignored. Peter Thiel (2014) describes this in terms of discovering and sharing a secret. Using "secret" as a metaphor for innovation is apt because it implies that innovation occurs against the background of a community of agents who apply similar methods in pursuing similar goals. Innovation involves deviating from those common methods or goals.

What does an innovator sacrifice? The innovator sacrifices fitting in with the rest of the group. She sacrifices the comfort associated with following common and predictable patterns. She also risks failing, being wrong, in addition to the risk of being disliked. As a species, we tend to detect, follow, and enforce norms. We might be alarmed when we see someone deviate from norms. An innovator has to be willing to face negative judgment. As Thiel said:

> If your goal is to never make a mistake in your life, you shouldn't look for secrets. The prospect of being lonely but right—dedicating your life to something that no one else believes in—is already hard. The prospect of being lonely and wrong can be unbearable. (Thiel, 2014, p. 98)

I include a discussion of innovators, not because they are related to rules and rule-violation, but because innovation (violating a norm) should be distinguished from rule-violation. The distinction between norms and rules is highlighted when we consider the consequences of imitating cheaters, rebels, and innovators. Imitating a cheater can make you a cheater; imitating a rebel can make you a rebel; but, imitating an innovator does not make you an innovator. Even an innovator who imitates her own past is no longer an innovator. She is now adhering to a new norm that she has set for herself. Norms are established, for individuals and groups, by repetition and imitation. Innovation takes place against the background of stable norms.

To summarize, in our imagined game, we distinguished between three ways of violating the beliefs and expectations of the other players: covert violation of a rule, overt violation of (or rebellion against) a rule, and violation of a norm. The three types of violations are typically associated with different goals, outcomes, and risks. I described what may be pursued in each form of violation, as well as what may be sacrificed. If we exclude the social context of these actions, we would be unable to understand them.

4.5   Types of Participation within Goal Hierarchies

The performance of an honest participant, who has sufficient understanding of an activity, is an expression of a goal hierarchy. A goal hierarchy, which might appear static in our descriptions, is given dynamic expression through actions. In this section, I will go through the three types of "deviant" participation, this time with explicit reference to the concept of goal hierarchy.

In the case of cheating, we have a conflict between the person's relation to superordinate and subordinate levels of the hierarchy. The person wishes to adhere to the superordinate goals, such as "try to win", but cannot fulfill that goal with the appropriate set of subordinate goals, such as "playing each move according to the rules." Therefore, cheating involves the violation of subordinate goals. Because we have already associated "basic-level" goals with visibility and interpersonal interaction and because we have already associated cheating with pretense, it is easy to conclude that a cheater pretends to adhere to basic-level goals. Cheaters maintain their appearance as honest participants. We can repeat that idea with a reference to goal hierarchies: Cheating can go unnoticed when the cheater's subordinate intentions—the way in which a cheater enacts the basic-level intention—are not examined by others. If people are assured of not being scrutinized, as they are in many experimental studies of cheating, then they are more likely to cheat (Ting, 2018).

In the case of a rebel, basic-level goals are violated. A rebel targets relatively visible levels of the goal hierarchy, or she renders them visible through rebellion. In contrast to cheating, subordinate goals are less relevant. It does not matter that the woman in Fig. 4.1 is standing on a pillar or walking. We do not pay as much attention to these details as we do to her refusal to cover her hair. What is more important is that she, through her act of civil disobedience, is signaling a set of goals and values (individual liberty, women's rights) that are in conflict with the goal hierarchy enforced by the law. A rebel may wish to change or overthrow an existing hierarchy. It is also possible that she is driven by a goal hierarchy distinct from the one against which she is rebelling.

In the case of innovation, the person might be using an existing subordinate goal to achieve new superordinate goals or pursuing an existing superordinate goal with new subordinate goals. In the case of Richard Fosbury, and the "Fosbury flop", the goal of competing in high-jumping was not changed. Instead, the existing subordinate features of fulfilling the goal were replaced with more effective features.

Notice how an innovation can change the visible (basic-level) goals of an activity. Prior to seeing the Fosbury flop, people might have been paying attention merely to whether or not the bar was hit by the athlete. The athlete's orientation (facing vs. not-facing the bar) during the jump was a negligible subordinate goal. After seeing the innovative technique, however, orientation became the target of attention. In a game of chess, an innovative queen sacrifice can become temporarily more visible than the relatively superordinate goal of winning the game (cf. Bilalić, McLeod, & Gobet, 2008). Innovations remind us that the methods we use to pursue our basic-level goals can change.

There is no sharp boundary between rebellion and innovation, although I focused on what is distinct about each of them. A rebel's ultimate goal might be to preserve and improve a goal hierarchy, or to merge two hierarchies, which is to say a rebel's superordinate goal might be to innovate. On the other hand, an innovator who faces resistance from others might use rebellion as a subordinate strategy. By standing on a pillar, holding her veil in the form of a flag, the Iranian woman turned her stance into a visual symbol, which we could see an act of innovation in the service of her rebellion. She gave others a way of remembering and imitating her action. Thus, rebellion and innovation can be associated as parts of the same goal hierarchy.

4.6   Experimental Studies of Lying and Rule-Breaking

To be a part of an experiment, either as a research participant or as an experimenter, involves being part of a goal hierarchy. From the point of view of a researcher, when we think about superordinate goals of an experiment, we might think about gathering new knowledge, finding interesting results, or succeeding in one's career. Relatively lower on the hierarchy, we might think about testing particular hypotheses, collecting data, exploring a particular paradigm, or evaluating and prioritizing research questions. Basic-level intentions of researchers might include, in addition to the aforementioned, writing grant proposals, training students, conducting a study, writing a research paper, or conducting a pilot study. Subordinate goals include, for example, trouble-shooting an experiment, instructing or debriefing a group of participants, giving participants feedback during their performance (verbally or through automated messages of an experiment), or constructing a graph of the results.

What is salient to participants is different from what is salient to researchers. From the point of view of research participants, basic-level intentions might include understanding an experimenter's instructions, following those instructions, finding out what the experiment is testing, and completing the experiment as efficiently as possible. From the point of view of an experimenter, the participant's performance is described in terms of entirely different, often technical, basic-level goals. These include "categorizing visual objects", "associative learning", "orienting of attention", and "ignoring distractors" (especially in the case of subtle and barely visible distractors), which are most likely subordinate goals for a research participant. These are subordinate to the basic-level goal of completing the experiment and receiving compensation (course credit or money).

Recall the difference between a novice and an experienced chess player. A combination of moves would appear as a subordinate category for the novice player, while it would appear as a basic-level category for the experienced player. Similarly, details of performance, which serve as basic-level categories for experienced researchers, are likely to be subordinate categories for research participants. In a visual cueing experiment, participants might focus on responding correctly to a target, being more or less unaware of the presence of a transient cue, while the experimenters are aware of cue-target compatibility on the current trial, the previous trial, and the overall proportion of cue-target compatible trials across the experiment (Ansorge et al., 2017; Schumacher & Hazeltine, 2016). Participants notice their correct responses and mistakes, and perhaps think about how long the experiment will last, whereas the experimenter talks about the participant's "attention bias toward/against the cued location" and "conflict adaptation" over a sequence of trials.

The discrepancy between the two perspectives is especially important when rule-following and rule-violation are the target of investigation. The participants' task and the research findings are described primarily in terms of what is visible, what is basic-level, from the researchers' perspective. What is visible for research participants is, consequently, placed in the background, even though the investigation is framed in reference to the participants' intention to break a rule. We tend to ignore participants' compliance with the instructions. An action might be described as "following instructions" by the research participants, while described as "lying", "dishonest", or "rule-violating" by the experimenter (Foerster et al., 2018; Foerster, Wirth, Herbort, Kunde, & Pfister, 2017; Foerster, Wirth, Kunde, & Pfister, 2017; Pfister, Wirth, Schwarz, Foerster, et al., 2016; Pfister, Wirth, Schwarz, Steinhauser, & Kunde, 2016; Sartori, Agosta, Zogmaister, Ferrara, & Castiello, 2008; Van Bockstaele et al., 2012; Van Bockstaele, Wilhelm, Meijer, Debey, & Verschuere, 2015; Verschuere et al., 2009; Wirth, Foerster, Herbort, Kunde, & Pfister, 2018; Wirth, Pfister, Foerster, Huestegge, & Kunde, 2016).

Consider, for instance, the so-called lie effect, which refers to the observation that truthful responses are, on average, faster and more accurate, compared to untruthful responses (Sartori et al., 2008; Van Bockstaele et al., 2012, 2015). This effect is demonstrated in tasks that present participants with a series of yes/no questions. Participants are instructed to respond to each question, truthfully or untruthfully, either based on a rule at the beginning of an experimental block or based on transient cues provided throughout an experiment (Foerster et al., 2018; Foerster, Wirth, Herbort, et al., 2017; Foerster, Wirth, Kunde, & Pfister, 2017). Researchers have examined the modulating effect of the ratio of the untruthful to truthful responses (Van Bockstaele et al., 2012, 2015). They have also disentangled the "lie effect" from the cost of switching from a truthful response to an untruthful response (Debey, Liefooghe, De Houwer, & Verschuere, 2015). These experimental designs have been considered as potential methods of lie detection (Sartori et al., 2008; Van Bockstaele et al., 2015), although their validity and reliability have been questioned (Verschuere et al., 2009).

In everyday language, being truthful is an implied principle, on which we rely in understanding each other's behavior and speech (Grice, 1975), similar to how we rely on the "honest participant" principle in understanding the behavior of players in a game. The type of experiments that investigate the "lie effect" turns the assumption of truthfulness into an explicit rule. Moreover, they include a set of superordinate rules that determine when to apply and when to violate the truthfulness rule. We can call these superordinate rules "recursive rules" or "meta-rules" (rules about rules). By strategically neglecting those recursive rules, we can then conflate the meaning of "lying" in an experiment with its meaning in everyday language.

In Sect. 4.2, we noted that cheating/lying involves maintaining a discrepancy between appearance and reality, which makes it vulnerable to inspection. In the tasks used to measure the "lie effect", the experimenters are aware of which responses are "truthful" and which are "untruthful" because the two types of response are determined by the experimenters' recursive rules. As a result, participants do not need to hide any part of their performance or be concerned about vulnerability to inspection.

The reason for the "lie effect" (i.e., relative inefficiency of instructed untruthful responses, compared to instructed truthful responses), might be the unequal strength of the two goals corresponding to the two types of response: (1) making a truthful response and (2) making an untruthful response. The two goals must be maintained simultaneously, and it is reasonable to assume that the goal of making a truthful response is, for the most part, more dominant and more accessible, partly because of the role it plays outside the laboratory. It has been argued that the goal of responding untruthfully is identified by participants with reference to (and as a negation of) the goal of responding truthfully, which means activating the first goal requires activating both goals (Debey et al., 2015; Wirth et al., 2018). If this assumption holds, then even when truthful and untruthful responses are equally frequent, the goal of responding truthfully is activated twice as many times as the goal of responding untruthfully.

The dominance of one goal (responding truthfully) over another goal (responding untruthfully) could be reduced through various manipulations, such as repeated activation of the less dominant goal (Van Bockstaele et al., 2012; Wirth et al., 2018), reminding the participants (Van Bockstaele et al., 2015), association with reward (Hommel et al., 2017), and elaboration of the less dominant goal (Foerster, Wirth, Herbort, et al., 2017). For example, Van Bockstaele et al. (2015) included reminders at the beginning of each trial, using a cue ("TRUTH" / "LIE"), before the participant was presented with a yes/no question. They found that the reminders can ameliorate the disadvantage of untruthful responses. These results are consistent with the idea that the "lie effect" is not due to lying per se, but to the relative dominance and accessibility of one goal over another.

The role of goal dominance was examined by Foerster, Wirth, Herbort, et al. (2017), who varied dominance by means of elaboration. Their study had three phases. In the first phase, participants were instructed to perform a set of activities in a room (e.g., "drawing geometric figures on a piece of paper"). In the second phase, they were told that they were participating in an experiment designed to examine lying and lie-detection. To prepare to tell lies, they were asked to imagine alternative activities (e.g., "sending an email") that they could have done using the objects in the room but did not actually do. These alternative activities (alibis) would have to be confirmed in the case of the upcoming untruthful responses. In the third phase, they were presented with yes/no questions and were instructed to respond truthfully or untruthfully, based on the cues on each trial. The researchers found that untruthful responses, associated with an alibi, were more efficient than the truthful responses, associated with the participants' activities. Their results suggest, again, that the advantage of truthful responses over untruthful responses is due to the relative accessibility or dominance of the truthful responses, which could be manipulated via elaboration.

There might be some overlap between performing an untruthful response in these experimental tasks associated with the "lie effect" and behaving untruthfully in everyday situations, but there are also important differences. The meaning of lying depends on whether it involves deceiving another person, maintaining a discrepancy between reality and appearance, and becoming vulnerable to inspection. In most cases, when a participant is lying or violating a rule according to an experimenter's instruction, these actions do not involve any of these factors. Moreover, the behavioral differences associated with the "lie effect" can be attributed to the dominance and accessibility of one goal over the other, which renders the truthful/untruthful distinction superfluous as part of an explanation.

The relative dominance and accessibility of goals can change by changing their relationship to a given superordinate goal. The set of studies by Roland Pfister and colleagues is relevant to this point, as it examined the effect of describing an action as rule-violation (Pfister, Wirth, Schwarz, Foerster, et al., 2016; Pfister, Wirth, Schwarz, Steinhauser, & Kunde, 2016; Wirth et al., 2016). Instead of identifying two actions as merely two alternatives, consistent with a single superordinate goal, the researchers described one as "rule-following" and the other as "rule-breaking." In so doing, they included a rule-following goal (G_r) and a rule-breaking goal (not-G_r). Both goals, G_r and not-G_r, were embedded within the goal of completing the experiment (Fig. 4.2). Moreover, the latter goal (not-G_r) is a recursive rule that requires understanding, and reference to, G_r. Let us consider these studies in detail.

Participants in Pfister, Wirth, Schwarz, Steinhauser, and Kunde's (2016) experiments had to move a cursor from a starting position to one of two target positions. The correct target position was determined on each trial by a combination of recursive rules that were described differently across participants. Participants were divided into two groups, both of which received a set of nominal task rules. Those in the "reversal" group were instructed to occasionally perform the task in a manner

Fig. 4.2 A rule can be recursively related to task instructions such that the superordinate rule of completing an experiment requires breaking a basic-level rule

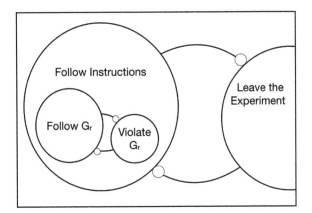

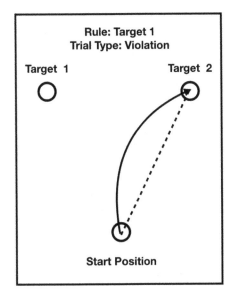 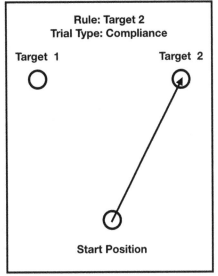

Fig. 4.3 Shows the basic features of Pfister, Wirth, Schwarz, Steinhauser, and Kunde's (2016) method, in which participants performed a movement task, from a starting position to one of the target positions. Target position was determined by the combination of the rule and trial type (whether the rule was supposed to be violated or followed). The left panel shows a trial in which the rule dictated moving to Target 1 and it had to be broken. The right panel shows a trial in which the rule dictated moving to Target 2 and it had to be followed

that reverse the task rules. By contrast, participants in the "violation" group were instructed to occasionally violate the task rules (Fig. 4.3). Thus, the correct target position was determined by (a) the nominal rules and (b) whether the rules had to be followed or reversed/violated (trial type). Several dependent measures were used to test the efficiency (initiation and completion of the movements) and the trajectory of movements (systematic deviation from a straight target-directed path).

Movements on reversal/violation trials were, on average, performed more slowly and their path deviated toward the target associated with the rule. Importantly, these performance costs were higher in the "violation" group, who presumably framed the task in terms of a single set of rules, than in the "reversal" group, who were more likely to frame the task in terms of two sets of rules. Pfister, Wirth, Schwarz, Steinhauser, and Kunde (2016) interpreted the performance cost in the "violation" trials as the cognitive conflict inherent in rule-violation. To break a rule, they reasoned, one has to first consider the rule and then, and only then, deviate from it.

In Experiment 1 of Pfister, Wirth, Schwarz, Steinhauser, and Kunde (2016), participants chose, at the beginning of each trial, either to follow or to reverse/violate the task rule. "Violation" was chosen, on average, in about 40% of the trials, whereas "reversal" was chosen in about 48% of the trials. That is to say, labeling an action as a "violation" reduced its frequency, compared with labeling it as a "reversal." Furthermore, frequency of violation was associated with the cost of rule-violation, suggesting that the cost was higher for people who violated the rule less frequently. We should note that about 5% of trials, as well as the immediately following trials, were excluded from analysis because participants had not acted in accordance with their choice (e.g., they had decided to follow the rule, at the onset of the trial, but had instead violated it). Thus, when we consider the entire set of rules, and their recursive relationship, only trials in compliance with the instructions were included in the investigation.

In Experiment 2, participants were instructed, at the beginning of each trial, to follow (75% of trials) or reverse/violate (25%) the rules. This design ensured that the difference between the two groups was not because of the relatively less frequent voluntary violations, compared to reversals (Pfister, Wirth, Schwarz, Steinhauser, & Kunde, 2016). The results showed a higher cost of rule-violation, relative to rule-reversal, even when the two were equally frequent. About 4% of the trials, as well as the immediately following trials, were excluded because participants did not follow/reverse/violate the rule according to the experimenters' instructions (i.e., when they violated the recursive rules). These exclusions is necessary if we wish to study the performance attributes of deliberate rule-violation, and if we wish to clearly distinguish violations from rule-following and from mistakes. On the other hand, maintaining such a degree of control over participants' task, to the point that even their rule-violation represents compliance with task instruction, creates a gap between what we would ordinarily call rule-violation (e.g., cheating in a game) and what is under laboratory investigation in these studies.

In a similar study, Pfister, Wirth, Schwarz, Foerster, et al. (2016) used a virtual "egg-factory" game. Playing this game involves a left/right key-press response every time a chicken appears on the left/right side of the screen. The left/right key brings a cup on the left/right side, and the rule is to place the cup under the chicken. At the beginning of each trial, participants reported whether they intended to follow the factory rule. Next, they had to execute their decision upon the appearance of the chicken. With respect to the initial decision, participants chose to follow the rule at an above-chance level, in about 63% of the trials. With respect to performing the decision, participants were faster to follow than to violate the rule. Event-related potentials, locked to the onset of the chicken, showed a delayed and attenuated posterior P300 on violation trials. Pfister, Wirth, Schwarz, Foerster, et al. (2016) interpreted this finding as the cost of translating the stimulus (chicken) to a response (key-press) in the violation condition. The findings are also consistent with a relative dominance and accessibility of the goal of following the rule, compared with the goal of breaking the rule.

Extending the above findings, later studies asked whether a history of rule-violation can reduce its cost. Wirth et al. (2016, 2018) found that repetition, over two consecutive trials, does not eliminate the cost of rule-violation. If, however, rule-violation is performed frequently (in 75% of the trials) *and* recently (in the immediately preceding trial), then its cost can be eliminated. What we ought to consider, in this case, is that a frequent action in a given context can result in the generation of its own task, which would make it directly accessible—without the mediation of the nominal task rules—and as salient as the original task. When an action is performed frequently in a given context, we tend to treat it as a norm (Tworek & Cimpian, 2016). The explicit instructions, which distinguished compliance and rule-breaking, might have been undermined through the frequent demand to break the rules (Ting, 2018). As experimenters, we might continue to refer to the two conditions as "rule-following" and "rule-breaking", but that does not mean the participants agree with our distinction. The meaning assigned to the two actions from the participants' perspective might change because of their ratio.

Another study about the role of rule-violation history was conducted by Jusyte et al. (2017), who compared participants with a criminal record to a control group without a criminal record. They reasoned that a history of rule-breaking might be associated with the reduced dominance of rule-following goals, relative to rule-violating goals, rendering rule-breaking more accessible and efficient in participants with a history of rule-breaking. The results from the control group replicated the previous findings: Rule-violation was less efficient (delayed initiation and longer movement time) than rule-following, and the path of rule-violating movements curved toward the path of rule-following (Fig. 4.3). For the "unlawful" participants, the path of rule-violating movement did not show the same curve toward rule-following, which might indicate that a history of breaking rules is associated with reduced conflict associated with rule-violation.

The findings of Jusyte et al. (2017) was based on an elegant hypothesis and fit other studies on the effect of practice in the efficiency of lying (Van Bockstaele et al., 2012) and rule-violation (Wirth et al., 2018). But the presence of a strong hypothesis and the agreement with similar research should not stop us from considering an important alternative interpretation. If we examine the time it took for participants to initiate and complete the movements, we find similar patterns in "unlawful" and control participants—both were relatively more efficient to follow than to break the rules. Moreover, the time to initiate movements was, overall, *delayed* in the "unlawful" group. Why is this delay crucial? Because there is substantial literature on the interaction between the timing of movements and the way movements curve toward distracting locations (Al-Aidroos & Pratt, 2010; Buetti & Kerzel, 2009; Gozli, Chow, Chasteen, & Pratt, 2013; Tipper, Howard, & Jackson,

1997; Welsh & Elliott, 2004). When a non-target location is salient, and participants do not have enough time to inhibit that location, movements curve toward the salient non-target location. If, however, participants have enough time to inhibit the salient non-target, movements begin to curve *away* from the non-target location. The extra time taken by the "unlawful" participants might have eliminated the movement curvatures, which means the between-group difference in movement trajectories might have been an artifact of the difference in their initiation time.

What is under investigation in the studies by Pfister, Wirth, Jusyte et al., reviewed in this section? Participants do not deviate from the instructions (they would be excluded if they do), they are not vulnerable to scrutiny, and they do not find new subordinate methods of achieving the superordinate goal of completing the experiment. Therefore, what is being investigated is neither cheating nor innovation. If there is innovation involved, and I believe there is, it is the *experimenters'* innovation, who set up tasks with recursive rules. The cost of following a recursive rule can then be reduced upon sufficient repetition (Wirth et al., 2018), or upon adopting a strategy (Verschuere et al., 2009). These studies are informative and interesting, not with respect to rule-violation per se, but with respect to recursive rules, unequal dominance and accessibility of competing goals, the effects of frequency, recency, and so forth.

4.7   Experimental Studies of Cheating

Despite my earlier skepticism (Gozli, 2017a), I have been persuaded that cheating behavior can, in principle, be studied experimentally (Pfister, Wirth, Weller, Foerster, & Schwarz, 2019; Ting, 2018). Perhaps it would be more accurate to say that, rather than discovering cheating behavior, we can guide participants toward cheating with certain design manipulations. For example, Fischbacher and Föllmi-Heusi (2013) asked each participant to roll a die and report the outcome. To set up the condition for cheating, (1) different outcomes were associated with different rewards, and (2) only the participant herself could see the outcome. Researchers reassured participants of the secrecy of their choice and their anonymity as research participants. Although this method does not allow tracking honesty at the level of a single trial, it does allow estimating the frequency of cheating over many trials (Hilbig & Hessler, 2013; Hilbig & Thielmann, 2017). What can we find using such a method? We can find, rather unsurprisingly, that *some people act dishonestly sometimes*. Moving beyond this crude statement is difficult, because many factors influence the decision to lie, including prior experience with the game (Fischbacher & Föllmi-Heusi, 2013), the amount of reward (Hilbig & Thielmann, 2017), or participants' interpretation of the task (Bryan et al., 2013).

What we find in an experiment is, in part, determined by the design of the experiment (Gozli, 2017a). Consider Hilbig and Thielmann's (2017) Experiment 1, in which the reward of cheating in a die-roll game increased over time. The authors found that they could divide the participants into three categories: those who did not lie ("incorruptibles"), those who lied after the reward of lying passed a certain threshold ("corruptibles"), and those who lied regardless of the reward ("brazen liars"). In their Experiment 2, however, with a change of design, they managed to find a fourth category, "small sinners", including those who lied only to gain small rewards. What about other possible categories? What if, for instance, we introduce two kinds of reward: *monetary* reward and *social* reward (e.g., the ability to dictate another person's action). Doing so would open another dimension. Perhaps "corruptibles" could now be divided into "corruptible money-seekers" and "corruptible power-seekers". The point is that how we structure an experiment determines what we can find. If our participants receive money for their cheating behavior, then we can describe their motivation and their frequency of cheating with reference to money.

With regard to the "corruptibles" and the "small sinners", we can perhaps more confidently say that their performance depended on money because their cheating behavior changed as a result of changing the amount of monetary reward. With regard to the "brazen liars", we cannot decipher motives so easily. We cannot uniquely associate what they do with money, because their behavior is not sensitive to changes in the amount of money. Toward the end of the article, Hilbig and Thielmann (2017) wrote, "the brazen liars have a price and it is very low" (p. 22), neglecting the possibility that a subset of participants might have had motives other than money. Perhaps a subset of the "brazen liars" simply wanted to see what would happen if they kept cheating (explorative rule-breaking); perhaps some of them detected the experimenters' subtle invitation to cheat and, thus, their performance should be considered as a type of compliance; perhaps some of them wanted to show their superiority over the experimenter, by showing that they were not following the rules (rebellious rule-breaking). In short, their behavior was ambiguous and open to multiple interpretations. What appears to narrow down the scope of interpretation is a set of already-determined factors included in the design of the experiments (e.g., monetary reward).

4.8   Implications

The behavior of participants is guided within an experiment because hypothesis testing requires the outcome of an experiment to be within a predetermined range. Experiments on cheating involve guiding participants' decisions toward cheating, by emphasizing the secrecy of the choices and reassuring them that they will not be scrutinized. In these experiments, researchers can keep track of cheating frequency over a large number of choices and at the group level (Fischbacher & Föllmi-Heusi, 2013; Hilbig & Hessler, 2013; Hilbig & Thielmann, 2017).

Experiments that compare performance features of rule-following and rule-violation actions also guide participants' behavior using a two-layered task, which include recursive rules (rules about rules, Fig. 4.2). The nominal, or basic-level, rule is followed/broken at different times, based on the superordinate rules. Comparing performance features in these experiments requires us to unambiguously categorize a behavior as "compliance" or "violation". These requirements preclude, for the most part, the study of cheating. What counts as rule-violation is already predetermined by the experimenters, which also precludes the study of rebellion or innovation. Because so much is already determined by the experimenters, what is left to be investigated are details of performance, such as the timing to initiate and complete a movement, the path and curvature of movements, the effect of repetition, recency, and so forth (Pfister et al., 2019; Wirth et al., 2016, 2018).

At the beginning of this chapter, I noted that rules can help coordinate behavior in situations where multiple goals, or multiple agents, could be in conflict (Lewis, 1969). In experimental psychology, certain uniformities are required in the behavior of participants. To participate in an experiment, people enter contexts of meaning that are constructed, and communicated to them, by experimenters (Gozli, 2017a). Without such a shared context of meaning, the meaning of behavior would not be so transparent. We might forget that this transparency is maintained by the experimenters' effort (Smedslund, 2009). We might think of the participants' behavior without keeping in mind the experimental setting. Neglecting the presence of the experimenters and, more generally, the social nature of an experiment might lead researchers to claim, for example, that "we were able to isolate cognitive mechanisms that process (non-) conformity even in *non-social* settings" (Wirth et al., 2016, p. 850, emphasis added).

Part of what makes rule-violation interesting is that it highlights the presence of rules and the nature of rule-governed behavior. In our present discussion, this means a focus on the rules that govern the behavior of participants in an experiment. In this chapter, we reviewed how experimenters study "lying" or "rule-breaking" by setting up tasks with recursive rules, requiring participants to monitor basic-level rules and occasionally break them, fulfilling the superordinate rule in order to complete an experiment. These observations reveal that the experimental task itself is partly out of focus. Once we bring the task into focus, we recognize that the meaning of concepts, such as lying and rule-breaking, in experimental research must be distinguished from how we use these concepts in everyday language. We also notice the differences between performance in a pre-specified task and psychologically interesting concepts such as honesty, cheating, rebellion, and innovation (Giorgi, 2013).

References

Al-Aidroos, N., & Pratt, J. (2010). Top-down control in time and space: Evidence from saccadic latencies and trajectories. *Visual Cognition, 18*(1), 26–49.

Ansorge, U., Gozli, D. G., & Goller, F. (2017). Investigating the contribution of task and response repetitions to the sequential modulations of attentional cueing effects. *Psychological Research* (Online first).

Bilalić, M., McLeod, P., & Gobet, F. (2008). Why good thoughts block better ones: The mechanism of the pernicious Einstellung (set) effect. *Cognition, 108*(3), 652–661.

Blass, T. (1999). The Milgram paradigm after 35 years: Some things we now know about obedience to authority. *Journal of Applied Social Psychology, 29*, 955–978.

Bryan, C. J., Adams, G. S., & Monin, B. (2013). When cheating would make you a cheater: Implicating the self prevents unethical behavior. *Journal of Experimental Psychology: General, 142*(4), 1001–1005.

Buetti, S., & Kerzel, D. (2009). Conflicts during response selection affect response programming: Reactions toward the source of stimulation. *Journal of Experimental Psychology: Human Perception and Performance, 35*(3), 816–834.

Caspar, E. A., Cleeremans, A., & Haggard, P. (2018). Only giving orders? An experimental study of the sense of agency when giving or receiving commands. *PLoS One, 13*(9), e0204027.

Debey, E., Liefooghe, B., De Houwer, J., & Verschuere, B. (2015). Lie, truth, lie: The role of task switching in a deception context. *Psychological Research, 79*(3), 478–488.

Dennett, D. C. (1991). *Consciousness explained.* New York, NY: Little, Brown.

Dennett, D. C. (2004). *Freedom Evolves.* London, UK: Penguin.

Fischbacher, U., & Föllmi-Heusi, F. (2013). Lies in disguise—An experimental study on cheating. *Journal of the European Economic Association, 11*(3), 525–547.

Foerster, A., Pfister, R., Schmidts, C., Dignath, D., Wirth, R., & Kunde, W. (2018). Focused cognitive control in dishonesty: Evidence for predominantly transient conflict adaptation. *Journal of Experimental Psychology: Human Perception and Performance, 44*(4), 578–602.

Foerster, A., Wirth, R., Herbort, O., Kunde, W., & Pfister, R. (2017). Lying upside-down: Alibis reverse cognitive burdens of dishonesty. *Journal of Experimental Psychology: Applied, 23*(3), 301–319.

Foerster, A., Wirth, R., Kunde, W., & Pfister, R. (2017). The dishonest mind set in sequence. *Psychological Research, 81*, 878–899.

Freud, S., & Breuer, J. (1895). *Studies in hysteria.* London, UK: Penguin.

Giorgi, A. (2013). Reflections on the status and direction of psychology: An external historical perspective. *Journal of Phenomenological Psychology, 44*(2), 244–261.

Gozli, D. G. (2017a). Behaviour versus performance: The veiled commitment of experimental psychology. *Theory & Psychology, 27*, 741–758.

Gozli, D. G. (2017b). The lackluster role of misperceptions in an enactivist paradigm. *Constructivist Foundations, 13*, 133–135.

Gozli, D. G., Chow, A., Chasteen, A. L., & Pratt, J. (2013). Valence and vertical space: Saccade trajectory deviations reveal metaphorical spatial activation. *Visual Cognition, 21*, 628–646.

Grice, H. P. (1975). Logic and conversation. In P. Cole & J. Morgan (Eds.), *Syntax and semantics* (Vol. 3). Cambridge, MA: Academic.

Hilbig, B. E., & Hessler, C. M. (2013). What lies beneath: How the distance between truth and lie drives dishonesty. *Journal of Experimental Social Psychology, 49*(2), 263–266.

Hilbig, B. E., & Thielmann, I. (2017). Does everyone have a price? On the role of payoff magnitude for ethical decision making. *Cognition, 163*, 15–25.

Hommel, B., Lippelt, D. P., Gurbuz, E., & Pfister, R. (2017). Contributions of expected sensory and affective action effects to action selection and performance: Evidence from forced- and free-choice tasks. *Psychonomic Bulletin & Review, 24*(3), 821–827.

Jusyte, A., Pfister, R., Mayer, S. V., Schwarz, K. A., Wirth, R., Kunde, W., & Schönenberg, M. (2017). Smooth criminal: Convicted rule-breakers show reduced cognitive conflict during deliberate rule violations. *Psychological Research, 81*, 939–946.

Köhler, W. (1947). *Gestalt psychology.* New York, NY: Liveright Publishing.

Lewis, D. (1969). *Convention.* Cambridge, MA: Harvard University Press.

Milgram, S. (1963). Behavioral study of obedience. *Journal of Abnormal and Social Psychology, 67*, 371–378.

Perry, G. (2013). *Behind the shock machine: The untold story of the notorious Milgram psychology experiments.* New York, NY: The New Press.

Pfister, R., Wirth, R., Schwarz, K., Steinhauser, M., & Kunde, W. (2016). Burdens of nonconformity: Motor execution reveals cognitive conflict during deliberate rule violations. *Cognition, 147*, 93–99.

Pfister, R., Wirth, R., Schwarz, K. A., Foerster, A., Steinhauser, M., & Kunde, W. (2016). The electrophysiological signature of deliberate rule violations. *Psychophysiology, 53*, 1870–1877.

Pfister, R., Wirth, R., Weller, L., Foerster, A., & Schwarz, K. A. (2019). Taking shortcuts: Cognitive conflict during motivated rule-breaking. *Journal of Economic Psychology, 71*, 138–147.

Piaget, J. (1965). *The moral judgment of the child*. New York, NY: Free Press.

Sartori, G., Agosta, S., Zogmaister, C., Ferrara, S. D., & Castiello, U. (2008). How to accurately detect autobiographical events. *Psychological Science, 19*(8), 772–780.

Schumacher, E. H., & Hazeltine, E. (2016). Hierarchical task representation: Task files and response selection. *Current Directions in Psychological Science, 25*(6), 449–454.

Smedslund, J. (2009). The mismatch between current research methods and the nature of psychological phenomena: What researchers must learn from practitioners. *Theory & Psychology, 19*(6), 778–794.

Stapel, D. (2016). *Faking science: A true story of academic fraud* (N. J. L. Brown, Trans.). https://errorstatistics.files.wordpress.com/2014/12/fakingscience-20141214.pdf

Thiel, P. (2014). *Zero to one: Notes on startups, or how to build the future*. London, UK: Penguin.

Ting, C. (2018). The feedback loop of rule-breaking: Experimental evidence. *The Social Science Journal* (Online first).

Tipper, S. P., Howard, L. A., & Jackson, S. R. (1997). Selective reaching to grasp: Evidence for distractor interference effects. *Visual Cognition, 4*(1), 1–38.

Tworek, C. M., & Cimpian, A. (2016). Why do people tend to infer "ought" from "is"? The role of biases in explanation. *Psychological Science, 27*(8), 1109–1122.

Van Bockstaele, B., Verschuere, B., Moens, T., Suchotzki, K., Debey, E., & Spruyt, A. (2012). Learning to lie: Effects of practice on the cognitive cost of lying. *Frontiers in Psychology, 3*, 526.

Van Bockstaele, B., Wilhelm, C., Meijer, E., Debey, E., & Verschuere, B. (2015). When deception becomes easy: The effects of task switching and goal neglect on the truth proportion effect. *Frontiers in Psychology, 6*, 1666.

Verschuere, B., Prati, V., & Houwer, J. D. (2009). Cheating the lie detector: Faking in the autobiographical implicit association test. *Psychological Science, 20*(4), 410–413.

Welsh, T. N., & Elliott, D. (2004). Movement trajectories in the presence of a distracting stimulus: Evidence for a response activation model of selective reaching. *The Quarterly Journal of Experimental Psychology Section A, 57*(6), 1031–1057.

Wirth, R., Foerster, A., Herbort, O., Kunde, W., & Pfister, R. (2018). This is how to be a rule breaker. *Advances in Cognitive Psychology, 14*, 21–37.

Wirth, R., Pfister, R., Foerster, A., Huestegge, L., & Kunde, W. (2016). Pushing the rules: Effects and aftereffects of deliberate rule violations. *Psychological Research, 80*, 838–852.

Chapter 5
What Is a Task?

Let us take a step back from the question "What is a task?" and begin with a different question: What are the possible reasons behind the goal of understanding a task? We might want to be able *count* the number of tasks someone is performing. Counting would be easier if we know what we are counting. We might want to distinguish a task (e.g., setting up the chess pieces on the board) from a non-task (e.g., spilling tea all over the chessboard). We might want to be able to identify when two tasks are equivalent, or to distinguish *differences among tasks* from *different ways of performing* the same task. The goal of this chapter is to clarify the nature of experimental tasks and their role in the production of knowledge. I will rely on the work of other experimental psychologists who have made similar attempts to explicate the concept of task (Dreisbach, 2012; Hazeltine & Schumacher, 2016; Künzell et al., 2017; Schumacher & Hazeltine, 2016), although my overarching aim is different from theirs.

Despite their central role in experimental psychology, tasks themselves are not usually the focus of attention and investigation (De Houwer, 2011). Why are tasks important to experimental psychologists? There are several reasons. First, certain lines of research, such as research on "task-switching," require some understanding of tasks (Kiesel et al., 2010; Künzell et al., 2017). In these cases, having a working definition—which makes minimal commitment to necessary and sufficient properties of tasks—is unavoidable. Second, some experimental findings are difficult to explain without an explicit reference to tasks (Dreisbach, 2012; Hazeltine & Schumacher, 2016). In these cases, a change in performance has to be explained with reference to task properties, thus illuminating properties of experimental tasks. In both cases, explicit discussion of tasks constitutes a step toward better understanding experimental design and data. When we shift our attention to the tasks themselves (e.g., cognitive control task), and away from what the tasks are designed to investigate (e.g., cognitive control), it is often for the purpose of returning to the target of investigation with a clearer understanding of the role played by our method of investigation (Gozli, 2017; Valsiner, 2017).

© Springer Nature Switzerland AG 2019
D. Gozli, *Experimental Psychology and Human Agency*,
https://doi.org/10.1007/978-3-030-20422-8_5

In our present discussion, "What is a task?" is also related to other questions, including "What are the necessary conditions for experimental psychology?" or "How do those conditions shape the knowledge produced by experimental research?" Although it might be impossible to define a task in terms of necessary and sufficient properties, we can adopt a style of noticing, as much as possible, properties that can be associated with experimental tasks, without committing to a final definition (Strawson, 1992). To do so, we shall continue to explore, as we did in the preceding chapters, both through ordinary language and through experimental research.

Imagine two friends playing a game. The first (P1) says, "A bus, carrying ten passengers, arrives at a stop. Two passengers exit the bus and three enter. At the next stop, two passengers exit and four enter…." After going through several more stops, P1 asks, "How many times did the bus stop?" The second person (P2), who was keeping track of the number of passengers on the bus, cannot give the correct answer. We can think about the discrepancy between what P2 was doing and what she was supposed to do to answer P1's question as a discrepancy between two tasks.

In order to know the current number of passengers, P2 prepares and enacts a set of subordinate goals: remembering the most recent number of passengers, selectively attending to information about passengers exiting and entering the bus, updating the number of passengers by adding the entries and subtracting the exits. By the time she is about to hear the description of the fourth or fifth bus stop, she is prepared to perform specific operations (adding and subtracting) on a subset of the incoming information (number of passengers), while ignoring those parts of P1's description that she regards as irrelevant. In a more technical language, when you adopt a task, "your response dispositions are reconfigured such that your intended action is usually triggered by the stimulus condition specified in the instruction or intention" (Goschke, 2000, p. 331).

Before the bus game, P2 was capable of selecting and ignoring parts of a verbal description, just as she was capable of performing additions and subtractions. Performing the bus game demands that these operations are organized ("reconfigured") in response to the ongoing descriptions of the bus, in order to fulfill a superordinate goal. It is required, in general terms, that "new couplings between stimuli and action schemata be set into readiness, that skills be recombined into new behavioral sequences, and that a specific mode of interaction between various processing systems be established" (ibid, pp. 331–332).

We should note that P1 is also performing a task, which involves misdirecting her friend's attention toward a different task (keeping track of the number of passengers on the bus) and away from P1's intended task (keeping track of the number of stops). To increase the likelihood of misdirection, P1 has to be careful about the emphasis she places on the parts of her description. P1's goal might be to hear her friend say "I don't know!" seeing her surprise, or teaching her friend about selective attention. If P2 already knows about this game, or if she identifies the task correctly, then P1 cannot fulfill these goals.

To begin with a minimal working definition, therefore, we could say a task involves "performing some specified mental operation or action in response to stimulus input" (Kiesel et al., 2010, p. 850). Adding and subtracting numbers in response to hearing about passengers entering and exiting the bus. Counting the number of passes in a basketball game is another example (Simons & Chabris, 1999). We ought to supplement the note about performing specific operations with a note about the superordinate goals that necessitate those operations. Adding and subtracting the number of passengers serves the goal of keeping track of the current number of passengers, which itself serves the goal of solving the puzzle or playing one's part well in the game (Künzell et al., 2017; Schumacher & Hazeltine, 2016). Similarly, counting the number of passes in a basketball game serves the goal of knowing the total number of passes, which itself serves the goal of participating well in an experiment.

Performing a task involves attention to parts of the situation. Counting the number of passes in the basketball game means ignoring other details about the scene, such as the location and number of players, or a "gorilla" walking into the scene (Bilalić, McLeod, & Gobet, 2008; Simons & Chabris, 1999). While counting, a left-to-right pass is equivalent to a right-to-left pass. Similarly, passes made early in the task are equivalent to those at the end of the task. A pass, regardless of its direction, force, or time, counts as one. We could describe this feature of tasks as abstraction. Our abstractions are imposed, not only on stimuli but also on behavior. Imagine, for instance, two people (P2 and P3) both listening to the bus game. One (P2) is keeping track of the number of passengers on the bus, and the other (P3) is keeping track of the number of sentences uttered by P1. In so far as we are concerned with performance in this task, P2 and P3's performances are equivalent—they both fail to fulfill the requirement of the task.

The term "performance", which is closely related to task, also conveys the idea of abstraction. It is useful to distinguish two different senses in which we use the term performance. We use it, first, to refer to *types* of behavior. In this sense, what we mean by performance is rule-governed behavior, or behavior that can be evaluated according to some set of standards. Examples of performance-as-type include running in a marathon, playing J. S. Bach's famous chaconne in D minor on the violin, or participating in an experiment that measures reaction time.

A second use of "performance" has to do with an *attribute* of behavior, usually referring to a measurable attribute, such as frequency, force, speed of initiation, movement duration, and trajectory (Bergner, 2016; Ossorio, 2006). These attributes are not meaningful on their own. Compare "a hand motion that transports an object from one location to another" with "handing the scalpel to the surgeon" or with "fulfilling one's task as a surgical assistant". What makes performance-as-attribute (hand movements; time of completion) meaningful and open to evaluation is performance-as-type (assisting a surgeon; running a marathon). Once we know the type of behavior, then we can focus on the standards of evaluating attributes of behavior. In this sense, experimental psychology relies on recognized types of behavior (performance in the first sense), and the corresponding standards of inclusion and evaluation, according to which some attributes of behavior can be evaluated (performance in the second sense), while other attributes can be ignored (Gozli, 2017; Smedslund, 2009).

Our emphasis has been on selective attention or abstraction imposed by a task, which gives the impression that a task only removes parts of the situation from view. To demonstrate why that is not the case, think of a surgical assistant, who responds to single words uttered by a surgeon ("scalpel," "scissors," "forceps," etc.). Out of their context, it would be unclear what one should do in response to these words. In their appropriate context, however, each word triggers an action that has already been prepared for by the assistant (Goschke, 2000; Hommel, 2000; Wittgenstein, 1953). "Scalpel" is short for "hand me the scalpel". The assistant's knowledge specifies the meaning of single words. A task, therefore, involves adding meaning to stimuli. Similar remarks can be said about the bus game (hearing the number of passengers exiting the bus can trigger the operation of "subtraction") and the basketball game (seeing a pass triggers the operation "increment by 1"). By giving meaning to otherwise-ambiguous events, tasks facilitate communication and interaction.

5.1   Basic-Level Intentions and Social Transfer of Tasks

It is useful to think of tasks in relation to basic-level goals (Chap. 3). Basic-level goals are easily identified, compared to their associated superordinate or subordinate goals. Tasks seem to have this feature, too. If I ask a research participant what she did in an experiment, she might tell me, "I watched a video and counted the number of passes in a basketball game," but is less likely to say, "I fulfilled the role of being a good research participant" (participant's superordinate goal), or "I kept looking at the basketball as it was passed among the players, maintained and updated the total number of passes in memory" (participant's subordinate goal), or "I participated in an experiment about inattentional blindness" (researcher's superordinate goal). Thus, our description of a task corresponds to some basic-level goal that is itself embedded in a broader context of goals and activities.

As we discussed in Chap. 3, basic-level goals play a role in communication. In determining how to interact with people, knowing their superordinate goal ("being a good father") is not as helpful as knowing their basic-level goal ("picking up children from school"). If I know Jim is on his way to pick up his children from school, I will keep our conversation brief. Knowing that he wants to be a good father, on the other hand, would not have an immediate effect on our interaction. Thus, identifying a task in terms of a basic-level goal facilitates interaction by being more easily communicable than relatively super/subordinate goals.

The two attributes—ease of identification and communication—are particularly salient in the tasks used in experimental research. Experimental tasks are, as a matter of design, overly specific and unambiguous (Wachtel, 1973). They usually involve setting clear boundaries around what should be done. Consequently, they set clear standards for what counts as task performance, excluding any behavior that fails to meet those standards. This is the case even in experiments that are designed to study deviation from rule-governed or normative behavior, such as dishonesty and rule-violation. Even in these experiments, participants follow specific instructions, such as "In this condition, provide *untruthful* responses to the questions" (Chap. 4). When participants do not follow instructions, we cannot categorize their behavior with respect to experimental conditions ("dishonesty" or "rule-violation") (Gozli, 2017).

What about behavior outside the lab? When are we inclined to describe an activity as a task? For example, is having lunch with your friends a task? We are not inclined to use the word "task" in this case, partly because having lunch with friends can correspond to a wide range of acceptable behavior. It would seem awkward to describe people as succeeding or failing at having lunch with their friends. Someone might fail to remember a lunch appointment, or fail to find the meeting location, but our concern is with having lunch per se and not with remembering or navigating. Showing up for the lunch meeting does involve a narrow range of acceptable behavior (being in the right place at the right time), but the behavior during lunch, assuming that one is among friends, is not subject to strict standards of evaluation, success, or failure.

What if someone instructs you to have lunch with your friends? A man might be instructed by his therapist to do so. In that case, having lunch reflects his cooperation with the therapist, and it is an expression of their shared goal. The shared goal gives them a set of criteria for evaluating a lunch meeting. If, for instance, the goal is to have more positive social interactions, then the lunch meetings will be evaluated based on the interactions during lunch. If the man gets into a hostile argument with his friends during the lunch, then the lunch counts as a "failure" with respect to their goal. Similarly, if the goal is to have a better diet by eating with friends who eat healthy food, then the lunch meetings will be evaluated based on the improvement in the man's choice of food.

In the same way, asking for directions might not seem like a task. If you ask a stranger for directions and he does not help you, either because he is in a rush or because he is also unfamiliar with the area, we would not be inclined to call your interaction a "failure". These possible outcomes are within the acceptable range of such interactions. By contrast, when a language teacher instructs her students to go out and ask strangers for direction—in order to practice talking to native speakers of the language—it turns the activity into a task. Let us pause and point to features that seem to give us the inclination to call something a task.

- A task is identified more readily in terms of a basic-level goal ("taking one's children to school") than the associated superordinate and subordinate goals, even though the latter goals cannot be separated from the task.
- By virtue of its association to a basic-level goal, a task plays a role in communication and interaction (knowing someone's task can guide our interactions).
- There is an identifiable superordinate goal that the task is fulfilling (e.g., being a good father, increasing one's positive social interactions, improving one's diet, practicing speaking in a second language).
- There is an identifiable set of standards for evaluating whether the task is successful (e.g., ensuring that the children arrive at the school on time, quality of

social interaction, choice of food, effective communication). These standards tell us where to look to evaluate performance in the task.

The above features are consistent with the observation that a task is usually *assigned* to someone (Künzell et al., 2017). That does not mean that one cannot assign a task to oneself. It means that the relation between a task and its associated goal has priority over the person who performs the task. For example, it would seem plausible that the therapist has assigned the "therapeutic lunch" to other clients before or will assign it to future clients, by virtue of the presumed relation between the task and its effects. The task is an expression of a belief that can apply to other clients. Similarly, the language teacher has assigned the "asking for directions" task to other students or will assign it to future students, by virtue of a presumed relation between interacting with native speakers and improving one's language skills. Following these observations, we can continue our list of task features:

• Justification for the task is provided or presupposed by the person assigning the task.
• The person performing the task can be replaced by someone else because what is being expressed is a regular and predictable relation between performing the task and fulfilling a superordinate goal (Künzell et al., 2017; Wachtel, 1973).

Recognizing the role of someone who assigns a task and distinguishing it from the role of performing the task discourages us from thinking that a task is fully "represented" inside the mind of a single individual. Rather than thinking of the task as in the mind of the person, it is more accurate to think of the person performing the task as part of a larger whole, a goal hierarchy, of which the person is partially aware (Noë, 2009, 2015). This idea will become clearer when we discuss the organization of shared tasks. For now, it suffices to recognize that the two roles of assigning and performing a task involve different perspectives on the task. The roles pay attention to different parts of a task. The person assigning the task (e.g., therapist) is concerned with relatively superordinate goals (e.g., improving the client's social life or diet) and is likely indifferent to subordinate goals. On the other hand, the person performing the task is concerned with relatively subordinate goals (engaging in small talk during lunch, choosing from the menu) and might be indifferent or even suspicious of the superordinate goals. The two perspectives meet at the level of a shared basic-level goal, which enables the common description of the task.

Therefore, tasks do not necessarily belong to a single person. They are embedded in contexts that include relationships, interactions, and shared goals. Think of a father and his task of taking his son to school. He can inform his wife, who is rushing to go to work and is worried about their son's transportation; he can inform his son, who does not want to go to school; he can inform the police officer, who stops him for going over the speed limit; he can inform his boss, who notices his late arrival at work. The task plays different roles in each interaction, based on the goals of the interaction partners. From the wife's perspective, the task indicates that the man is a responsible father. For his son, it might indicate that he is an overly controlling father. For the police officer and his boss, the task might offer a poor excuse for his fast driving and lateness for work. In each case, communicating that he is taking his son to school serves the function of bringing his perspective into alignment with theirs.

Similar to everyday tasks, the tasks used in experimental psychology can also be viewed from different perspectives. Consider a graduate student instructing a research participant on a task. If you ask the graduate student, she might describe the task with reference to her doctoral thesis or a particular hypothesis. If you ask the student's advisor, she might describe the task with reference to a research project or a research grant. Some supervisors might not care about the details of the experiments conducted in their lab, as long as their lab is active. If you ask the research participant, she might say she is fulfilling a course requirement to receive the credit. Because of their different overarching concerns, the three perspectives highlight different ways of looking at the task. The graduate student's perspective reveals the place of the task in a line of research with its associated history, debates, methods, data, and theories; the supervisor's perspective reveals the place of the task in the context of her academic career with its associated political and power relations; the participants' perspective reveals the place of the task in the education-research institute and its requirements from students. Each perspective highlights a subset of what is associated with the experimental task and brings into view a different hierarchy of goals, including a different basic-level goal. Completion of the task is, at the same time, a move toward fulfilling the participant's goals (receiving course credit, taking an item off her to-do list), the graduate student's goals (collecting data, making progress on her thesis, testing a hypothesis), and the supervisor's goals (maintaining an active lab).

In this chapter, we are interested in the perspectives within experimental psychology, including how researchers characterize experimental tasks. For this reason, we continue our discussion with the help of recent contributions from experimental psychologists.

5.2   Goal-Directed Schema

Schumacher and Hazeltine (2016) proposed that we understand a task by comparing it to a memory schema. Like a schema, a task is an abstraction; unlike a schema, they argued, a task is goal-directed. Something does not seem right about this comparison. Can we really assume that a memory schema is goal-free? Since a memory schema is an abstraction, the question arises as to what has guided the abstraction. What has determined which parts of the situation ought to be regarded as relevant, and included, in the schema?

There are ways of addressing this problem without abandoning Schumacher and Hazeltine's proposal. First, rather than denying the presence of goals in memory schemas, perhaps the authors' comparison is a matter of goals being either in the foreground or in the background. According to this view, goals are implicit in memory schemas, whereas they become explicit in tasks. A second way to address the problem has to do with variability of goals. A memory schema can be attached to many possible goals. Without denying that a schema must be attached to some goal(s), we can recognize the possibility of associating different goals with the same schema. I can have a schema of a lecture hall, which can be used for the purpose of giving a lecture, attending a lecture, walking around the lecture hall, and leaving the lecture hall. The goals can change, without altering the lecture-hall schema. Thus, I believe Schumacher and Hazeltine's (2016) distinction between a schema and a task is not about whether goals are present or absent but about whether or not goals are specified and stable. When I use the lecture-hall schema—which can be associated with different goals—for the specific purpose of delivering a lecture, I am engaging in a task.

I must note that the schema vs. task comparison was not presented as the core of Schumacher and Hazeltine's (2016) argument. It appeared on the final page where the authors concluded: a task "is more than a memory schema […], which essentially is an abstract affordance representation dissociated from the goals and intentions of the organism" (Schumacher & Hazeltine, 2016, p. 453; see also, Hazeltine & Schumacher, 2016). You might wonder, then, why I am focusing on an apparently minor part of their proposal. The reason has to do with the risk of identifying a task with a single goal. If we think that a schema is goal-free ("dissociated from goals and intentions"), we might forget that the creation of a schema depends on goals. It is true that one and the same schema can be associated with different goals, but possible variation in goals should not be taken as absence of goals. Similarly, as we move from a schema to a task, identifying a basic-level goal might further encourage ignoring other goals, including superordinate and subordinate goals associated with the task (Chap. 3).

We have already pointed out that basic-level goals depend on the perspective we adopt for a given activity, which leads to the question: What are the basic-level goals of an experimental task? We are now talking about basic-level goals that are the topic of discussion when researchers communicate with each other. What goals attached to a memory schema might, in Schumacher and Hazeltine's proposal, turn the schema into a task? These goals are captured in the term "response selection". Indeed, response selection was central in Hazeltine and Schumacher's (2016) argument, described as "operation of producing a response to a stimulus according to the current task goals" (p. 196).

The crucial role of a memory schema is that it helps us avoid thinking of response selection merely in terms of the stimulus. Recall Kiesel et al.'s (2010, p. 850) minimal definition, according to which a task involves "performing some specified mental operation or action in response to stimulus input", or Goschke (2000), who pointed out that once we adopt a task an action can be triggered by its designated stimulus. When we describe a task in these terms, we might focus only on stimulus–response associations in the process of response selection. It turns out, however, that response selection, in general, cannot be adequately explained without considering *all* possible responses in a task and the way those responses are *organized* in relation to each other, and in relation to their corresponding stimuli (Adam, Hommel, & Umiltà, 2003, 2005; Hazeltine & Schumacher, 2016). To illustrate this point with an example, consider having to respond to the presentation of a blue square (by saying aloud the word "square") in the following tasks:

- Task A: stimulus set consists of four possible objects: a blue square, a green square, a blue diamond, or a green diamond (Fig. 5.1). Participants respond based on the stimulus *shape*, with "square" (for square) and "diamond" (for diamond).
- Task B: stimulus set is identical to that of Task A. In this task, participants respond based on the stimulus *color*, with "square" (blue) and "diamond" (green).
- Task C: stimulus set is identical to that of Tasks A and B. In this task, responses are determined based on shape-color conjunction (Fig. 5.2). If the object is a blue square, participants respond with "square"; if it is a green diamond, they respond with "diamond"; otherwise, the participants withhold from responding.

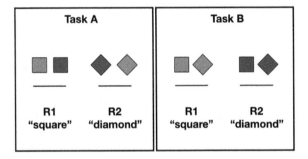

Fig. 5.1 Two tasks with 4-to-2 stimulus–response mapping, both of which require responding to a blue square by saying aloud "square". Task A involves responding to shape, ignoring color, and Task B involves responding to color, ignoring stimulus shape. Grouping stimulus–response events is easier in Task A compared to Task B, due to the similarity of features *within* each stimulus–response event and the dissimilarity of features *between* events

Fig. 5.2 A go/no-go discrimination task, with four stimuli and two "go" responses. Correct response is determined based on color-shape conjunction

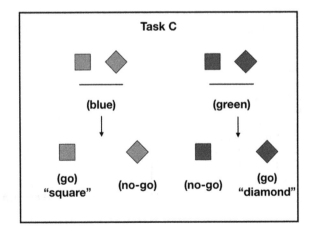

Let us first compare Tasks A and B. Even though the same response ("square") is selected when seeing a blue square, in both tasks, we would expect faster performance, on average, in Task A compared to Task B (Fitts & Seeger, 1953; Hommel, Müsseler, Aschersleben, & Prinz, 2001; Kornblum, Hasbroucq, & Osman, 1990). In Task A, stimulus features easily form groups with their corresponding responses. That is not only because of the similarity *within* each stimulus–response event but also because of the dissimilarity *between* stimulus–response events (e.g., blue diamond → "diamond" and green square → "square"). By contrast, in Task B, there are dissimilarities within events that should be bound together according to the task rules, and there are similarities between stimulus–response events that should be kept separate (e.g., blue diamond → "square" and green square → "diamond") (Prinz, 2018).

Task C has additional properties, which enable us to pay a closer attention to how stimulus–response events might be organization in tasks. We can think about the organization of Task C in various ways. We might think of it as a two-step task, the combination of (1) a color (or shape) discrimination task and (2) a go/no-go task. It is conceivable that, after seeing a visual object, participants evaluate the color of the object, and then evaluate whether or not they should make a response (Fig. 5.2). In that case, the grouping by color is stronger than, and has primacy over, grouping by response type. Alternatively, it is conceivable that grouping based on response type (go vs. no-go) is stronger than, and has primacy over, grouping by color (Fig. 5.3). In that case, participants first evaluate whether or not the current trial is a "go" trial, and then they evaluate whether the stimulus is a blue square or a green diamond.

How could we know whether the actual organization (or schema) of Task C matches Fig. 5.2 or Fig. 5.3? One way to find out is by comparing the benefit, in performance speed and accuracy, of (a) knowing in advance the stimulus color and (b) knowing in advance whether the trial will be a "go" trial. If the benefit of the former is greater than the benefit of the latter, it confirms that the stimulus–response events are primarily grouped based on stimulus color. If, on the other hand, the benefit of knowing response type ("go" vs. "no-go") is larger, it confirms that

Fig. 5.3 A different organization of Task C (compare with Fig. 5.2), according to which stimulus–response events are grouped primarily based on response type (go vs. no-go), and then based on discrimination task, with four stimuli and two "go" responses. Correct response is determined based on color-shape conjunction

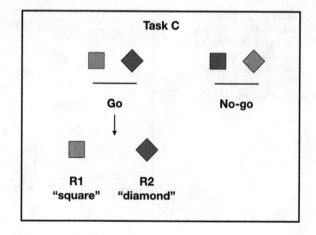

Fig. 5.4 The left panel shows a set of dots that can be grouped based on their various features. Identifying the dots based on their position in the upper and lower halves provides a stronger basis for grouping than identifying their colors

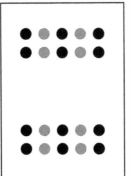
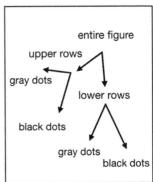

stimulus–response events are primarily grouped based on response type. If this idea seems a little confusing, it might help to describe it with reference to Fig. 5.4. On the left panel, we see a group of 20 circles, with various features that we could use to group them. What does it mean, in this case, to say that grouping the upper and lower halves is stronger, and has primacy over, say, grouping based on color? It means, among other things, that it is easier to pay attention only to the upper columns, ignoring the lower columns, than to pay attention to the black dots, ignoring the gray dots. Knowing in advance that one has to pick one circle from the upper rows more effectively excludes half of the circles, by relying on the most salient basis for grouping the dots. By contrast, it would be less helpful to know in advance that one has to pick one of the black dots. Paying attention to the black dots, which are linked to the gray dots on the basis of the most salient grouping feature, is less effective in excluding half of the circles. Applying this idea to Task C helps clarify the role of grouping: If responses are primarily grouped on the basis of response type (go vs. no-go), then prior knowledge of response type would be more effective in ruling out half of the possible events in the task.

Understanding that stimulus–response events are organized in groups, and that some features serve as a relatively more dominant basis for grouping, is key in understanding tasks. This idea, which has its roots in gestalt psychology, was discussed in two key contributions by Adam et al. (2003, 2005) and is crucial in understanding the main points in the discussions by Hazeltine and Schumacher (2016) and Schumacher and Hazeltine (2016). To clarify the idea of grouping and organization of stimulus–response events, let us see how it applies to other tasks.

Using the same stimulus set in Tasks A–C, we can design a task in which the relevant stimulus dimension (shape vs. color) switches from trial to trial (Fig. 5.5). We might give participants two response keys, each key corresponding to a color and a shape. Thus, we have two (sub)tasks, four stimuli, and two motor actions (Kiesel et al., 2010; Meiran, 1996; Monsell, 2003). Figure 5.6 shows a possible organization of this type of task with respect to an associated goal hierarchy (left panel) and with respect to a "decision tree" (right panel). The decision tree is not meant to suggest sequential processing. That is, I am not claiming that stimulus features cannot be selected or processed before a task is selected. The figure simply

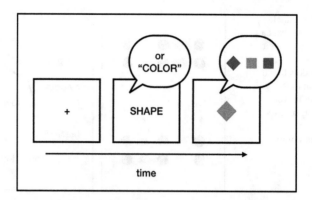

Fig. 5.5 Schematic view of a task in which the relevant stimulus dimension can switch from trial to trial ("task-switching"). Participants first view a cue ("SHAPE" or "COLOR"), indicating the relevant stimulus dimension, and then they see the stimulus. Correct response is determined based on the combination of the cue and the stimulus

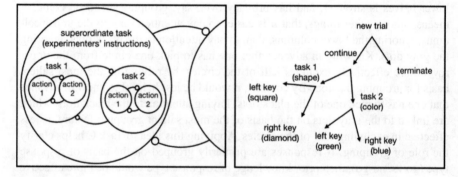

Fig. 5.6 Organization of goals (left panel) and decisions (right panel) in task-switching

indicates relative primacy and salience of grouping on the basis of stimulus–response events (Task 1, respond to shape, vs. Task 2, respond to color) over grouping by shape, grouping by color, or grouping by response key.

In the research literature on task-switching, the term "task" describes stimulus–response events at a particular level of the goal hierarchy, which is to say tasks are regarded as the basic-level category in the hierarchy of goals (Fig. 5.6). Because this is so common, I find it unavoidable to sometimes use "task" in this sense, particularly when discussing task-switching research, although I have done my best to make this clear. At the same time, my overarching view is that a task corresponds to multiple levels of a goal hierarchy. It is maintained by the superordinate goal, "follow the experimenters' instructions," and it is enacted by the subordinate goals, such as "press the left key!" (Dreisbach, 2012; Gozli & Dolcini, 2018; Hazeltine & Schumacher, 2016; Künzell et al., 2017; Schumacher & Hazeltine, 2016). Such a view makes it easier to think about tasks, not only in terms of stimulus–response associations but also in terms of *how stimulus–response associations are organized in relation to each other.*

Assuming that a task is organized in a particular manner leads to certain predictions, including predictions about the effect of repetition of task features. In choice-reaction time tasks, in which the relevant stimulus dimension does not vary from trial to trial, repetition is associated with performance improvement (Hyman, 1953; Logan, 1990). What happens if, in the task depicted in Figs. 5.5 and 5.6, a motor action is repeated from trial n to trial $n + 1$? In general, repetition of a motor response (subordinate goal) is beneficial only when the task (the relatively superordinate goal) is also repeated (Hommel, 1998; Kleinsorge & Heuer, 1999; Meiran, 1996). In the case of the task depicted in Figs. 5.5 and 5.6, repetition of a motor action can be costly if one responds to shape on trial n and to color on trial $n + 1$. Thus, by examining the benefit of repeating and switching various task features, we can infer how the features are organized in a hierarchy.

Another prediction, which I briefly mentioned before, has to do with the effect of prior knowledge about the upcoming response selection. Consider, for instance, a task used by Rosenbaum (1980). Participants place their left and right index fingers on the starting positions (Fig. 5.7). The task is to move one index finger to a target location, defined as the square that is illuminated on that trial. Each response can be described in terms of three binary dimensions: hand (left vs. right), direction (forward vs. backward), and distance (near vs. far). Prior to seeing a target, participants were sometimes given prior knowledge of one of the response dimensions. They could be informed, for instance, that the response is going to be made with the right hand, or that it would involve moving forward, or that it would be made to a near target. Which type of prior knowledge would result in fastest response selection? Rosenbaum found that advance knowledge of the responding hand was more advantageous than knowing the response direction, which was in turn more advantageous

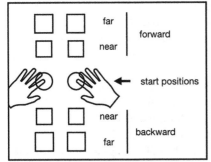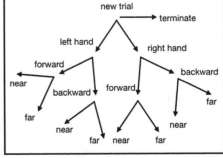

Fig. 5.7 The left panel shows a target-directed reaching task (Rosenbaum, 1980). Eight possible responses are defined in terms of three binary features: left/right, forward/backward, and near/far. The right panel depicts the grouping of the responses based on the response feature. This is meant to indicate, not sequential processing, but that grouping of responses based on hand/side is more dominant than grouping based on movement direction, which in turn is more dominant than grouping based on hand-to-target distance

than knowing the hand-to-target distance. Hence, to reduce the time it takes to initiate a response by means of a single cue, it would be most effective to have advance knowledge of the responding hand and least effective to have advance knowledge of hand-to-target distance.

According to one interpretation of Rosenbaum's (1980) findings, when selecting a response, selection of hand is more time-consuming, compared to selection of direction, which in turn is more time-consuming than selection of distance. According to this view, advance knowledge of hand is more effective in reducing response time because hand selection is the most time-consuming component of response selection. Once the most time-consuming component of selection is completed, specifying the remaining attributes of the movement would take less time. There is, however, another way to interpret the findings.

The alternative way to interpret the findings has to do with the organization and grouping of the eight possible responses with respect to each other (Adam et al., 2003; Reeve & Proctor, 1984). Recall how the circles in Fig. 5.4 are grouped first and foremost with respect to upper vs. lower halves, which does not in any way imply that selecting the upper half in the Fig. 5.4 is the most time-consuming component of selecting a circle. Similarly, the findings of Rosenbaum (1980) suggest that the eight possible responses (Fig. 5.7) are grouped first and foremost with respect to hand/side (left vs. right). Next, within each side, the possible responses are grouped with respect to direction (forward vs. backward). Why is advance knowledge of hand relatively more effective in reducing response time? Because it is more effective to eliminate half of the possible responses on the basis of the most dominant response-grouping feature. In the decision tree shown in Fig. 5.7 (right panel), this is reflected by placing the dimension at the highest (superordinate) level of response specification. By contrast, knowing that the target would be at a "near" location is less effective in eliminating half of the responses, as it refers to response grouping at the subordinate level. In this case, resolving the competition among the superordinate groups must await the target.

The hierarchical organization of responses depicted in Fig. 5.7 cannot be described in terms of stimulus–response associations alone. This is why Schumacher and Hazeltine (2016) evoked the idea of memory schema. They rightly pointed out the limitation of an approach based on simple (unmediated) stimulus–response associations. Response selection emerges as the result of resolving competition among multiple levels of a goal hierarchy, which means selection of a given response feature has to be considered with regard to the place of the response within the task organization and in relation to other responses. Hazeltine and Schumacher (2016) reviewed a wide range of evidence to support the importance of understanding task organization. Rather than repeating their examples here, let us apply the idea of task organization to the domain of *joint* task performance.

In a series of studies, Yamaguchi, Wall, and Hommel (2017a, 2017b, 2018, 2019) asked whether we are sensitive to tasks performed by our co-actors. More specifically, using two-person tasks, they asked whether observing a co-actor would cause the observer to follow along and covertly adopt the co-actor's task. To answer this question, we must have a method for detecting sensitivity to the other's task

performance. Yamaguchi et al. (2017b) used variants of the task-switching paradigm (Fig. 5.5). For the sake of simplicity, I have presented modified versions of
their tasks in Fig. 5.8. In one experiment (Fig. 5.8, top row), each participant was
given two response keys (left key and right key). On each trial, a cue signaled the
relevant stimulus dimension (color *vs.* shape), and another cue signaled the actor
who should perform the task (person 1 *vs.* person 2). Thus, a response was considered correct if it was based on the relevant stimulus dimension and performed by the
correct actor.

A task-switching cost was defined as the reduction in performance efficiency
(increased response time and/or error rate) when the relevant stimulus dimension
was switched (color → shape or shape → color), compared to when it was repeated
(color → color or shape → shape). Yamaguchi et al. (2017b) reasoned that the task-
switching cost on trial $n + 1$ can be taken as an indication that one was engaged with
the task on trial n. Crucially, if the response on trial n was performed by one's co-
actor, *and* a switch cost is observed, it would indicate that observing one's co-actor
can cause one to also engage in the task. The authors, however, found a task-
switching cost only when the same actor had performed on the previous trial. No
switch cost was found when the actors switched from trial n to trial $n + 1$. Thus,
task-switching cost did not survive actor-switching, which the authors interpreted as
evidence against shared task representation.

To demonstrate that task-switching cost can be observed in such a complex task,
with multiple cues and switches along multiple dimensions, the authors conducted
a control experiment, in which participants performed the task alone (Fig. 5.8,

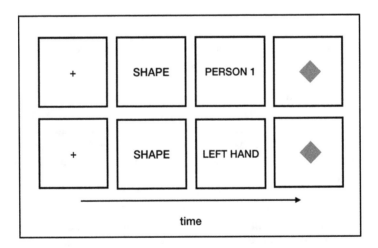

Fig. 5.8 A task-switching procedure, in which one response is performed upon seeing a target
stimulus (here, the diamond). Prior to seeing the target, a cue indicates the relevant stimulus
dimension ("task": shape *vs.* color). In the joint version of the task (top row), another cue indicates
who should perform the response (person 1 *vs.* person 2), while in the individual version of the
task, a cue indicates which hand (left hand *vs.* right hand) should respond (based on Yamaguchi
et al., 2017b)

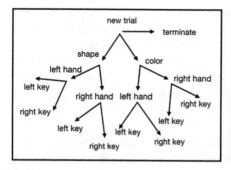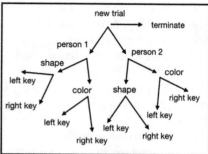

Fig. 5.9 A possible organization of tasks used by Yamaguchi et al. (2017b), which can explain why switch costs were observed with individual performers (hand-switching) but not with joint performers (person-switching)

bottom row). In addition to switching the relevant stimulus dimension, participants sometimes had to switch hands. Each hand was linked to a pair of keys, and the keys on the left side were equivalent to the keys on the right side. Participants had to wait for a cue that signaled the relevant stimulus dimension (color *vs.* shape) and another cue that signaled the responding hand (left *vs.* right). A switch cost (color → shape or shape → color) was found when participants performed the two consecutive responses with the same hand *and* when they switched hands. In short, task-switching cost survived hand-switching. Yamaguchi et al. (2017b) reasoned that the absence of task-switching, when the actors switch, suggests that one does not represent a co-actor's task (cf. Sebanz, Knoblich, & Prinz, 2003, 2005).

I suggest we should interpret Yamaguchi et al. (2017b) findings, not in reference to task representation, but in reference to task organization. An important difference between the joint version and the individual version of the task (Fig. 5.8) is about whether task selection (color *vs.* shape) is superordinate or subordinate, in relation to the other to-be-selected feature (hand/actor) (Fig. 5.9). In joint performance, actor selection must have been superordinate to task selection, which is why repeating the task (color → color) was not beneficial if the actors switch. By contrast, in individual performance, hand selection must have been subordinate to task selection, which can explain why task-switching cost survived hand-switching. Both observations can be taken to confirm the same principle: repeating a subordinate task feature does not benefit performance if a superordinate feature is switched (Badre, 2008; Kleinsorge & Heuer, 1999).

There are important differences in an interpretation based on task *representation* and an interpretation based on task *organization*. Representational accounts regard tasks as internal to the actor, whereas organizational accounts consider tasks to be larger wholes in which actors take part. Actors' internal (neural) organization, readiness to perform particular responses, and their sensitivity to stimulus set are parts of a larger organization that goes beyond the actor's body (Morris, 2005; Noë, 2009). Representational accounts imply an either/or style of thinking with regard to engagement with tasks. We either represent our co-actor's task, or we do not. By

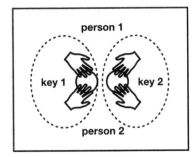 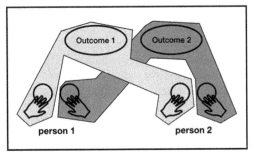

Fig. 5.10 Possible ways to make response selection (key 1 *vs.* key 2) superordinate to actor selection. The left panel shows an arrangement in which co-actors share two keys, such that grouping based on key becomes more salient than grouping based on actor (dashed lines indicate such grouping-by-key). The right panel shows a conceptually similar design, in which responses are grouped on the basis of common outcome (Janczyk & Kunde, 2014; Yamaguchi et al., 2017a). This arrangement can turn response selection (outcome 1 *vs.* outcome 2) into a more salient basis for grouping than actor selection (shaded areas indicate grouping-by-outcome)

contrast, organizational accounts ask, "What part of the task (the larger whole) is selectively attended to by the actors?".

Other findings by Yamaguchi et al. confirm the interpretation based on task organization. In particular, Yamaguchi et al. (2019) modified their joint task, such that each actor was linked to one of the two responding keys. In this arrangement, each actor was responsible for one shape feature (e.g., square) and one color feature (e.g., blue), while the other actor was responsible for the remaining two features. In this experiment, a task-switching cost was found both with and without switching actors. This is unsurprising in light of the present interpretation. If we link actor 1 with the left key and actor 2 with the right key, then actor selection will coincide—and form a group—with response selection (a subordinate feature). Consequently, task selection (color *vs.* shape) rises to a level that is superordinate, relative to actor selection, and task-switching cost can be obtained despite switching actors.

It is also possible to give the same two response keys ("left" and "right") to two co-actors (Fig. 5.10, left panel). With this arrangement, both actors would place their hands on the same two keys. For the moment, let us forget about possible stimuli and just think about the four possible responses, distinguished based on the two actors and the two keys. Which of the two features would be a more salient basis for grouping the responses? While actors tend to be the more salient basis for grouping responses when they have their separate keys (Yamaguchi et al., 2017b), it is possible that sharing the keys would make key selection superordinate to actor selection. If so, the actors might be more sensitive to each other's response, compared with when they respond with separate keys, which would be reflected in shared task-switching cost. While, to the best of my knowledge, this particular design has not been tried, a conceptually similar design was implemented by Yamaguchi et al. (2017a). In that study, the responding keys were not physically shared, but they were made equivalent by producing the same *outcome* (Fig. 5.10, right panel; see also, Elsner & Hommel, 2001; Janczyk & Kunde,

2014). In such a condition, pressing a left key, by either actor, would produce the same sensory outcome (e.g., a high-pitched tone), and pressing the right key, by either actor, would produce another sensory outcome (e.g., a low-pitched tone). Using such a design, Yamaguchi et al. (2017a) found task-switching cost with and without switching actors, which is consistent with an account based on hierarchical task organization, and the idea that the transfer of switching cost from one actor to another depends on the status of actor selection in the hierarchy.

For an analogy from the world outside the lab, imagine a husband and wife preparing breakfast together, one of them making toast and the other making coffee. Are they sharing a task? Of course, they are jointly engaged with the (superordinate) task of preparing breakfast, but that does not require them to perform the same actions. Jointly preparing breakfast requires coordination and cooperation, which involves staying out of each other's way, and letting go of a subtask once one knows that the other is taking care of it (Sellaro, Treccani, & Cubelli, 2018). This is far from a perfect analogy for laboratory task-sharing, since in this scenario the couple can spontaneously organize their actions, dividing the subtasks, and they can improvise with respect to the subordinate goals (adding cream to coffee, or spreading butter on toast). Nonetheless, the example illustrates the point that task-sharing is not about two co-actors sharing common "internal representations" but rather about taking part in an organized whole that includes the actors and their shared environment (Hibberd, 2014; Noë, 2009, 2015).

Regardless of whether it is performed jointly or alone, a task simplifies the situation. It guides the actors' expectation and prepares them to react to pre-specified stimuli (Goschke, 2000; Hommel, 2000). Engaging in a task that is sufficiently stable and well-specified also involves knowing what part of the situation can be ignored. This inattention could be either because of the irrelevance of a particular event or feature to the task (Eitam, Shoval, & Yeshurun, 2015; Eitam, Yeshurun, & Hassan, 2013) or because a co-actor is dealing with it (Sellaro et al., 2018). To elaborate our discussion of tasks in relation to ignoring irrelevant parts of the situation, we turn to another important contribution by Gesine Dreisbach (2012).

5.3   Persistence, Flexibility, and Defense Against Distractors

Dreisbach's (2012) contribution is important, in part, because she examined the nature of tasks with respect to their costs and benefits. Before outlining her main claims, we should note what is being compared and contrasted with tasks. When something is *not* a task, what is it? Similar to Schumacher and Hazeltine (2016), Dreisbach compared and contrasted tasks with an unorganized, ungrouped, or non-hierarchical set of stimulus–response pairs. It may not be fair to call such sets completely unorganized because stimulus–response pairs, although they may not be organized along a multi-level hierarchy, are nonetheless organized along a single level. To clarify this point, we shall borrow an example from the author (Dreisbach, 2012; Dreisbach, Goschke, & Haider, 2007).

Imagine having to respond to a sequence of stimuli, using two keys, such that the left key responds to any member of the first stimulus set, {3, 7, K, M}, and the right key responds to any member of the second stimulus set, {4, 8, A, E} (Dreisbach, 2012, p. 228; Dreisbach et al., 2007). In this task, there are two superordinate event types. Each event type corresponds to one stimulus set and one response key. Let us call this organization of stimulus–response events the *single-layered organization*. Now, let us modify the description of this task, and regard it in terms of additional features. Notice that the stimulus sets consist of numbers, {3, 4, 7, 8}, and letters, {A, E, K, M}. The numbers are odd or even number, {{3, 7}, {4, 8}}, and the letters into vowels or consonants, {{A, E}, {K, M}}. With these features in mind, we now re-organize the task, based on stimulus type (number *vs.* letter), and then within-group features (odd *vs.* even; vowel *vs.* consonant). Let us call this organization of events the *two-layered organization*.

The difference between the two task organizations has to do with the grouping and layers of stimulus–response events, not with which better represents tasks. If we compare the two organizations, we are not comparing a task with a non-task; we are not comparing rule-governed performance with rule-free performance. It is somewhat puzzling, therefore, that Dreisbach (2012) associated the two-layered organization with task rules and the single-layered organization with stimulus–response associations. It is true that, in the two-layered organization, responses to numbers (odd *vs.* even) can be distinguished from responses to letters (consonant *vs.* vowel) in terms of two separate subtasks, but even when these two subtasks are not identified, participants would still be performing a task.

There is a conceptual advantage in the two-layered organization of our example. Identifying stimulus sets in terms of distinct categories (numbers *vs.* letters, colors *vs.* shapes, etc.) provides a clear basis for grouping stimulus–response events, which are applicable over a wide range of stimuli. Given the single-layered organization, a participant would not know how to respond to a new stimulus, such as "G" or "9," whereas the rules involved in the two-layered organization can be extended to these stimuli (Dreisbach, 2012). Indeed, in the absence of explicitly provided stimulus categories, participants might generate their own categories, such as "things I like" *vs.* "things I dislike" (Dreisbach, 2012), spontaneously moving from a single-layered organization into a two-layered organization.

Based on these observations, Dreisbach (2012) put forth the following claims. First, engaging with a (sub)task helps us ignore events that are irrelevant to the (sub) task. That is, if we clearly demarcate subtasks of a task, such as the color and shape subtasks shown in Figs. 5.5 and 5.6, or the two-layered organization of the number/letter task, it becomes easier to persist in one of the subtasks (e.g., color) and ignore the alternative subtask (e.g., shape). As such, organizing a task into subtasks can facilitate continual engagement, or *persistence*, in a particular subtask, while shielding our attention against currently irrelevant subtasks and their associated features (Dreisbach & Wenke, 2011). Second, Dreisbach pointed out, if we clearly demarcate subtasks of a task, then switching from one of the subtasks (e.g., color) into another (e.g., shape) involves a performance cost (Dreisbach et al., 2007). Organizing a task into subtasks, which then requires regularly switching between the subtasks, is described as requiring cognitive *flexibility*. Persistence and flexibility, in Dreisbach's approach, are conceived as antagonistic modes of control (see also, Hommel, 2015). This approach, therefore, not only accounts for the costs and benefits of task organizations but also identifies two distinct modes of cognitive control. After this brief summary, we can now contextualize Dreisbach's claims within the present framework.

The meaning of *persistence, flexibility*, and *shielding* changes when they are placed in the framework I have been developing (starting in Chap. 3). Recall our discussion of the "task-switching" paradigm (Figs. 5.5 and 5.6). Performance in such a task involves selection of responses along multiple response features, including stimulus category (color, shape, number, letter, etc.), and the responding key (left key, right key, etc.). Those features are organized in a hierarchy, such that a feature can be superordinate relative to some features and subordinate relative to others. In reference to Fig. 5.6, what Dreisbach et al. described as *persistence* results from having to switch between the subordinate response features (e.g., left key → right key), while *not* having to switch between (sub)task 1 and (sub)task 2 (e.g., color → shape). Sufficient repetition in one subtask, which demands ignoring features related to the alternative (sub)task, helps shield against irrelevant distractors (Bilalić et al., 2008; Eitam et al., 2013, 2015). Flexibility, on the other hand, results from having to switch between relatively superordinate features of response, which implies not being able to ignore a superordinate group of responses.

Thus, what some authors (Dreisbach, 2012; Dreisbach & Fröber, 2018; Hommel, 2015) have described as "persistence" and "flexibility" are not antagonistic modes of response selection but rather selection involving relatively subordinate and relatively superordinate switches within a task hierarchy. Furthermore, what we call a flexible mode of performance is a matter of perspective. If we are concerned about whether or not someone is thinking about leaving the experiment, then switching between the color/shape subtasks constitutes persistence, as long as the participant is following task instructions. In this case, the participant is persistent on the overall task, while being flexible with respect to the subtasks. If, on the other hand, our concern is with whether or not someone is engaged with one of the two subtasks (color *vs.* shape), then switching between the two left/right response keys constitutes persistence, as long as the participant remains within a subtask. In this case, the participant is persistent on the relevant stimulus category (e.g., color), while being flexible with respect to response keys. In short, our judgments about persistence or flexibility change if we change our perspective, and if we change what we regard as the basic-level goal of the task. In their everyday use, the words "persistence" and "flexibility" are ambiguous, and their ambiguity is indeed useful and reflects their range of application. By turning them into technical words, we would rigidly and inaccurately narrow their meaning.

Let me offer an additional point in support of my approach to hierarchical task organizations. In a more recent article, Dreisbach and Fröber (2018) once again distinguished persistence and flexibility as two antagonistic modes of cognitive control, and then proposed two hypotheses for explaining how cognitive flexibility is achieved: (a) lowering the updating threshold and (b) maintaining multiple tasks in working memory. Dreisbach and Fröber saw these two hypotheses as mutually inconsistent, associated with different empirical predictions. Within the approach I have been defending, the two hypotheses are consistent. They describe different types of cognitive flexibility. Flexibility at a higher level of the goal hierarchy (Fig. 5.6: "remain in the experiment" *vs.* "leave the experiment prematurely") can sensitize participants toward a wide range of goals both in and outside of the lab. This would appear, in Dreisbach and Fröber's terms, as a general lowering of goal-updating threshold. Flexibility at a mid-level (Fig. 5.6: "color" *vs.* "shape"), on the other hand, would sensitize participants to the demands of both subtasks, without necessarily sensitizing them to the goals outside of the experimental session. This would appear as maintaining multiple tasks in working memory. Hence, the two hypotheses are not incompatible. They can both be confirmed under different circumstances and as a result of different performance strategies. Importantly, they both fit in the hierarchical view of task organization (Schumacher & Hazeltine, 2016).

As discussed in this section, an important advantage of viewing a task in terms of a hierarchically organized set of goals is that it enables us to stop thinking about tasks as "internally represented" in the minds of actors and think of them instead as larger wholes in which actors take part. Accordingly, actors' awareness of tasks is partial and incomplete. Someone who is following instructions may not be fully aware of the superordinate goals associated with his or her task performance (recall the client following the therapist's instructions, the student following the instruction of his language teacher, and a research participant following the researcher's instructions). This point will be further explicated as we turn to our next target contribution.

5.4   Goals Without Actors

In their article, "What is a task? An ideomotor perspective", Künzell et al. (2017) distinguished *tasks* from *goals* and *actions*. Following the ideomotor approach (Hommel, 2013; Shin, Proctor, & Capaldi, 2010), they defined *goals* as desired future states, dividing them into relatively concrete and relatively abstract goals. *Actions*, they wrote, are movements that attempt to fulfill a concrete goal. In writing an email, for instance, the visual appearance of words and sentences on the screen serve as concrete goals. The abstract goal of "writing an email" limits the current concrete goals (Powers, 1998). Similarly, in the task-switching paradigm (Figs. 5.5 and 5.6), responding to stimulus shape is a relatively abstract goal, whereas responding to a diamond-shaped stimulus is a relatively concrete goal. Finally, finger movements that push down response keys are actions that fulfill the concrete goals.

Within the framework I have outlined, Künzell et al.'s (2017) "actions", "concrete goals", and "abstract goals" roughly correspond to "subordinate goals", "basic-level goals", and "superordinate goals". I do not think they would find my terminology problematic because it acknowledges the hierarchical nature of goals.

They also treat "concrete" and "abstract" as relative terms, noting that more than two levels of goal can be identified in a given activity. Moreover, by adopting the ideomotor approach, the authors accepted that there is no clear dividing line between *goals* and *actions* (Hommel, 1997; Hommel et al., 2001). By describing all levels of the hierarchy with respect to *goals*, we acknowledge that they all involve anticipation. The tactile sensation of fingers against the keyboard, the appearance of words on the screen, and knowing that one has sent an email can all be anticipated. All three can be pursued at the same time, as parts of the same task (Powers, 1998). A superordinate (abstract) goal does not disappear after shaping the current basic-level (concrete) goals and actions.

What about *tasks*? Intriguingly, Künzell et al. defined tasks as "depersonalized goals". The difference between a task and a goal, they wrote, "is that a goal is personal, meaning that it is bound to a specific person striving for this goal" (Künzell et al., 2017, p. 6). In contrast to a goal, the authors continued, "a task is not bound to a specific person, because it describes what has to be done by any participant" (ibid). If someone adopts a task, then "the depersonalized task becomes a personal goal of that specific person" (ibid).

Are goals so entangled with particular people that, in order to separate the two, we need the help of an additional concept? In ordinary language, goals are not tied to particular persons, which is why we can talk about a goal without talking about who pursues the goal. When we read Wittgenstein (1953, p. 42), for instance, who wrote, "what is inexact attains its goal less perfectly than what is more exact", we are not thinking about the goal of a particular person, although the statement is meaningful to us. When we talk about the goal of being accurate, being objective, we are not talking about the goal of a particular person. We are, in fact, referring to the outcome of an analysis that has already separated the goal from the person or people who might be contemplating, pursuing, approving, or condemning the goal. This is why the phrase "personal goal" is not redundant. A goal does not have to be attached to a particular person.

But Künzell et al. might have been proposing that goals are factually, not conceptually, attached to particular persons, whereas tasks are factually detached from particular persons. This claim would be problematic because—as we saw in the previous sections—it is generally difficult to describe a task without stating how the task is organized. And, the way a task is organized can change based on the participants' understanding of the task (Dreisbach et al., 2007; Freedberg, Wagschal, & Hazeltine, 2014), which is to say a task cannot be defined without at least an implicit reference to a subject-centered view of the task. Does this not contradict the claim that tasks are depersonalized goals? In what sense, then, are persons removed from the tasks? In what sense is Künzell et al.'s description of tasks correct?

Although it does not seem reasonable to say, "a goal = a person + a task", it seems reasonable to say that a goal, compared to a task, provides easier ground for us to pay attention to the person. Removing the person—or treating the person as replaceable—requires not just the act of abstraction but also choosing the type of goal that allows for such an abstraction. To say that a task is a depersonalized goal is to say that the goal has been described so clearly and thoroughly that we can set aside the possible differences among participants' interpretation of the goal (Wachtel, 1973). In everyday life, goals tend to imply something about people who pursue them, someone who aims for a major achievement is an ambitious person, someone who frequently chooses comfort and short-term pleasures is a hedonist, and so forth (Bergner, 2016, 2017). Succeeding or failing to fulfill a goal affects the person who is pursuing the goal. Failure tends to result in disappointment, frustration, or change of plans. The goals assigned in experimental tasks do not have these features. Experimental research participants are usually university students, who are required to participate in order to obtain course credit. Aside from this general statement, which says more about the institutional structures in which psychological science takes place, we cannot infer much about research participants based on their goals *within* an experiment.

Rather than having to assume goals without actors, therefore, we need to assume that it is possible to identify or create basic-level categories of goal that enable us to treat the actors pursuing those goals as replaceable. This approach, of course, entails regarding people as means to some end, and it entails an asymmetry with which a task shapes the behavior of those who assign it and those who perform it. In the case of experimental tasks, participants' behavior is shaped by the task, and we could not infer much about the personal characteristics of the participants based on their participation. On the other hand, the researchers' behavior is not shaped by the tasks they assign to their participants, but we could infer something about them on the basis of the tasks, such as their research interests, methods, and so on. Within the hierarchy of goals associated with an experimental task, participants' performance is subordinate to the goals of the researcher.

Of course, people who participate in an experiment have concerns and goals outside of the lab. By setting aside those concerns, by treating participants as replaceable, we would describe their performance only with reference to the goals within the experiment. Recall the study by van Steenbergen (Van Steenbergen, Langeslag, Band, & Hommel, 2014, discussed in Chap. 3), who primed their participants to think about their romantic relationships before asking them to perform an experimental task. The researcher then claimed that a higher level of passionate love (measured using a questionnaire) might be associated with reduced cognitive control (measured as the influence of distractors on performance). Such a claim is the outcome of neglecting the participants' goals, including the goals related to their romantic relationship, which is implicit in regarding the tasks as depersonalized goals. By regarding a task as depersonalized, we might take a further step and regard research participants as lacking goals beyond the experimental task (e.g., "if they are distractible during an experiment, it *must* be because they lack cognitive control").

Let us return to the claim, "a goal = a person + a task". After removing the performing person from view, is a task merely a goal? Throughout the previous chapter and the present chapter, we saw how rules and relevance are intrinsic to tasks. A task is *organized* around a set of goals, but it is not identical to those goals (Mammen & Mironenko, 2015; Noë, 2015). Someone who cheats in a game is violating the rules of the game, and might be consequently excluded from the game, despite sharing with other players the goal of winning. Identifying a goal is, therefore, insufficient to identify a person's mode of participation in an activity. What is required is to specify an organized goal hierarchy. The goal hierarchy, in the case of the game, dictates winning without rule-breaking. The goal hierarchy consists of multiple goals at different levels. When we describe a task, what we describe is part of a larger goal hierarchy.

There is, at least, one further aspect of Künzell et al. (2017) that requires our attention, and that is their remarks on the cost of multi-tasking. The authors argued that it is more accurate to describe the cost of multi-tasking as a competition among multiple competing *actions*, as opposed to multiple *tasks*. We should unpack this claim, especially since, both in my present approach and in Künzell et al.'s ideomotor approach, goals and actions are subject to a common logic, one involving the anticipation and bringing about of desired states. When we describe the difficulty of resolving competition among multiple actions (left key *vs.* right key), we are referring to the difficulty of choosing among subordinate goals. By locating the source of difficulty at this level, Künzell et al. identified "switching cost" as a failure of *persistence* on the superordinate goal (cf. Dreisbach & Fröber, 2018; Hommel, 2015). However, we could also describe the difficulty of multi-tasking as the difficulty of switching or maintaining multiple, incompatible ways of organizing stimulus–response events (e.g., simultaneously keeping track of the number of passengers on the bus and the number of stops). Recognizing the hierarchical organization of tasks, therefore, helps us recognize that "switching cost" can also be a failure to flexibly adopt a superordinate goal. As such, we cannot in principle reduce the cost of switching among goals, at various levels of the hierarchy, to the cost of switching among actions, which confines actions to a narrower, subordinate range of the goal hierarchy.

It is worth asking, nevertheless, why we might be inclined to equate the cost of multiple tasks with the cost of multiple actions. I suspect that this inclination is grounded in the fact that the person performing the task is, for all intents and purposes, ignoring the superordinate goals associated with the task and focusing ("persisting") on the subordinate actions. Recall the example of the therapist who asked his client to have lunch with friends. The division of control in that example was that the therapist determined the superordinate goal and the client was in control of the subordinate goals (actions). Similar to how actors in *joint* task performance might let go of what the other is doing (Sellaro et al., 2018; Yamaguchi et al., 2017b), the client might also let go of thinking about, questioning, and re-considering the superordinate goals associated with the task assigned to him. In such special cases, we would not expect performance cost—for the client, or any other actor who assumes a relatively subordinate place in a goal hierarchy—based on a competition among superordinate goals. On the other hand, just because people can engage in tasks, we would not deny their capacity for conflict at superordinate levels of control (competition among superordinate goals). The fact that competition among multiple actions is possible and costly does logically lead to the conclusion that multi-tasking or task-switching costs are reducible to conflict among multiple actions. Recognizing higher levels of control means recognizing the possibility of conflict at those levels.

5.5   The Task of Being an Experimental Psychologist

In my first year as a doctoral student, I asked a senior graduate student why he was interested in "attentional control" tasks. He seemed upset with my unrefined view of his scientific ambition. "I am not interested in the tasks," he said, "I am interested in *consciousness*!" A task is often designed to engage specific cognitive or behavioral capacities and is not itself the ostensive target of investigation. By finding out the factors to which task performance is sensitive, we infer something about those underlying capacities (van der Heijden & Stebbins, 1990). On the rare occasions when researchers turn to tasks themselves, the aim of their discussion is either (a) to explain some empirical findings which could not be explained without an explicit reference to tasks or (b) to clarify *task* as a central concept of a research program, such as research on "task-switching" and "task-sharing."

By contrast, my aim in this chapter was to provide an analysis that can begin to highlight the role of tasks as *engines of research production*. By thinking about experimental tasks in this way, we can regard them as tools for extending, magnifying, and re-organizing the human capacities for perceiving, paying attention, thinking, and acting (Bruner, 1964). A task not only helps to reveal something about our psychological capacities but may also influence those capacities. For example, when reviewing the research by Yamaguchi et al. (2017a, 2017b, 2019), we saw how various tasks encourage more or less sensitivity to a co-actor's performance. Rather than adopting an attitude of discovery ("Are we sensitive to what our co-actor does?"), we can adopt an attitude of design and intervention ("How can we change the design of this task such that participants are more/less sensitive to their co-others' performance?"). From this perspective, the idea that cognitive structures and functions are stable, waiting to be discovered through the lens of tasks, is implausible (Gozli & Deng, 2018; Kingstone, Smilek, & Eastwood, 2008).

In the example at the beginning of this chapter ("the bus game"), we had two friends, one of whom presented a puzzle to the other, designed to misdirect the friend's attention to irrelevant features of the description of the bus. The game was not designed to discover something about the friend's attention and responses. It was designed to guide the friend's responses along a pre-determined path. It was designed to obtain a desired *effect*. Something similar happens in the work of experimental psychologists. If a student is interested in using the Stroop task (Stroop, 1935), the Simon task (Simon, 1990), or the flanker task (Eriksen & Eriksen, 1974), we would usually encourage him or her to first design the basic conditions in which the effect is obtained. Then, and only then, the student could move on to investigate whether and how these effects are sensitive to other factors. If an experiment involving the Stroop effect fails to find the Stroop effect in all of the experimental conditions, it would be difficult to interpret the results because we cannot assume that the basic pre-conditions for the study were present.

In addition to highlighting the role of tasks in a creative process, the purpose of my analysis was to offer a view of tasks that is applicable, not only to the behavior of research participants but also to the behavior of researchers. Describing tasks with respect to a hierarchically organized set of goals opens the scope for including experimenters and their concerns. Experimental psychology is embedded within a social-cultural context, and it would be naïve to regard the larger context as neutral with respect to the activities of researchers (Danziger, 1997).

Every student of experimental psychology soon learns that there are "proper" ways of talking about research (Billig, 2013). We learn to regurgitate, for instance, that we "study the mind," or we study "how the mind works." We choose an experimental task, introduce some new variations, publish the results, and repeat. At the same time, we learn and internalize the practice of salesmanship, which involves packaging our work under the best possible light. What is neglected in this process is theoretical reflection regarding the meaning and relevance of the experimental research, whether the chosen empirical method is appropriate for the research question, and whether or not empirical investigation is necessary at all (Hibberd & Gozli, 2017; Smedslund, 1991).

The current norms and practices in our profession are not inherently corrupt. The danger comes from having placed them at the top of the goal hierarchy: collecting new empirical data, finding effects, and publishing results are viewed as our highest goals, ends in themselves, goals in relation to which we become subordinate. Similar to how persistence in a subtask shields the actor's attention against irrelevant distractors (Dreisbach, 2012; Hommel, 2015), persistence in the normative practices of experimental research and mindlessly following the standards of career success, would shield our attention against other important goals, such as theoretical synthesis, societal relevance, and questions about the meaning of research findings.

A simple and, I believe, effective remedy for the current situation consists of embedding our research practices within an additional layer of critique and reflection. This is the type of activity, in which I have attempted to engage in this book. The goal is to have a layer of reflection and dialog in which we (a) articulate our goals and activities of researchers, (b) extend our awareness of our activities, including the tasks we perform and the tasks we assign to our research participants, and (c) recognize our active roles (rather than in terms of discovery), in terms of design, creation, and intervention. As such, critique is an open-ended goal that can bring awareness to our activities, the ways in which those activities are organized, and the possibility of re-organizing them (Gozli & Dolcini, 2018; Noë, 2015).

References

Adam, J., Hommel, B., & Umiltà, C. (2005). Preparing for perception and action (II): Automatic and effortful processes in response cueing. *Visual Cognition, 12*(8), 1444–1473.

Adam, J. J., Hommel, B., & Umiltà, C. (2003). Preparing for perception and action (I): The role of grouping in the response-cuing paradigm. *Cognitive Psychology, 46*(3), 302–358.

Badre, D. (2008). Cognitive control, hierarchy, and the rostro-caudal organization of the frontal lobes. *Trends in Cognitive Science, 12*, 193–200.

Bergner, R. M. (2016). What is behaviour? And why is it not reducible to biological states of affairs? *Journal of Theoretical and Philosophical Psychology, 36*, 41–55.

Bergner, R. M. (2017). What is a person? What is the self? Formulations for a science of psychology. *Journal of Theoretical and Philosophical Psychology, 37*(2), 77–90.

Bilalić, M., McLeod, P., & Gobet, F. (2008). Why good thoughts block better ones: The mechanism of the pernicious Einstellung (set) effect. *Cognition, 108*(3), 652–661.

Billig, M. (2013). *Learn to write badly: How to succeed in the social sciences*. Cambridge, UK: Cambridge University Press.

Bruner, J. S. (1964). The course of cognitive growth. *American Psychologist, 19*(1), 1–15.

Danziger, K. (1997). *Naming the mind*. London, UK: Sage Publications.

De Houwer, J. (2011). Why the cognitive approach in psychology would profit from a functional approach and vice versa. *Perspectives on Psychological Science, 6*(2), 202–209.

Dreisbach, G. (2012). Mechanisms of cognitive control: The functional role of task rules. *Current Directions in Psychological Science, 21*, 227–231.

Dreisbach, G., & Fröber, K. (2018). On how to be flexible (or not): Modulation of the stability-flexibility balance. *Current Directions in Psychological Science, 28*(1), 3–9.

Dreisbach, G., Goschke, T., & Haider, H. (2007). The role of task rules and stimulus–response mappings in the task switching paradigm. *Psychological Research, 71*, 383–392.

Dreisbach, G., & Wenke, D. (2011). The shielding function of task sets and its relaxation during task switching. *Journal of Experimental Psychology: Learning, Memory, and Cognition, 37*, 1540–1546.

Eitam, B., Shoval, R., & Yeshurun, Y. (2015). Seeing without knowing: Task relevance dissociates between visual awareness and recognition. *Annals of the New York Academy of Sciences, 1339*, 125–137.

Eitam, B., Yeshurun, Y., & Hassan, K. (2013). Blinded by irrelevance: Pure irrelevance induced "blindness". *Journal of Experimental Psychology: Human Perception and Performance, 39*, 611–615.

Elsner, B., & Hommel, B. (2001). Effect anticipation and action control. *Journal of Experimental Psychology: Human Perception and Performance, 27*, 229–240.

Eriksen, B. A., & Eriksen, C. W. (1974). Effects of noise letters upon the identification of a target letter in a nonsearch task. *Perception & Psychophysics, 16*(1), 143–149.

Fitts, P. M., & Seeger, C. M. (1953). S-R compatibility: Spatial characteristics of stimulus and response codes. *Journal of Experimental Psychology, 46*(3), 199–210.

Freedberg, M., Wagschal, T. T., & Hazeltine, E. (2014). Incidental learning and task boundaries. *Journal of Experimental Psychology. Learning, Memory, and Cognition, 40*(6), 1680–1700.

Goschke, T. (2000). Intentional reconfiguration and involuntary persistence in task set switching. In S. Monsell & J. Driver (Eds.), *Control of cognitive processes: Attention and performance XVIII* (pp. 331–355). Cambridge, MA: MIT Press.

Gozli, D. G. (2017). Behaviour versus performance: The veiled commitment of experimental psychology. *Theory & Psychology, 27*, 741–758.

Gozli, D. G., & Deng, W. (2018). Building blocks of psychology: On remaking the unkept promises of early schools. *Integrative Psychological and Behavioral Science, 52*, 1–24.

Gozli, D. G., & Dolcini, N. (2018). Reaching into the unknown: Actions, goal hierarchies, and explorative agency. *Frontiers in Psychology, 9*, 266.

Hazeltine, E., & Schumacher, E. H. (2016). Understanding central processes: The case against simple stimulus-response associations and for complex task representation. In B. H. Ross (Ed.), *Psychology of learning and motivation* (Vol. 64, pp. 195–245). Amsterdam, The Netherland: Academic Press.

Hibberd, F. J. (2014). The metaphysical basis of a process psychology. *Journal of Theoretical and Philosophical Psychology, 34*(3), 161–186.

Hibberd, F. J., & Gozli, D. G. (2017). Psychology's fragmentation and neglect of foundational assumptions: An interview with Fiona J. Hibberd. *Europe's Journal of Psychology, 13*, 366–374.

Hommel, B. (1997). Toward an action-concept model of stimulus-response compatibility. In B. Hommel & W. Prinz (Eds.), *Theoretical issues in stimulus-response compatibility* (pp. 281–320). Amsterdam, The Netherland: Elsevier.

Hommel, B. (1998). Automatic stimulus-response translation in dual-task performance. *Journal of Experimental Psychology: Human Perception and Performance, 24*, 1368–1384.

Hommel, B. (2000). The prepared reflex: Automaticity and control in stimulus-response translation. In S. Monsell & J. Driver (Eds.), *Control of cognitive processes: Attention and performance XVIII* (pp. 247–273). Cambridge, MA: MIT Press.

Hommel, B. (2013). Ideomotor action control: On the perceptual grounding of voluntary actions and agents. In W. Prinz, M. Beisert, & A. Herwig (Eds.), *Action science: Foundations of an emerging discipline* (pp. 113–136). Cambridge, MA: MIT Press.

Hommel, B. (2015). Between persistence and flexibility: The Yin and Yang of action control. In A. J. Elliot (Ed.), *Advances in motivation science* (Vol. 2, pp. 33–67). New York, NY: Elsevier.

Hommel, B., Müsseler, J., Aschersleben, G., & Prinz, W. (2001). The theory of event coding (TEC): A framework for perception and action planning. *Behavioral and Brain Sciences, 24*, 849–878.

Hyman, R. (1953). Stimulus information as a determinant of reaction time. *Journal of Experimental Psychology, 45*(3), 188–196.

Janczyk, M., & Kunde, W. (2014). The role of effect grouping in free-choice response selection. *Acta Psychologica, 150*, 49–54.

Kiesel, A., Steinhauser, M., Wendt, M., Falkenstein, M., Jost, K., Philipp, A. M., & Koch, I. (2010). Control and interference in task switching—A review. *Psychological Bulletin, 136*(5), 849–874.

Kingstone, A., Smilek, D., & Eastwood, J. D. (2008). Cognitive ethology: A new approach for studying human cognition. *British Journal of Psychology, 99*(3), 317–340.

Kleinsorge, T., & Heuer, H. (1999). Hierarchical switching in a multi-dimensional task space. *Psychological Research, 62*(4), 300–312.

Kornblum, S., Hasbroucq, T., & Osman, A. (1990). Dimensional overlap: Cognitive basis for stimulus-response compatibility—A model and taxonomy. *Psychological Review, 97*, 253–270.

Künzell, S., Broeker, L., Dignath, D., Ewolds, H., Raab, M., & Thomaschke, R. (2017). What is a task? An ideomotor perspective. *Psychological Research, 82*(1), 4–11.

Logan, G. D. (1990). Repetition priming and automaticity: Common underlying mechanisms? *Cognitive Psychology, 22*(1), 1–35.

Mammen, J., & Mironenko, I. (2015). Activity theories and the ontology of psychology: Learning from Danish and Russian experiences. *Integrative Psychological and Behavioral Science, 49*(4), 681–713.

Meiran, N. (1996). Reconfiguration of processing mode prior to task performance. *Journal of Experimental Psychology: Learning, Memory, and Cognition, 22*, 1423–1442.

Monsell, S. (2003). Task switching. *Trends in Cognitive Sciences, 7*(3), 134–140.

Morris, D. (2005). Animals and humans, thinking and nature. *Phenomenology and the Cognitive Sciences, 4*(1), 49–72.

Noë, A. (2009). *Out of our heads: Why you are not your brain, and other lessons from the biology of consciousness*. London, UK: Macmillan.

Noë, A. (2015). *Strange tools: Art and human nature*. New York, NY: Hill and Wang.

Ossorio, P. (2006). *The behavior of persons*. Ann Arbor, MI: Descriptive Psychology Press.

Powers, W. T. (1998). *Making sense of behavior*. Montclair, NJ: Benchmark Publications.

Prinz, W. (2018). Contingency and similarity in response selection. *Consciousness and Cognition, 64*, 1–248.

Reeve, T. G., & Proctor, R. W. (1984). On the advance preparation of discrete finger responses. *Journal of Experimental Psychology: Human Perception and Performance, 10*(4), 541–553.

Rosenbaum, D. A. (1980). Human movement initiation: Specification of arm, direction, and extent. *Journal of Experimental Psychology: General, 109*(4), 444–474.

Schumacher, E. H., & Hazeltine, E. (2016). Hierarchical task representation: Task files and response selection. *Current Directions in Psychological Science, 25*, 449–454.

Sebanz, N., Knoblich, G., & Prinz, W. (2003). Representing others' actions: Just like one's own? *Cognition, 88*(3), B11–B21.

Sebanz, N., Knoblich, G., & Prinz, W. (2005). How two share a task: Corepresenting stimulus-response mappings. *Journal of Experimental Psychology: Human Perception and Performance, 31*(6), 1234–1246.

Sellaro, R., Treccani, B., & Cubelli, R. (2018). When task sharing reduces interference: Evidence for division-of-labour in Stroop-like tasks. *Psychological Research*, 1–16. https://doi. org/10.1007/s00426-018-1044-1

Shin, Y. K., Proctor, R. W., & Capaldi, E. J. (2010). A review of contemporary ideomotor theory. *Psychological Bulletin, 136*(6), 943–974.

Simon, J. R. (1990). The effects of an irrelevant directional cue on human information processing. In R. W. Proctor & T. G. Reeve (Eds.), *Stimulus-response compatibility: An integrated perspective* (pp. 31–86). Amsterdam, The Netherland: Elsevier.

Simons, D. J., & Chabris, C. F. (1999). Gorillas in our midst: Sustained inattentional blindness for dynamic events. *Perception, 28*(9), 1059–1074.

Smedslund, J. (1991). The pseudoempirical in psychology and the case for psychologic. *Psychological Inquiry, 2*(4), 325–338.

Smedslund, J. (2009). The mismatch between current research methods and the nature of psychological phenomena: What researchers must learn from practitioners. *Theory & Psychology, 19*(6), 778–794.

Strawson, P. F. (1992). *Analysis and metaphysics*. Oxford, UK: Oxford University Press.

Stroop, J. R. (1935). Studies of interference in serial verbal reactions. *Journal of Experimental Psychology, 18*(6), 643–662.

Valsiner, J. (2017). *From methodology to methods in human psychology*. New York, NY: Springer.

van der Heijden, A. H., & Stebbins, S. (1990). The information-processing approach. *Psychological Research, 52*(2–3), 197–206.

Van Steenbergen, H., Langeslag, S. J., Band, G. P., & Hommel, B. (2014). Reduced cognitive control in passionate lovers. *Motivation and Emotion, 38*, 444–450.

Wachtel, P. L. (1973). Psychodynamics, behavior therapy, and the implacable experimenter: An inquiry into the consistency of personality. *Journal of Abnormal Psychology, 82*, 324–334.

Wittgenstein, L. (1953). *Philosophical investigations*. New York, NY: Macmillan.

Yamaguchi, M., Wall, H. J., & Hommel, B. (2017a). Action-effect sharing induces task-set sharing in joint task switching. *Cognition, 165*, 113–120.

Yamaguchi, M., Wall, H. J., & Hommel, B. (2017b). No evidence for shared representations of task sets in joint task switching. *Psychological Research, 81*(6), 1166–1177.

Yamaguchi, M., Wall, H. J., & Hommel, B. (2018). Sharing tasks or sharing actions? Evidence from the joint Simon task. *Psychological Research, 82*(2), 385–394.

Yamaguchi, M., Wall, H. J., & Hommel, B. (2019). The roles of action selection and actor selection in joint task settings. *Cognition, 182*, 184–192.

Chapter 6
Free Choice

The topic of this chapter requires at least a passing reference to existential philosophy, in particular, the question of how we ought to think about human freedom and free actions. One way to think about human freedom is in terms of detachment, withdrawal, and negation (Sartre, 1956; cf. Berlin, 2002). According to this view, we are free when we say no to social conventions, the demands of our relationships, the expectations that come with adopting social roles, and in general the normative pressures of our environments. A more positive way of thinking about freedom is possible, however, that does not contradict our attachments (Marcel, 1962). According to this view, we are free when we are engaged in activities that reflect our highest values and commitments. Our freedom is realized as we enact and express our deepest personal or communal values. We can clarify the distinction between the two existentialist perspectives on freedom with reference to a Hollywood movie.

The movie, *The Truman Show* (1998), tells the story of Truman Burbank (Jim Carrey), who is living a seemingly ordinary life. He is married, lives in a small town (Seahaven Island), and works at an insurance company. Like all people, Truman's life is constrained. He fantasizes about leaving his town, but he continually faces obstacles. First, his aquaphobia prevents him from sea travel. When he attempts to travel by other means, he meets severe inconveniences, which disguise the fact that he is being intentionally controlled to stay in Seahaven Island. Unbeknownst to him, Truman's town is a very large set of a television show, and his actions must remain within a pre-determined range. The creator of the show, the person who has been in control of all the major events of Truman's life, including his learned aquaphobia, is a man named Christoff. When Truman finally becomes aware of the reality of his circumstances, he rebels, nearly dying in the process of escape.

The Truman Show highlights the idea that our available choices depend on the degree to which we are aware of our circumstances. With a change in our awareness comes a change in how we think about the exercise of our freedom (Dennett, 2004). When Truman becomes aware of his circumstance, he becomes an active participant in a drama. He discovers something new, something fundamental, about what it means for him to live freely. We might describe the story of Truman as the story of

© Springer Nature Switzerland AG 2019
D. Gozli, *Experimental Psychology and Human Agency*,
https://doi.org/10.1007/978-3-030-20422-8_6

someone who is not initially free, but becomes free as the story unfolds. This interpretation is more in line with the negative approach to freedom. Truman withdraws from his controlled life story, the one that was imposed on him by Christoff. His freedom, according to this interpretation, is most strongly expressed in his act of escape.

We could interpret the story from a different perspective, according to which Truman is free all throughout the story. His freedom does not increase. Rather, the meaning of his freedom changes as he becomes aware of his condition. This interpretation is salient when we notice that Truman is, as the story begins, the only person in his community who is not a television actor. He believes in what he does, his role in the community, his relationships, and his career. His colleagues, his best friend, and his wife are all actors in the show. They are all detached from their roles the way an actor is detached from his or her acting role. Truman, on the other hand, does not have the same distance from his role. His role is his life. By virtue of his belief, his engagement with his role, his life history is real to him, and he is truly living it. With this interpretation, we see Truman as a free person, both at the beginning of the movie (before his discovery of "the Truman Show") and in the end (when he escapes). This interpretation is in line with the positive understanding of freedom.

While performing the role of Truman, it is said that Jim Carrey kept improvising and deviating from the script, causing conflict with the director. Was Jim Carrey, the actor, exercising his freedom? The negative approach tells us that he was free because he was deviating from the pre-written script. The positive approach, on the other hand, tells us that he was free because he was engaging with the role of Truman according to what he believed to be the best way of expressing it. He would not have been free were he to break away from the script due to forgetfulness or an emotional outburst. From the perspective of a creative artist, the freedom to merely deviate from the script, without serving any other goal, is not a freedom worth wanting (Dennett, 2004; Marcel, 1962). The freedom that is valued by an artist is one that would allow him to deviate from the script *for the sake* of improving it. Rather than requiring arbitrary detachment, therefore, a positive approach to freedom requires commitment, engagement, and goals.

The positive and the negative approaches to freedom can, of course, be regarded as complementary, but when regarded in isolation they set different standards for deciding whether an action is free. The negative view judges an action as free when the situational factors fail to provide a sufficient explanation for the action. A person is free to the extent that he or she is *not* constrained by his or her situation. Dennett (2004, p. 101) has described this as a requirement for "moral levitation"—the ability to transcend whatever could be used to explain our actions. The positive view, on the other hand, judges an action as free when the action is an expression of the actor's intentions and values, when it is integrated into the actor's hierarchy of goals. While the negative view of free action is grounded in a strict separation between the subject and the world, and the subject's struggle to stand out against the pressures of the environment, the positive view of freedom is grounded in the relation between the subject and the world, and the subject's struggle to understand his or her place in the world.

Notice that we are not asking whether human freedom is real or illusory. We are, instead, considering different ways of thinking about freedom and free action. It so happens that experimental psychology of free choice has implicitly adopted the negative view of freedom, in which an action is free when it lacks any compelling reason for its selection. This is a convenient approach if we are going to regard research participants as replaceable and disregard their concerns and characters outside of the laboratory (Chap. 4). If we do not know a person's own goals, what we are left with—as a criterion of free choice—is deviation from pre-determined scripts and action against external influence. This is the first of two important features of experimental research on free-choice action: Free choice is defined as a negation, detachment, or moral levitation. The other feature of the experimental work is that the two categories of "free-choice" and "forced-choice" actions are distinguished prior to conducting a study and based on a pre-existing definition. Even though this is a fundamental limitation, we should first understand it as a solution to a difficult problem: How can we look at an action and decide whether it is performed freely?

We could turn to a philosophical thought experiment involving an evil manipulator (Kukla & Walmsley, 2006). The thought experiment is designed to highlight the potential similarity between acting based on one's own choice and acting based on enforced instructions. The evil manipulator, in our version of the thought experiment, uses the promise of reward or threat of punishment to force someone else's actions. Using this method, he might force someone (Jim) to tell a joke at a gathering. Our question is: Can we observe Jim's behavior and infer whether he is acting freely or being forced by the manipulator?

Our problem is not unlike Truman Burbank's problem of finding out the true identity of his significant others. We might think that performing forced actions can be distinguished from free actions, not based on *what* action is being performed, but based on *how* an action is performed. We might, in the case of our thought experiment, check to see whether or not the person is happy. But happiness—or positive affect—is not a reliable criterion. People who voluntarily sacrifice short-term pleasures for the sake of long-term goals might seem unhappy. We are not necessarily enthusiastic when we make free choices (e.g., refusing to eat dessert). Positive affect cannot be a reliable sign of free action.

Alternatively, we might assume that someone who is being forced to perform an action is pursuing a different set of goals, compared to someone who is acting out their own volition (Marken, 2014). As such, the two are differently vulnerable to interference. A free actor, we might assume, will adjust his performance in response to the changing context. We might decide to interfere with the actor and see the manner in which he persists or gets back on track. Failing to interrupt an action, which would presumably be interrupted if it were freely chosen, can be a sign that the actor is following orders. If Jim is telling a joke of his own volition, then his action would be interrupted if, say, we ask his audience to leave the room. If he continues, despite facing an empty room, we might conclude that he is following orders.

Judging an actor's sensitivity to disruption, similar to judging the actor's affective state, is an inadequate way of finding out the presence of the evil manipulator.

That is because our manipulator can give his instructions at different levels of the goal hierarchy. He might force Jim to tell a particular joke, enforcing a relatively subordinate goal, but he might also force Jim to try to entertain his friends by any means possible, enforcing a relatively superordinate goal. The manipulator ultimately can turn the actor's volition into an instrument. That is, Jim's volition—his capacity to choose among alternative actions—can be exploited by the manipulator, just as his capacity to utter words, perform movements, and follow instructions can be exploited. In principle, therefore, there is no limit to what our manipulator can do. Whatever test we devise could be predicted by the manipulator and his instructions could be adjusted accordingly (Kukla & Walmsley, 2006; Verschuere, Prati, & Houwer, 2009).

You might raise the following objection: involuntary actions, which are the complete opposite of free actions, cannot be equated with actions enforced by our evil manipulator. An involuntary action is, at least in everyday language, one that is caused by non-personal factors, factors with which the acting person does not identify (Haggard, 2008). These may include actions during sleep-walking, reflexes, the outcome of direct neural stimulation, or perhaps even actions elicited by methods of subliminal persuasion. The evil manipulator, in our version of the thought experiment, is not using any method that circumvents Jim's awareness. He is merely presenting Jim with a set of rules (promise of rewards and/or threat of punishments). As such, his force is mediated through Jim's volition.

Although the above objection is valid, and although it offers a better way to distinguish free and non-free actions, it does not correspond to the distinction adopted in experimental research. Rather than comparing voluntary and involuntary actions, the research we shall discuss in this chapter defines free and forced choice, respectively, as stimulus-based and stimulus-independent choice.

I included the evil manipulator thought experiment for two reasons. The first reason is that it demonstrates the difficulty in distinguishing free and forced actions, which to some extent justifies researchers' *a priori* definitions. In addition, the thought experiment shows that both the "free" and "forced" categories—as defined in certain experimental studies—are often expressions of reflective, personal choice (rather than non-personal causes). To sum up, the research discussed in this chapter has the following two features:

- In light of the philosophical problems of deciding whether an action is free, researchers tend to settle on operational definitions. Whereas in "forced-choice" tasks, we instruct participants to perform a specific response, R1, whenever they see a specific stimulus, S1 (1-to-1 stimulus–response mapping); in a "free-choice" task, we instruct them to choose either R1 or R2 whenever they see S3 (1-to-2 mapping; Fig. 6.1).
- In both free- and forced-choice tasks, participants are aware of their response selection and of their role as the agent of selection (Frith, 2013). In both cases, the person would presumably reply, "Yes," if asked, "Did you perform the action voluntarily?"

Fig. 6.1 Stimulus–
response mapping in a task
that combines free- and
forced-choice response
selection. Participants are
instructed to perform R1
when they see the first
stimulus S1, perform R2
when they see S2, and
choose freely either R1 or
R2 when they see S3

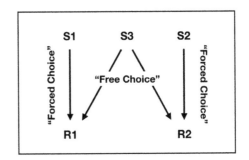

6.1 Free-Choice Experimental Tasks

The research discussed in this section can be traced back to Berlyne (1957). Consider
a simple task with two stimulus–response pairs. In Berlyne's experiments, participants would sometimes see one stimulus ("forced choice") and sometimes both
stimuli ("free choice"). When both stimuli are presented, participants choose either
of the responses. It is also possible to introduce a third stimulus, which is paired
with free-choice responses (Fig. 6.1). This procedure, in its various modifications,
has been used in different topics of research. I will discuss three of them. First, in
research that shows both free- and forced-choice responses are susceptible to selection bias through external factors (priming). Second, in research that aims to pinpoint features that can distinguish free-choice responses from forced-choice
responses. This research is in part motivated by the observation that free-choice
responses, on average, take longer to execute than forced-choice responses. Third,
in research that examines the role of outcome anticipation in response selection, and
whether anticipation plays a dominant role in free-choice response selection. I will
go through these topics one by one.

6.1.1 Priming

In a task that involves free-choice responses, which should presumably depend only
on the whim of the participants, it would be impressive to show biases in response
selection linked to external factors in the participants' environment. It would be
even more impressive if research participants did not consciously perceive the
events that bias their selection. This is the basic idea behind subliminal priming of
free-choice responses. This line of research is considered important because it challenges our intuitions about free choice. It suggests that free-choice responses should
perhaps be subsumed in the category of forced-choice responses.

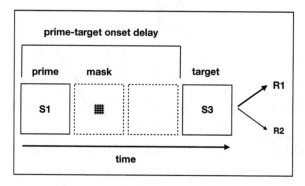

Fig. 6.2 Schematic view of experimental procedures used for priming free-choice responses. The procedure requires a mix of forced- and free-choice responses. Following Fig. 6.1, it is assumed that S1–R1 and S2–R2 are stimulus–response pairs in the forced-choice component of the task, whereas S3 signals to the participants that they should freely choose either R1 or R2. Prior to a free-choice stimulus, participants could be presented with a "prime," which is perceptually similar to S1 (or S2), thus biasing the free choice toward the corresponding response. Other features of the task include a mask, which limits perceptual access to the prime, and the delay between the onset of the prime and the onset of the target

In our selective review of the findings, we are going to stay with the schematic in Fig. 6.1. Free-choice responses are usually performed in a task that includes forced-choice responses, and we shall see why this is a practical requirement for research. The sequence of events in such an experiment is shown in Fig. 6.2. Participants are instructed to wait to see a target stimulus, which could be S1, S2, or S3. In the case of S1 or S2, participants perform forced-choice responses, whereas in the case of S3, participants perform a free-choice response. Before seeing the target stimulus, participants may be presented with a "prime" stimulus, which might resemble one of the forced-choice stimuli (S1/S2). Researchers use a "mask" to limit or eliminate participants' awareness of the prime. Nevertheless, prime stimuli have been shown to influence selection of free-choice responses (Kiesel et al., 2006; Schlaghecken & Eimer, 2004). Such a priming effect can be reflected in *performance speed* (responses that are congruent with the prime are performed faster than those that are incongruent with the prime; R1 in Fig. 6.2) and/or *response frequency* (responses that are congruent with the prime are performed more frequently than those that are incongruent with the prime; R2 in Fig. 6.2).

Imagine using arrows as the stimuli used in the forced-choice component of the task (< < and > >) and an ambiguous stimulus (< >) to signal free choice. In addition to appearing as target stimuli, S1 and S2 could also appear as primes at the beginning of a trial. This was done in a study by Schlaghecken and Eimer (2004). An important feature of their study was the inclusion of blocks in which participants always performed free-choice response and blocks in which free- and forced-choice responses were intermixed. When free-choice responses were mixed with forced-choice responses, they were susceptible to priming effect. But when free-choice responses were performed alone, priming effect was not observed. These results are important because they showed the role of having established the forced-choice task (S1–R1 and S2–R2) in generating a priming effect for free-choice responses. We could argue that associating responses with the target stimuli enables the stimuli to activate their corresponding responses, which produces bias in free-choice response selection (Hommel, 2000). Without the stimulus–response grouping, imposed by the forced-choice component of the task, the similarity between the prime and the responses of the free-choice task was insufficient to influence response selection (Schlaghecken & Eimer, 2004). That is why mixing free- and forced-choice responses within the same task may be a practical necessity for researchers who wish to further examine priming of free-choice responses.

We can take the role of stimulus–response grouping one step further. We already considered, in Chap. 5 (Fig. 5.1), that stimulus–response groups are stronger in some tasks than others. If the forced-choice component of the task involves a relatively strong stimulus–response grouping, and we assume that priming of free-choice responses depends on the stimulus–response associations, we should expect a relatively large priming effect in the selection of free-choice responses. This was observed by Kiesel et al. (2006), who used two different stimulus sets across separate experiments. In their Experiment 1, they used numbers (S1 = "4," S2 = "6," S3 = "0") and in their Experiment 2, they used arrows. Although numbers and locations can be grouped, due to the implicit association between space and magnitude (small numbers associated with left; large numbers associated with right; Dehaene, Bossini, & Giraux, 1993), the associations between response locations and arrows, which are explicitly spatial, are stronger (Ristic & Kingstone, 2006).

When using numbers, Kiesel et al. (2006) found that free-choice responses that were congruent with the prime (R1 in Fig. 6.2) were about 8% more frequent than incongruent responses (R2). However, when they used arrows instead of numbers (Experiment 2), the difference increased from 8% to about 18%. The difference between the two experiments is consistent with the idea that stronger stimulus–response grouping in the forced-choice component of the task can increase the susceptibility of free-choice responses to a priming effect.

Similarly, Mattler and Palmer (2012) used three different stimulus sets across different experiments. While responses were defined spatially (left vs. right) in all three experiments, the stimuli could be arrows (left vs. right), arbitrary shapes (square vs. diamond), and physical location (left vs. right). The authors found a reliable priming effect on free-choice responses when the stimuli were explicitly spatial (arrows and location), presumably because these stimuli were more easily grouped with the responses. When the stimuli were arbitrary shapes, not readily grouped with response locations, the primes were relatively ineffective in biasing free-choice responses.

We could describe the effectiveness of prime stimuli in these studies as the inability to de-couple the responses (R1/R2) from the forced-choice stimuli. After all, participants are asked to perform randomly when they face the free-choice stimulus (S3), and doing so requires—among other things—decoupling the two responses from their corresponding forced-choice stimuli. Fulfilling this requirement would be easier when the stimulus–response grouping is relatively weak (Fig. 6.3, left panel). If you recall from Chap. 5, the strength of stimulus–response

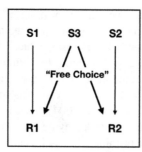 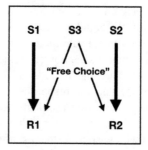

Fig. 6.3 In a task involving a mix of forced- and free-choice responses, it is possible to weaken (left panel) or strengthen (right panel) the grouping among stimulus–response pairs. For instance, with left and right key-press, respectively, as R1 and R2, using arbitrary shapes (S1 = diamond, S2 = square) would result in weaker grouping, relative to spatial features (S1 = left-pointing arrow, S2 = right-pointing arrow)

grouping is not merely the outcome of *what* stimulus and what responses are selected and *how* they are paired but also the outcome of a performance history. Having just enacted a given set of stimulus–response group tends to strengthen the group, compared to just having switched from one way of grouping to another (Dreisbach & Fröber, 2018).

When we refer to target stimuli of forced-choice responses (S1/S2 in Figs. 6.1, 6.2, and 6.3), we are referring not only to entire perceptual objects but also to certain relevant features of the perceptual objects. By implication, when we talk about stimulus–response groups, we are talking about the grouping between the task-relevant feature of the stimuli and the task-relevant feature of the response (Chap. 5). A study by Heinemann, Pfister, and Janczyk (2013) provides a demonstration of this point. Similar to the aforementioned studies, Heinemann et al. (2013) used a task that included both forced- and free-choice responses. The free-choice component of the task required producing a random number between 1 and 9. The forced-choice component of the task required judgment of a tone. Importantly, the relevant feature of the tone changed from trial to trial. Participants sometimes responded to tone volume (low vs. high) and sometimes to tone duration (short vs. long), and responses were spatially defined (left vs. right). The procedure was designed such that the tones could serve as primes for free-choice responses. Given that magnitude (volume/duration) is associated with space, it could be hypothesized that low and short tones (associated with *left*) could prime the generation of smaller numbers, whereas high and long tones (associated with *right*) could prime the generation of larger numbers in the free-choice task (Dehaene et al., 1993; Fischer, 2001; Walsh, 2003). This hypothesis was confirmed by Heinemann et al., though with two additional qualifications.

First, Heinemann et al. (2013) found a priming effect from the relevant stimulus feature, but not the irrelevant feature. When participants were required to judge the volume of the tone, a high-volume tone, on average, resulted in producing larger numbers than a low-volume tone, but tone duration did not affect the number-generation task. On the other hand, when participants judged tone duration, a long tone, on average, resulted in producing larger numbers than a short tone, but tone volume did not affect the number-generation task. In both cases, therefore, the relevant (but not the irrelevant) tone feature affected free-choice responses. Second, the influence of tone judgment on the free-choice task was found to depend on the response set. When responses were spatially defined along the horizontal axis (left vs. right) and consistently paired with tone features (*left* always mapped onto low volume/short tones), the number-generation task was susceptible to priming by the tones. However, the priming effect was diminished when the responses were defined along the vertical axis (up vs. down) and inconsistently paired with tone features. The findings of Heinemann et al. are consistent with the idea that a stronger stimulus–response grouping in the forced-choice component of the task renders free-choice responses more susceptible to the priming effect.

Based on our discussion of task switching (Chap. 5), we can make an additional prediction that is presumably available from Heinemann et al.'s (2013) data, although not yet reported. In that study, in two consecutive trials, participants sometimes judged the same attribute (e.g., duration → duration) and sometimes switched between attributes (e.g., duration → volume). If we assume that repeating the relevant attribute strengthens stimulus–response groups, compared to switching the relevant attribute (Dreisbach, 2012; Dreisbach & Fröber, 2018), then priming of free-choice responses should be stronger on repeat trials, compared to switch trials. This prediction might seem paradoxical because participants are thought to be, in general, more susceptible to distraction when they switch between tasks (Dreisbach & Fröber, 2018). However, assuming that priming of free-choice responses is dependent on the strength of the stimulus–response grouping in the forced-choice component of the task, the effect of primes in eliciting their corresponding response should be stronger in repeat trials, compared to switch trials.

The studies reviewed so far have a feature in common. Namely, the primes are either identical to, or closely resemble, the target stimuli associated with the forced-choice responses. For instance, a left-pointing arrow (target) is used to call for a left response in the forced-choice component of the task, while another left-pointing arrow is used, as a prime, for priming a left response (Fig. 6.2). Is it necessary for prime stimuli to closely resemble target stimuli? A study by Bermeitinger and Hackländer (2018) helps us address this question. In that study, targets were arrows (left vs. right), while primes consisted of motion (left vs. right). Thus, despite the similarity between targets and primes, the targets and primes did not have common physical features. Nevertheless, Bermeitinger and Hackländer (2018) found a priming effect, suggesting that establishing stimulus–response groups, based on the forced-choice component of a task, results in the susceptibility of free-choice responses, not only to primes that physically resemble the targets but also to primes that are conceptually similar to targets and/or responses (Hommel, 1997; Hommel, Müsseler, Aschersleben, & Prinz, 2001).

In addition to external prime stimuli, participants' own performance history can bias their selection of free-choice responses. Khan, Mourton, Buckolz, Adam, and Hayes (2010) provided a demonstration of this type of bias. In their Experiment 1, participants selected one out of four responses, using the index and middle fingers of both hands. The task involved two steps. First, they selected one response (e.g., left index finger). Second, they either received a "go" signal, which required them to execute the planned response, or received a "switch" signal, which required them to switch hands and perform a free-choice response with the alternative hand (e.g., right middle finger or right index finger). Khan et al. (2010) found that participants were more likely to choose the corresponding finger on the alternative hand, meaning that, for example, *left-index* → *right-index* transition was more likely than *left-index* → *right-middle*. In their Experiment 2, the "switch" signal required participants to perform a free-choice response, not with the alternative hand, but with the alternative finger positions. That is, if they had selected the left index finger, they had to select either the left-middle or the right-middle finger. In this experiment, participants were more likely to switch into a finger of the same hand, meaning that, for example, *left-index* → *left-middle* was more likely than *left-index* → *right-middle*. These findings were replicated and extended by Janczyk and Kunde (2014).

Besides its relevance for priming research, Khan et al.'s (2010) study has implications for task organization. We could infer the hierarchical organization of a task, and the relative dominance of response features, from switch costs: switching a subordinate feature does not eliminate the benefit of already-selected superordinate features, whereas switching a superordinate feature should eliminate or even reverse the benefit of an already-selected subordinate feature (Chap. 5). Based on this asymmetry, how should we interpret the results of Khan et al. (2010)? What might be puzzling, at first glance, is that in Experiment 1, switching hands preserved the selected finger position, whereas in Experiment 2, switching finger position (index vs. middle) preserved the selected hand (left vs. right). In other words, whereas Experiment 1 suggests finger position was a superordinate feature relative to hand, Experiment 2 suggests the reverse.

The puzzle is resolved if we assume that the tasks were differently organized. This assumption is justified because in Experiment 1, finger selection was more stable throughout a trial. After selecting one of the index responses, participants could eventually perform an index response, regardless of whether they saw a "go" or a "switch" signal. In Experiment 2, by contrast, hand selection was more stable. In this experiment, after selecting one of the right-hand responses, participants could eventually perform a right-hand response. Superordinate features are, by definition, those that are relatively more stable over time. Although hand selection is, in general, a more effective basis for response grouping (Chap. 5; Rosenbaum, 1980), when other response features become more stable (less prone to switch), then hand selection can become relatively subordinate. Thus, we could assume that finger position was a more salient basis for grouping responses in Experiment 1, whereas hand selection was a more salient basis for grouping in Experiment 2.

There is one aspect to Khan et al.'s (2010) study that is, in fact, the primary reason I have included it in the present discussion. The study suggests that response type (free choice vs. forced choice) was treated as a subordinate feature, compared to the selection of finger position (Experiment 1) or hand (Experiment 2). We could infer this because switching from forced choice to free choice did not abolish the effect of having selected those response features, suggesting that the selection of hand or finger position was superordinate to response type. Taking note of this observation is important because it prevents overstating the distinction between the two response types. We cannot confidently claim that free- and forced-choice responses corresponded to two fundamentally different types of tasks. If they did, switching between them would have abolished the already-selected response features.

By mixing forced- and free-choice responses in a single experimental task, we encourage participants to adopt performance strategies that very likely reduce the differences between the two response types (Pfister, Kiesel, & Melcher, 2010; Schlaghecken & Eimer, 2004). The fact that the priming of free-choice responses can resemble, and be correlated with, the priming of forced-choice responses (Mattler & Palmer, 2012), and the fact that response features are preserved despite switching between free- and forced-choice response types (Hughes, Schütz-Bosbach, & Waszak, 2011; Khan et al., 2010) suggest that the two types of response, at least in the context of these experiments, are not as different as their names imply. The findings suggest the possibility of flexible performance strategies that can blend the two response types within a single task.

6.1.2 Selection Processes

A second group of studies aimed to determine what selection processes, if any, are unique to free-choice response. A starting point is the observation that free-choice responses tend to take more time than forced-choice responses (Berlyne, 1957). What is it that requires the extra time? It is possible that forced- and free-choice responses reflect two *qualitatively different types of decision*. Some might believe this necessarily follows, as a matter of definition, once we distinguish the two types of responses. As we shall see, however, neither evidence nor careful reflection on experimental procedures favors this possibility. It is also possible that the two types of response differ with regard to *what comes before the decision*. This includes, for instance, what is regarded as relevant perceptual evidence for the decision (Janczyk, Dambacher, Bieleke, & Gollwitzer, 2015; Janczyk, Nolden, & Jolicoeur, 2015; Naefgen, Dambacher, & Janczyk, 2018).

How would we test whether free- and forced-choice responses rely on common or distinct mechanisms? We might assume when two tasks require a common mechanism, performing them at the same time would result in larger interference, compared to two tasks that require different mechanisms (Baddeley, 2012). Rubbing your stomach and patting your head at the same time is difficult because these tasks rely on common spatial mechanisms, but rubbing your stomach and reading a sentence at the same time is easy because these tasks rely on distinct mechanisms. Following this logic, Janczyk, Nolden, and Jolicoeur (2015) reasoned that if selection of forced- and free-choice responses relies on distinct mechanisms, then they should be differently susceptible to interference from another task. In particular, performing two forced-choice tasks together should produce a larger interference, compared to performing a forced-choice task and a free-choice task together.

Janczyk, Nolden, and Jolicoeur (2015) used a visual task that included a mix of forced- and free-choice responses (Fig. 6.1) and an auditory task that included only forced-choice responses. Performance in the visual task was the primary measure, and the presence/absence of the auditory task was the primary manipulation. In the "single-task" condition, the visual task was performed on its own. In the "dual-task" condition, the visual and the auditory tasks were combined. Although performance in the visual task slowed down when it had to be performed alongside the auditory task, contrary to the distinct-mechanisms hypothesis, free- and forced-choice responses were equally prone to interference from the auditory forced-choice task. Replicating previous findings, Janczyk, Nolden, and Jolicoeur (2015) found free-choice responses to be slower than forced-choice responses, but both types of responses were equally slowed down as a result of dual-task interference (cf. Janczyk, Dambacher, et al., 2015). Based on these findings, we cannot conclude that the two types of responses require distinct selection mechanisms.

Another study that suggests similarity, rather than difference, focused on timing and, more specifically, how the two response types change when participants adopt a liberal (favoring speed) or conservative (favoring accuracy) decision criterion (Naefgen et al., 2018). In addition to two stimuli corresponding to the forced-choice component of the task, and one stimulus corresponding to the free-choice component, the authors included "catch" trials, in which no stimulus was presented. On catch trials, participants were required to withhold from responding. In order to induce changes in decision criterion, the authors manipulated the frequency of catch trials. Unsurprisingly, when catch trials were infrequent, participants adopted a relatively liberal strategy, resulting in faster performance; when catch trials were frequent, participants adopted a relatively conservative strategy, resulting in slower performance. The important observation was that changing the frequency of catch trials affected the speed of free- and forced-choice responses to the same extent. In additional experiments, Naefgen et al. (2018) used a response-deadline manipulation, which was also intended to change decision criterion. Again, when free- and forced-choice responses changed as a consequence of changing decision criteria, they followed the same pattern.

In another study, Naefgen, Caissie, and Janczyk (2017) tested whether forced- and free-choice responses are differently sensitive to compatibility effect from a neighboring task. They used the so-called *backward compatibility effect*, which is observed in tasks that require two consecutive responses (Hommel, 1998). On a given trial of these tasks, participants could see a single visual stimulus with two features (square/diamond appearing in red/green). Participants were instructed to first respond to stimulus color (Task 1) and then to shape (Task 2). In Naefgen et al.'s (2017) study, participants were instructed to perform Task 1 using key-press responses (left/right) and Task 2 using foot pedals (left/right). Thus, the two consecutive responses could be compatible (left → left) or incompatible (left → right). Compatibility of the two consecutive responses can facilitate responses, not only in Task 2 (*forward* compatibility) but also in Task 1 (*backward* compatibility). Naefgen et al. (2017) varied the type of response (free vs. forced choice) in Task 1, while Task 2 consisted only of forced-choice responses. The question was whether backward compatibility would differ for free- and forced-choice responses of Task 1.

Analyzing performance speed suggested that the compatibility effect was stronger in the forced-choice component of Task 1. Naefgen et al. (2017) then used a procedure in which Task 1 consisted of only forced-choice responses, and Task 2 included both response types. They found a similar pattern: forward compatibility effect on performance speed was larger for forced-choice responses than for free-choice responses. They concluded that when stimulus–response associations are strong (forced choice), then responses are more susceptible to influence from a neighboring task. This interpretation appears consistent with our review of the priming studies. There, too, we saw that stronger stimulus–response grouping *within* a task can increase the effect of response priming. We should, however, be careful in distinguishing the free- and forced-choice components as two separate tasks. As we saw previously, the stronger stimulus–response association in the forced-choice component of a task determines the degree to which the free-choice component of the task is susceptible to influence (Kiesel et al., 2006; Mattler & Palmer, 2012; Schlaghecken & Eimer, 2004). The positive correlation between, and the time-course similarity of, the priming effects on the two response types further discourage the idea that the two response types are differently susceptible to compatibility effects from a neighboring task (Mattler & Palmer, 2012). Finally, a closer inspection of Naefgen et al.'s findings would undermine our confidence in the claim that forced-choice responses are relatively more susceptible to a between-task compatibility effect.

When we consider selection frequency in Naefgen et al.'s (2017) results, we find evidence in favor of a stronger effect on free-choice responses. The proportion of free-choice responses that were compatible with the neighboring task ranged from 7% to 13% across their three experiments. Of course, free-choice responses can be selected in favor of between-task compatibility effect without committing an error. In contrast, selecting a forced-choice response in favor of the between-task compatibility effect can result in an error. Nevertheless, we should note that the proportion of erroneous forced-choice responses that were compatible with the neighboring task ranged from 1% to 3%, which is considerably lower than the corresponding effect on free-choice responses. This was acknowledged by Naefgen et al. (2017, p. 28). Part of the effect on free-choice responses might have been absorbed into response selection frequencies. Due to this possibility, we cannot make a strong claim with regard to different susceptibility of the response types.

Studies reviewed in this section suggest that, when paired with another forced-choice task, the two response types are equally susceptible to dual-task interference (Janczyk, Nolden, & Jolicoeur, 2015), and they are equally susceptible to between-task compatibility effect (Naefgen et al., 2017), suggesting similar, rather than different, selection processes for the two response types. Moreover, the two response types have been found to be equally sensitive to changes in decision criteria, which also suggests similar selection processes across the response types

(Naefgen et al., 2018). What we ought to keep in mind about these studies is that free- and forced-choice responses are intermixed and, hence, the former might have been strategically subsumed into the latter response type. This is particularly plausible given that free-choice responses are supposedly not based on anything, which enables participant to blend them with whatever task they happen to be concurrently performing. If that is the case, what we observe as characteristics of free-choice responses are, in part, the consequences of our own experimental design.

6.1.3 Anticipation

A third group of studies investigate whether anticipation plays a unique role in free-choice response selection. Before discussing those studies, a few brief remarks might be necessary about outcome anticipation as a topic of experimental investigation.

Anticipation of outcome is central to goal-directed action (Hommel, 2013; Shin, Proctor, & Capaldi, 2010). Goals, after all, are either as desired *future* states or as desired current states that are protected against *future* disturbance (Marken, 2014). In experimental tasks, the role of outcome anticipation was demonstrated by Kunde (2001). He measured performance efficiency while manipulating the relation between to-be-selected response features and anticipated outcomes. He found better performance in conditions where the two were compatible. For instance, when selecting between left and right key-press responses, participants on average performed faster when each key produced a sensory outcome at the corresponding side (right key → right light). Similarly, when selecting between soft and forceful key-press responses, participants were faster when the intensity of an auditory outcome was compatible with the intensity of the response (forceful key-press → loud tone) (Koch & Kunde, 2002; Pfister et al., 2010; Pfister, Janczyk, Gressmann, Fournier, & Kunde, 2014). These observations were qualified by further studies that showed response-outcome compatibility effects depend, at least to some extent, on the intention to produce the outcome (Ansorge, 2002; Zwosta, Ruge, & Wolfensteller, 2013).

A related line of investigation examines performance sensitivity to stimuli that are similar to response outcomes. These studies consist of two phases: an acquisition phase, in which new response-outcome associations are learned, and a test phase, in which stimuli that resemble the learned outcomes are presented as primes for response selection (Hommel, 1996). Elsner and Hommel (2001) used a version of this task, in which participants first learned that two key-press responses produced two distinct auditory outcomes. In the test phase, the tones were used as target stimuli. For one group of participants, tones were assigned to the responses that produced them during the acquisition phase (compatible). For the other group, stimuli were assigned to the responses that did not produce them (incompatible). Participants in the compatible condition performed better than those in the incompatible condition. Hence, a learned response outcome can serve as a prime, biasing selection of future responses (Elsner & Hommel, 2001, 2004; Wolfensteller & Ruge, 2011; Ziessler & Nattkemper, 2011; Ziessler, Nattkemper, & Frensch, 2004; Ziessler, Nattkemper, & Vogt, 2012). These studies provide indirect evidence for outcome anticipation during response selection, by showing learned associations between responses and sensory outcomes.

We can now turn to studies that test whether we could distinguish free- and forced-choice responses based on the degree of outcome anticipation. A first study to consider is by Herwig, Prinz, and Waszak (2007), Herwig and Waszak (2009), who modified Elsner and Hommel's (2001) design. Specifically, in the learning phase, participants in separate groups either performed forced-choice ("forced-choice group") or free-choice responses ("free-choice group"). Both groups received the same sensory outcomes following responses. The authors found evidence for response-outcome learning in the free-choice group, but not in the forced-choice group.

Herwig et al.'s results suggest that when a response is selected based on a target stimulus (which is *present* at the time of response selection), processes related to sensory outcomes (which are *absent* at the time of selection) are diminished. In a follow-up study, Pfister, Kiesel, and Hoffmann (2011) examined whether using a forced-choice task during the test phase, as was done by Elsner and Hommel (2001) and Herwig et al. (2007), could affect the results. When they included free-choice responses during the test phase, they found evidence of outcome learning even in participants who had performed forced-choice responses in the learning phase. Together, the findings have been taken as evidence that free-choice response selection might facilitate learning new sensory outcomes and/or involve a higher degree of anticipating learned sensory outcomes (Fig. 6.4).

Recall that mixing free-choice responses with forced-choice responses within the same task rendered free-choice responses susceptible to priming (Schlaghecken & Eimer, 2004). Given the evidence of outcome anticipation in pure free-choice

Fig. 6.4 The idea that free- and forced-choice responses differ in how much they involve processing the triggering stimulus (what is present at the time of response selection) and the outcome (what is absent at the time of response selection)

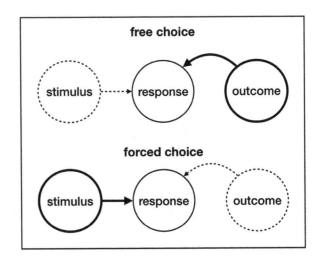

tasks, but not in pure forced-choice tasks, it is worth considering what would happen if the two response types were mixed within one task. Pfister et al. (2010) did exactly that and found evidence of outcome anticipation for forced-choice responses when they were intermixed with free-choice responses, but not when they were performed alone. This study confirms the idea that putting together the two response types can result in their strategic blending. Regardless of this point, it appears that we have finally arrived at a feature that might be more or less unique to free-choice responses, namely, anticipation of sensory outcome. Moreover, forced-choice responses might acquire this feature by virtue of being performed alongside free-choice responses (Pfister et al., 2010).

There is reason to doubt the idea that outcome anticipation is uniquely associated with free-choice response selection. That is because the strength of outcome antici-pation has been linked to other factors that can be manipulated in forced-choice responses. For example, Wolfensteller and Ruge (2014) used a forced-choice task in which response selection was either easy or difficult. The task involved four spa-tially defined response keys. In the easy condition, participants were presented with symbolic target stimuli, associated with responses based on the task rules, *and* an additional spatial signal that informed participants of the correct response. In the difficult condition, participants were presented only with symbolic target stimuli. The authors found stronger evidence for outcome anticipation in the difficult condi-tion, which suggests that the absence of response-outcome compatibility effects in forced-choice tasks might be due to the ease of selecting responses based on target stimuli.

My colleagues and I tested a similar idea about the relationship between response selection difficulty and outcome anticipation (Gozli, Huffman, & Pratt, 2016). We considered whether evidence for outcome anticipation can be found in forced-choice tasks if the task is sufficiently difficult to prevent reflex-like responses to target stimuli. In one experiment, our "easy" condition consisted of spatial compat-ibility between stimuli and responses (left target → left key, right target → right key). The "difficult" condition consisted of spatially incompatible mapping (left target → right key, right target → left key). In a second experiment, we used stimuli that were either easy or difficult to discriminate. In both experiments, we found an increased response-outcome compatibility effect under difficult conditions. Continuing this line of work, we found that response preparation can reduce the effect of outcome-related processes (Gozli & Ansorge, 2016; Huffman, Gozli, Hommel, & Pratt, 2018). Having prepared a response, participants can then narrow down the scope of sensory processes, simply waiting for the triggering stimulus.

In light of these findings, it might be useful to replace the categorical free- vs. forced-choice distinction with the distinction between prepared and unprepared responses, which is continuous. Free-choice responses, as defined in the experimental studies discussed above, are not uniquely associated with outcome anticipation. What increases outcome-related processes in free-choice responses might be a rela-tively wider and more ambiguous scope of what is perceptually relevant for response selection.

6.2   Free-Choice Tasks as Quasi-Forced-Choice Tasks

In the previous section, we considered if free-choice responses possess unique features that could distinguish them from forced-choice responses. We saw that, similar to forced-choice responses, free-choice responses are susceptible to priming effects, compatibility effects from neighboring tasks, and they follow a similar pattern of change as a function of decision criteria. Moreover, outcome anticipation, which might seem to be especially associated with free-choice responses, can be observed in forced-choice tasks with decreased response preparation or increased selection difficulty. In short, we did not find features that are unique to free-choice responses.

In this section, I attempt to show why the search for unique features of free choice is in vain, and why that should not surprise us. In particular, I argue that both types of responses, as conceived in experimental studies, are responses to external features of the situation. The difference in those features ("stimuli") constitutes the basic difference between the response types. In the case of the forced-choice task, response is based on an immediate target that can often be clearly perceived, presented within a thin slice of time. In the case of the free-choice task, response is based on a temporally extended impression. We will arrive at this conclusion if we carefully consider whether free-choice responses, addressed in experimental psychology, are truly free in the sense of being detached and withdrawn from the participants' situation.

Free-choice tasks are normative, which is to say there are good and bad ways of performing them. To be more precise, there is a range of good performances in the case of free-choice tasks, but there are also ways to perform the tasks poorly. Indeed, there are ways of performing free-choice tasks that would result in excluding the participant from the study (Gozli, 2017). Consider the first seven choices in a binary free-choice task, with the two choices represented as "A" and "B". The seven consecutive choices could be, for example, BAABABB, which is as good as ABBABAA. In comparison, the sequence AAAAAAA reflects poor performance. The sequence ABABABA would also raise experimenters' suspicion because it is following a simple, predictable pattern. Note the following instructions, which are typical of experiments on free choice.

> Written instructions emphasized [...], for the free choice trials, an even distribution of left and right responses as well as the avoidance of patterns in maintaining this distribution (Naefgen et al., 2018, p. 1043).

The authors state that "no erroneous responses can be made in free choice tasks" (ibid), but the no-error statement applies to single trials, considered in isolation, not to a sequence of trials considered as a whole. To perform the free-choice task well (to meet the inclusion criteria), participants should (1) maintain a roughly equal number of the two choices, (2) avoid repeating obvious patterns (ABABAB... AABBAA...).

To avoid patterns, the free-choice response, on any given trial, must be a response to the participants' history of previous responses (cf. Naefgen et al., 2018, p.1049).

The response is made such that, against the background of the participants' selection history, selections are evenly distributed and that the current sequence of responses appears spontaneous. Imagine a participant performing the first four trials of our binary free-choice task, choosing the same response on all four trials (AAAA…). On the fifth trial, if she is following the task instructions, her own selection history should bias selection toward B. This is not a matter of a random variable staying true to its distribution. It is, rather, a rule-governed attempt at acting *as if* one's choice is a random variable. Deviating from the criteria that characterize "good performance" on free-choice/random tasks often forces the researchers to exclude the participant from analysis because (according to this particular conception of free-choice performance) their performance cannot be counted as free choice.

> The data of participants whose free choice responses showed a strong bias towards one response option (> 80% of choices) were discarded and new data were collected from new participants. (Naefgen et al., 2018, p. 1043).

A participant's history of selection is not always as unambiguous as "AAAA…." The participants often face a history of mixed selection, against which a judgment of proportion is ambiguous. It is reasonable, therefore, to assume it is more difficult to respond to one's selection history than to respond to an easily identifiable target. In the former case, one is responding to the impression of a temporally extended sequence of events. By adjusting their responses based on that impression, participants "stay on track", continuing to act as if their responses are based on a random variable. The ambiguity of what participants respond to, in free-choice tasks, provides a clue as to why these tasks involve extraneous stimulus processing or distractibility (Herwig et al., 2007), usually take more time (Janczyk, Nolden, & Jolicoeur, 2015), and rely on memory (Naefgen & Janczyk, 2018).

Naefgen and Janczyk (2018) drew a connection between free-choice tasks and random generation tasks, but instead of regarding this idea as an insight about the operational definition of free choice, and how experimental design can pre-determine the findings, they treated it as an empirical question. After pointing out similar instructions for random-number generation and free-choice tasks, they went on to test whether the two rely on common mechanisms. They investigated whether both tasks rely on working memory. In their Experiment 1, participants were presented with different portions of their selection history. Specifically, they saw 0, 3, or 7 of their previous choices. Having the previous choices in front of them reduced the demand on their memory. The authors found faster and more evenly distributed ("random") responses when participants had visual access to their selection history, compared to when they did not. In Experiment 2, the researchers combined the free-choice task with another task which placed additional demands on memory. Experiment 2 found slower and less evenly distributed free-choice responses when participants had to remember information in order to perform a concurrent task. Therefore, Naefgen and Janczyk (2018) provided a nice demonstration that free-choice task relies on memory, and that the "stimulus" of a free-choice task consists of a temporally extended series of previous choices (selection history), the access to which requires memory. Their study also highlights the restricted manner in which free choice has been operationalized in experimental studies and the gap between that operational definition and the meaning of free choice in ordinary language.

In sum, while performance in forced-choice tasks requires satisfying relatively immediate constraints, performance in free-choice tasks requires satisfying relatively long-term constraints. Performance in both tasks is normative, subject to standards of inclusion and evaluation (Naefgen et al., 2018; Naefgen & Janczyk, 2018). Once we consider that selection history serves as a kind of stimulus for the current free-choice response, and once we recognize that this "stimulus"—given that it is extended over time—is often more difficult to judge than the target stimuli of the forced-choice task, we are faced with a straightforward way of explaining the extra time needed for free-choice tasks, relative to forced-choice task. This explanation is consistent with the idea that the difference between free- and forced-choice tasks has to do with perceptual processes, rather than response selection per se (Janczyk, Dambacher, et al., 2015; Janczyk, Nolden, & Jolicoeur, 2015; Naefgen et al., 2018). Furthermore, the same explanation tells us why performance in forced-choice tasks begins to resemble free-choice tasks, in terms of outcome anticipation, when the perceptual component of the task becomes demanding (Gozli et al., 2016; Wolfensteller & Ruge, 2014). Free-choice tasks are quasi-forced-choice tasks, performed in response to an ambiguous and demanding "stimulus," while maintaining evenness of distribution among responses and the appearance of simultaneity.

6.3 Implications

In this chapter, we have been discussing the experimental research of free-choice response selection. My aim has been to provide a context in which we can interpret the results of these experiments. First, the way in which free choice is operationalized in these tasks corresponds to a particular conception of free choice, which is based on detachment and negation (Sartre, 1956). To be free, according to this conception, is to act in a way that cannot be explained with reference to one's situation, social role, convention, or external pressure. To do so, in Dennett's (2004) term, is to perform "moral levitation." It is, however, possible to characterize free choice with reference to our attachment to what we truly value. What we want from our capacity for free choice is the pursuit of what is valuable and good to us (Berlin, 2002; Dennett, 2004). Our choices reveal who we are, which is why knowing a person well would enable us to anticipate their choices (Smedslund, 1997). By contrast, in experimental tasks, which require uniform treatment of research participants (Künzell et al., 2018), free-choice responses are supposedly not based on any reason, and not indicative of any personal characteristic of the people who perform them.

Once we have a set of operational definitions for free- and forced-choice responses, we have already narrowed down the scope of research questions. We are left with questions such as, "Can free-choice responses be influenced by subliminal primes?", "Can free-choice responses be influenced by a neighboring task?", "Are there features that can distinguish free-choice responses from forced-choice responses?". When we construct experiments in which these questions can be tested, the results of the experiments are determined, to a large extent, by the design of the experiments. For example, priming of free-choice responses has been found to depend on the forced-choice component of the experiment task, including the strength of stimulus–response grouping therein.

We might be surprised to find, at first glance, that free-choice responses can be influenced at all. This sense of surprise, however, is sustained by (a) a naïve view of freedom and free choice and (b) ignoring the research methods that lead to the findings. To highlight the first reason, note that we do not feel the same sense of surprise, nor do we shout "determinism!" when experimental findings show our *action* can bias our *perception* (Fagioli, Hommel, & Schubotz, 2007; Wykowska, Schubö, & Hommel, 2009). Finding that, for instance, preparing to grasp an object sensitizes the observer toward grasp-related visual features (distance-from-hand and object size) and away from grasp-unrelated features (color) would be framed as actions *guiding* our perception. By contrast, hearing that our *perception* can bias our *action*, in particular actions that supposedly ought to be dissociated from everything except for an "internal" will, appears surprising because it challenges the assumption that free actions must transcend all influence.

The second reason is equally important. Placing the surprising claim in a context that includes a description of methods would deflate the sense of surprise. With proper reference to methods and operational definitions, the claim becomes more accurate. Rather than stating "free choice can be influenced", we would state: when we instruct participants to randomly select among a set of alternatives, and continue to do so over a series of trials while trying to appear spontaneous, and also occasionally perform forced-choice responses, we could bias their choices through the presentation of primes. This would assume that the stimulus–response grouping in the forced-choice component of the task is sufficiently strong, and there is optimal delay between the presentation of the prime and the response. As a matter of fact, this approach re-orients us with respect to the role of priming effects. Instead of regarding the effects as a discovery, we could regard them as an indication of whether a given stimulus–response grouping is sufficiently strong, such that the stimuli could activate their corresponding responses (Smedslund, 2002).

The search for unique processes involved in free-choice response selection has proven elusive because it shares essential characteristics with forced-choice response selection. Both types of responses are selected on the basis of situational factors, which means free-choice responses have their own "stimuli." The difference between the stimulus of a forced-choice task and that of a free-choice task is that the former is often presented clearly at a point in time and space, and can be easily identified, whereas the latter is extended over time and is relatively ambiguous. That is why the two types of responses can be made to resemble each other through various experimental manipulations, such as reducing the ease and efficiency of forced-choice tasks (Huffman et al., 2018) and helping participants remember their previous selections in a free-choice task (Naefgen & Janczyk, 2018). Some of these experimental findings are almost pre-determined—they are guaranteed if participants follow the instructions (Smedslund, 1991). The idea that free-choice performance should resemble random-number generation, for instance, is correct because of the similarity in the methods of producing them (Naefgen & Janczyk, 2018).

If I am asked to make a random choice, a choice that is not based on anything, I am not asked to pursue an outcome that is of value to me. As such, I would probably not mind if someone tells me that they could influence my choice. If, on the other hand, my choice serves a purpose, then I would mind very much if someone influences my choice without my knowledge. If I decide about my relationships, my health, or my career, then I want my decision to be based on the right reasons. Such a purposeful decision is not really a "free" choice, in the sense of transcending all situational factors. It is based on appropriate engagement, and it is constrained by a set of beliefs and values (Stam, 1990; Strawson, 1992). The quality of my choices is, thus, based on how well I perceive those relevant constraints and how well I respond to them. To the extent that I do not identify with a given goal, including goals that are assigned to me by experimental psychologists, and to the extent that I participate in, and enact, an imposed hierarchy, I am participating in a forced-choice task, and that includes tasks that are conventionally described as "free choice."

References

Ansorge, U. (2002). Spatial intention-response compatibility. *Acta Psychologica, 109*(3), 285–299.

Baddeley, A. (2012). Working memory: Theories, models, and controversies. *Annual Review of Psychology, 63*, 1–29.

Berlin, I. (2002). Two concepts of liberty. In H. Hardy (Ed.), *Liberty*. Oxford, UK: Oxford University Press.

Berlyne, D. E. (1957). Conflict and choice time. *British Journal of Psychology, 48*, 106–118.

Bermeitinger, C., & Hackländer, R. P. (2018). Response priming with motion primes: Negative compatibility or congruency effects, even in free-choice trials. *Cognitive Processing, 19*, 351.

Dehaene, S., Bossini, S., & Giraux, P. (1993). The mental representation of parity and number magnitude. *Journal of Experimental Psychology: General, 122*(3), 371–396.

Dennett, D. C. (2004). *Freedom evolves*. New York, NY: Penguin Books.

Dreisbach, G. (2012). Mechanisms of cognitive control: The functional role of task rules. *Current Directions in Psychological Science, 21*, 227–231.

Dreisbach, G., & Fröber, K. (2018). On how to be flexible (or not): Modulation of the stability-flexibility balance. *Current Directions in Psychological Science, 28*, 3.

Elsner, B., & Hommel, B. (2001). Effect anticipation and action control. *Journal of Experimental Psychology: Human Perception and Performance, 27*, 229–240.

Elsner, B., & Hommel, B. (2004). Contiguity and contingency in the acquisition of action effects. *Psychological Research, 68*, 138–154.

Fagioli, S., Hommel, B., & Schubotz, R. I. (2007). Intentional control of attention: Action planning primes action-related stimulus dimensions. *Psychological Research, 71*(1), 22–29.

Fischer, M. H. (2001). Number processing induces spatial performance biases. *Neurology, 57*(5), 822–826.

Frith, C. (2013). The psychology of volition. *Experimental Brain Research, 229*, 289–299.

Gozli, D. G. (2017). Behaviour versus performance: The veiled commitment of experimental psychology. *Theory & Psychology, 27*, 741–758.

Gozli, D. G., & Ansorge, U. (2016). Action selection as a guide for visual attention. *Visual Cognition, 24*, 38–50.

Gozli, D. G., Huffman, G., & Pratt, J. (2016). Acting and anticipating: Impact of outcome-compatible distractor depends on response selection efficiency. *Journal of Experimental Psychology: Human Perception and Performance, 42*, 1601–1614.

Haggard, P. (2008). Human volition: Towards a neuroscience of will. *Nature Reviews Neuroscience, 9*(12), 934–946.

Heinemann, A., Pfister, R., & Janczyk, M. (2013). Manipulating number generation: Loud + long = large? *Consciousness and Cognition, 22*(4), 1332–1339.

Herwig, A., Prinz, W., & Waszak, F. (2007). Two modes of sensorimotor integration in intention-based and stimulus-based actions. *The Quarterly Journal of Experimental Psychology, 60*(11), 1540–1554.

Herwig, A., & Waszak, F. (2009). Intention and attention in ideomotor learning. *Quarterly Journal of Experimental Psychology, 62*(2), 219–227.

Hommel, B. (1996). The cognitive representation of action: Automatic integration of perceived action effects. *Psychological Research, 59*, 176–186.

Hommel, B. (1997). Toward an action-concept model of stimulus-response compatibility. In B. Hommel & W. Prinz (Eds.), *Theoretical issues in stimulus-response compatibility* (pp. 281–320). Amsterdam, The Netherlands: North-Holland.

Hommel, B. (1998). Automatic stimulus-response translation in dual-task performance. *Journal of Experimental Psychology: Human Perception and Performance, 24*, 1368–1384.

Hommel, B. (2000). The prepared reflex: Automaticity and control in stimulus-response transla-tion. In S. Monsell & J. Driver (Eds.), *Control of cognitive processes: Attention and perfor-mance XVIII* (pp. 247–273). Cambridge, MA: MIT Press.

Hommel, B. (2013). Ideomotor action control: On the perceptual grounding of voluntary actions and agents. In W. Prinz, M. Beisert, & A. Herwig (Eds.), *Action science: Foundations of an emerging discipline* (pp. 113–136). Cambridge, MA: MIT Press.

Hommel, B., Müsseler, J., Aschersleben, G., & Prinz, W. (2001). The theory of event coding (TEC): A framework for perception and action planning. *Behavioral and Brain Sciences, 24*, 849–878.

Huffman, G., Gozli, D. G., Hommel, B., & Pratt, J. (2018). Response preparation, response selec-tion difficulty, and response-outcome learning. *Psychological Research, 83*, 247.

Hughes, G., Schütz-Bosbach, S., & Waszak, F. (2011). One action system or two? Evidence for common central preparatory mechanisms in voluntary and stimulus-driven actions. *Journal of Neuroscience, 31*(46), 16692–16699.

Janczyk, M., Dambacher, M., Bieleke, M., & Gollwitzer, P. M. (2015). The benefit of no choice: Goal-directed plans enhance perceptual processing. *Psychological Research, 79*, 206–220.

Janczyk, M., & Kunde, W. (2014). The role of effect grouping in free-choice response selection. *Acta Psychologica, 150*, 49–54.

Janczyk, M., Nolden, S., & Jolicoeur, P. (2015). No differences in dual-task costs between forced- and free-choice tasks. *Psychological Research, 79*, 463–477.

Khan, M. A., Mourton, S., Buckolz, E., Adam, J. J., & Hayes, A. E. (2010). The influence of response grouping on free-choice decision making in a response selection task. *Acta Psychologica, 134*, 175–181.

Kiesel, A., Wagener, A., Kunde, W., Hoffmann, J., Fallgatter, A. J., & Stöcker, C. (2006). Unconscious manipulation of free choice in humans. *Consciousness and Cognition, 15*, 397–408.

Koch, I., & Kunde, W. (2002). Verbal response-effect compatibility. *Memory & Cognition, 30*(8), 1297–1303.

Kukla, A., & Walmsley, J. (2006). *Mind: A historical and philosophical introduction to the major theories*. Indianapolis, IN: Hackett Publishing.

Kunde, W. (2001). Response-effect compatibility in manual choice reaction tasks. *Journal of Experimental Psychology: Human Perception and Performance, 27*(2), 387–394.

Künzell, S., Broeker, L., Dignath, D., Ewolds, H., Raab, M., & Thomaschke, R. (2018). What is a task? An ideomotor perspective. *Psychological Research, 82*, 4.

Marcel, G. (1962). *Man against mass society* (G. S. Frasier, Trans.). South Bend, IN: St. Augustine Press.

Marken, R. S. (2014). *Doing research on purpose: A control theory approach to experimental psychology*. Chapel Hill, NC: New View.

Mattler, U., & Palmer, S. (2012). Time course of free-choice priming effects explained by a simple accumulator model. *Cognition, 123*(3), 347–360.

Naefgen, C., Caissie, A. F., & Janczyk, M. (2017). Stimulus-response links and the backward crosstalk effect—A comparison of forced-and free-choice tasks. *Acta Psychologica, 177*, 23–29.

Naefgen, C., Dambacher, M., & Janczyk, M. (2018). Why free choices take longer than forced choices: Evidence from response threshold manipulations. *Psychological Research, 82*, 1039.

Naefgen, C., & Janczyk, M. (2018). Free choice tasks as random generation tasks: An investigation through working memory manipulations. *Experimental Brain Research., 236*, 2263.

Pfister, R., Janczyk, M., Gressmann, M., Fournier, L. R., & Kunde, W. (2014). Good vibrations? Vibrotactile self-stimulation reveals anticipation of body-related action effects in motor control. *Experimental Brain Research, 232*(3), 847–854.

Pfister, R., Kiesel, A., & Hoffmann, J. (2011). Learning at any rate: Action-effect learning for stimulus-based actions. *Psychological Research, 75*(1), 61–65.

Pfister, R., Kiesel, A., & Melcher, T. (2010). Adaptive control of ideomotor effect anticipations. *Acta Psychologica, 135*(3), 316–322.

Ristic, J., & Kingstone, A. (2006). Attention to arrows: Pointing to a new direction. *The Quarterly Journal of Experimental Psychology, 59*(11), 1921–1930.

Rosenbaum, D. A. (1980). Human movement initiation: Specification of arm, direction, and extent. *Journal of Experimental Psychology: General, 109*(4), 444–474.

Sartre, J. P. (1956). *Being and nothingness*. New York, NY: Philosophical Library.

Schlaghecken, F., & Eimer, M. (2004). Masked prime stimuli can bias "free" choices between response alternatives. *Psychonomic Bulletin & Review, 11*, 463–468.

Shin, Y. K., Proctor, R. W., & Capaldi, E. J. (2010). A review of contemporary ideomotor theory. *Psychological Bulletin, 136*(6), 943–974.

Smedslund, J. (1991). The pseudoempirical in psychology and the case for psychologic. *Psychological Inquiry, 2*, 325–338.

Smedslund, J. (1997). *The structure of psychological common sense*. Mahwah, NJ: Lawrence Erlbaum.

Smedslund, J. (2002). From hypothesis-testing psychology to procedure-testing psychologic. *Review of General Psychology, 6*(1), 51–72.

Stam, H. (1990). What distinguishes lay persons' psychological explanations from those of psychologists? In W. J. Baker, M. E. Hyland, R. van Hezewijk, & S. Terwee (Eds.), *Recent trends in theoretical psychology* (Vol. 2, pp. 97–106). New York, NY: Springer-Verlag.

Strawson, P. F. (1992). *Analysis and metaphysics*. Oxford, UK: Oxford University Press.

Verschuere, B., Prati, V., & Houwer, J. D. (2009). Cheating the lie detector: Faking in the autobiographical Implicit Association Test. *Psychological Science, 20*(4), 410–413.

Walsh, V. (2003). A theory of magnitude: Common cortical metrics of time, space and quantity. *Trends in Cognitive Sciences, 7*(11), 483–488.

Wolfensteller, U., & Ruge, H. (2011). On the timescale of stimulus-based action–effect learning. *The Quarterly Journal of Experimental Psychology, 64*(7), 1273–1289.

Wolfensteller, U., & Ruge, H. (2014). Response selection difficulty modulates the behavioral impact of rapidly learnt action effects. *Frontiers in Psychology, 5*, 1382.

Wykowska, A., Schubö, A., & Hommel, B. (2009). How you move is what you see: Action planning biases selection in visual search. *Journal of Experimental Psychology: Human Perception and Performance, 35*(6), 1755–1769.

Ziessler, M., & Nattkemper, D. (2011). The temporal dynamics of effect anticipation in course of action planning. *The Quarterly Journal of Experimental Psychology, 64*(7), 1305–1326.

Ziessler, M., Nattkemper, D., & Frensch, P. A. (2004). The role of anticipation and intention in the learning of effects of self-performed actions. *Psychological Research, 68*(2-3), 163–175.

Ziessler, M., Nattkemper, D., & Vogt, S. (2012). The activation of effect codes in response preparation: New evidence from an indirect priming paradigm. *Frontiers in Psychology, 3*, 585.

Zwosta, K., Ruge, H., & Wolfensteller, U. (2013). No anticipation without intention: Response–effect compatibility in effect-based and stimulus-based actions. *Acta Psychologica, 144*(3), 628–634.

Chapter 7
Sense of Agency

In the previous chapter, we were concerned with a way of categorizing actions (free vs. forced). In this chapter, we are shifting our attention toward external events, distinguishing events as they relate to our own actions. Figure 7.1 provides a simple starting point. The division here is not based on objective causal relations, but on subjective judgment. First, there are self-caused events. For example, I call my cat and he comes to me. When reflecting on this event, I judge it as the cat responding to my call, thus perceiving a causal role for myself in the event. Second, there are events caused by others. The cat might come to me spontaneously. In this case, I have an unambiguous sense that the event is *not* caused by me. In contrast to the first two categories, there are ambiguous cases. My cat might come to me 5 s after I call him. In this case, I cannot tell whether or not he is responding to my call.

In the case of ambiguous events, we could orient our attention to aspects of them, or to some preceding events that are self-caused (Frith, 2005; Pacherie, 2008). In the example of calling a cat, regardless of whether I can clearly sense agency over the cat's coming to me, I can clearly sense agency over the act of calling him. Figure 7.2 illustrates this distinction. The proximal event (calling the cat) is unambiguously under my control in both cases, while my sense of agency differs with respect to the distal parts of the events (the cat's coming to me). When we talk about a person's sense of agency over an event, the event in question is the currently salient (basic-level) event, in a hierarchy of events. There are often proximal events of which the person feels in control. Being in control of those proximal or subordinate events is a prerequisite for surmising the person's agency over the relatively basic-level events. If I do not have control over my own voice, such that calling the cat is not possible for me, the question does not arise regarding my control over the cat's attention with my voice.

The question of agency can arise about an *actual* event, which has already happened, or *potential* events, which may or may not happen (Fig. 7.3). We might call these retrospective and prospective senses of agency (Chambon & Haggard, 2013). Of course, prospective agency is shaped by events in the past. If you ask me whether I am able to draw my cat's attention, and get him to come to me, I will answer based

© Springer Nature Switzerland AG 2019
D. Gozli, *Experimental Psychology and Human Agency*,
https://doi.org/10.1007/978-3-030-20422-8_7

Fig. 7.1 A division of
events based on their
sensed causal relation to
oneself: those that can be
unambiguously perceived
as self-caused (Event 1),
those that can be
unambiguously perceived
as *not* self-caused (Event
2), and those that are
ambiguous, which means
they can be perceived as
possibly self-caused

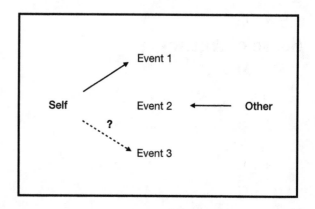

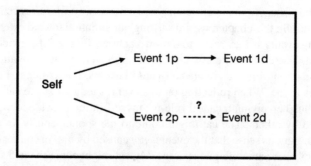

Fig. 7.2 When one perceives agency over a distal event (Event 1d), or faces ambiguity as to
whether the event is self-caused (Event 2d), one often has a sense of agency over some relatively
proximal (subordinate) event, including one's thought, intention, or body movement, which makes
it possible to surmise one's agency over the distal event

Fig. 7.3 Sense of agency
could be about events that
have actually occurred or
events that may or may not
occur

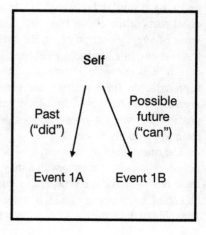

on my history of interactions with my cat. If you ask me the same question about a new cat, I will have to try calling the cat a few times. Perhaps the first time, the cat does not notice me, or ignores me. I will adjust my strategy and maybe try different tones and gestures. This is typical of new situations where the question of control arises. We do not form a judgment based on a one-off action. We explore. We search for ways of gaining agency in the situation (Gozli & Dolcini, 2018; Hills, Todd, Lazer, Redish, & Couzin, 2015). Exploration enables us to anticipate the outcome of our future actions, which is to say exploration makes it possible to form a prospective sense of agency. If I know that I can draw my cat's attention, then I can have a sense of agency over his attention, without actually calling him. I perceive, in my cat, the *affordance* of his attention (Gibson, 1986). The prospective sense of agency ("I can…", "I cannot…") may also serve as a background assumption in judging retrospective agency over particular events ("I did…", "I did not…"). If I have always failed to draw my cat's attention, his appearing to respond to my call on one occasion would not give me an unambiguous sense of agency over his attention and movement.

Sense of agency is a special subset of our understanding of causality (Frith, 2014; Gärdenfors, Jost, & Warglien, 2018; Hommel, 2017). It is special because it reflects an understanding of how our actions cause changes in the world, because it has significant affective and behavioral consequences (Maier & Seligman, 1976), and because it enables us to distinguish self-caused events from externally caused events. When animals face unpredictable and resource-scarce environments, they tend to engage in intense exploration, reward-seeking, and foraging (Anselme & Güntürkün, 2018; Ferster & Skinner, 1957), perhaps because they wish to secure, not only the resources necessary for their survival but also prospective control over their environment (Eitam, Kennedy, & Higgins, 2013; Karsh & Eitam, 2015).

The process of finding out that I am, or I am not, the cause of an event does not seem transparent from a third-person perspective, particularly if the action is performed within a complex situation, where discovering causal connections requires some understanding of what is relevant (Dennett, 1984). We appear to rely on certain presuppositions when we learn about the consequences of our actions (Hume, 1739; Kant, 1781/1998). For instance, if event E tends to consistently follows action A, and if E tends to not happen without A, then A is likely the cause of E. This is the principle of *contingency*, and it is used in research methods that involve learning new action–outcome associations (e.g., participants learning that two keys produce high- and low-pitch tones) (Elsner & Hommel, 2001).

Imagine actions A1 and A2 followed, respectively, by events E1 and E2. We might have participants learn these contingencies during a learning period. After the learning period, the contingencies would no longer be regular. When performing A1, we sometimes present participants with E1 (congruent with the learned contingencies), and sometimes with E2 (incongruent). Assuming that participants have learned the causal relations (A1 → E1, A2 → E2), we would expect them to have a stronger sense of agency when seeing congruent outcomes relative to incongruent outcomes (Caspar, Desantis, Dienes, Cleeremans, & Haggard, 2016; Gozli & Brown, 2011; Gozli, Aslam, & Pratt, 2016; Sidarus, Chambon, & Haggard, 2013).

In addition to contingency, *contiguity* plays a role in causal reasoning, in general, and sense of agency, in particular. If event E follows action A immediately, rather than following A after a delay, A is more likely the cause of E. The principle of contiguity (contiguity → sense of agency) is so central that its inverse can also be observed (sense of agency → contiguity). That is, when we feel agency over an event, we tend to perceive a shorter delay between our action and the event, compared to when we do not feel agency over the event. As we shall see, this phenomenon ("intentional binding") is used as an indirect measure of sense of agency.

Contingency and contiguity can have different effects on the subjective and immediate sense of agency versus the reflective and carefully reasoned judgment of agency (Wen, Yamashita, & Asama, 2015a). In certain situations, an experimental manipulation might selectively reduce the felt agency, or the sense of control over sensorimotor events, while leaving the explicit judgment of agency unaffected ("I know I caused that, but I did not feel like I did"), or vice versa ("I am not sure if I caused that, but it felt like I did"). For example, inverting the spatial relationship between the movements of a computer mouse and the movements of the cursor, such that a leftward mouse movement would now cause a rightward cursor movement, still gives the impression that the user is causing the movements of the cursor, but takes away the ability to accurately predict the moment-to-moment movements of the cursor (Gozli & Brown, 2011; Wolpert, 1997). With reference to the levels of control along a hierarchy, inverting the mouse–cursor relationship undermines a subordinate sense of agency, while preserving a relatively superordinate sense of agency. We will return to this issue when discussing sense of agency in shared tasks.

Another set of principles, recently discussed by Gärdenfors et al. (2018), has to do with how actions and effects ought to co-vary, assuming that they are both continuous variables. If more force is applied to an action, we tend to expect the corresponding effect to also increase in intensity. While pushing a table, for example, if I increase my force, I expect an increase (rather than a decrease) in the movement of the table. I would also expect small changes in my force to cause small changes in outcome, and not the other way around. We could extend this idea and consider the effect of action–outcome similarity. For instance, I face my cat and utter the phrase, "intentional binding," after which the cat meows. I then turn to my parrot and utter the same phrase, "intentional binding," after which the parrot repeats, "intentional binding." I might, in both cases, have the sense that my animal companions are responding to me, but the stark similarity of the parrot's response gives me a stronger sense that what he did was causally related to what I said (see Ebert & Wegner, 2010; Kawabe, 2013).

Although these principles seem to apply to our interactions with the physical world, they are less effective in accounting for our actions and agency in the social world. Pushing the table around a few times will establish my sense of agency over its motion because (assuming that my ability and the weight of the table are both constant) the causal relations between the table and I are reversible—I can move the table back and forth between two points as many times as I wish. By contrast, consider borrowing money from a friend. I can borrow money from a friend once or twice, while maintaining the sense that I can still borrow money from him. If I continue to ask for more money, however, I will begin to lose my prospective sense of agency regarding the exchange. This example illustrates how events within the social reality are irreversible (Mammen, 2017; Smedslund, 2016). By repeatedly borrowing money from my friend, I would not be gaining the ability to accurately predict the consequences of my future actions through observation and generalization. I would be changing my relationship, as well as the consequences of my future requests.

When we interact effectively with our physical or social environment, we may not pause and reflect on our sense of agency. When I call my cat and he comes to me, I do not withdraw from my interaction with him to reflect, "It was *I* who made him come to me". Similarly, when I tell a joke to my friends and they laugh, I do not take a step back to reflect on my causal power over their laughter, unless I have certain philosophical or social preoccupations. My sense of agency remains in the background, though available as a potential target of reflection (Gallagher & Zahavi, 2007). Assuming that I pose the questions "What made the cat come to me?" or "What made my friends laugh?", I can engage in a reflection, changing my way of engaging with the situation, and provide a report that would express my sense of agency. The explication of the sense of agency might itself be a factor that exerts change.

The above preliminary remarks could be summarized in three points. First, the capacity to experience agency over events can yield ambiguity. Such ambiguous cases are the primary focus of experimental research. Second, even in ambiguous cases ("did the cat come to me in response to my call?"), we can have a strong sense of agency over some proximal, intermediate event ("I called the cat"). As such, our overall sense of agency might change depending on where our attention goes. Third, to disambiguate the link between proximal and distal events, to test one's agency over the distal events, we need trial and exploration, relying on principles of causal reasoning. The opportunity to explore is usually not given to research participants during experiments that examine sense of agency. Instead, to construct and maintain ambiguity, participants are presented with one-off actions and outcomes, which makes it difficult to regard their judgments as correct or incorrect. It is precisely the ambiguous relationship between actions and subsequent events, occasionally perceived as the outcomes of those actions, that renders the participants' judgments of agency susceptible to various experimental manipulations.

7.1   Methods for Studying the Sense of Agency

Imagine we are concerned with whether a person's sense of agency is accurate. This can apply to patients with schizophrenia. The breakdowns of the sense of agency are often so profound that a formal test might not be necessary to detect them (Blakemore, Wolpert, & Frith, 2002; Frith, 2005). Still, let us ask what a valid test might be. What we want to test is whether the person can distinguish events that are caused by himself (Event 1 in Fig. 7.1) from events that are caused by external sources (Event 2 in Fig. 7.1). We construct an experiment in which the person performs an act (say the word "ring"). The act causes an outcome (a bell rings). In each condition, the experimenter gives the participant a signal. Upon receiving the signal, the participant has to either say the word "ring" or choose not to say it. Here are the conditions:

Condition 1: The bell rings immediately if, and only if, the participant says "ring". In this condition, the person has agency over the sound of the ring, and we expect him to report having a strong sense of agency.
Condition 2: The bell rings if, and only if, the participant does not say "ring". Although the contingencies are reversed compared to Condition 1, the participant has agency over *whether or not* the bell rings, and we might expect him to report at least a moderate sense of agency after sufficient exposure to the condition.
Condition 3: The bell rings 50% of the time, regardless of what the participant does. Put differently, the bell rings in roughly half of the trials when the participant says "ring". And, the bell also rings in roughly half of the trials when the participant does not say "ring". Here, the person has no agency over the bell, and we expect him to report little, if any, sense of agency.

To make the conditions as unambiguous as possible, the experimenter would offer as much time as the participant needs, allowing him to decide when he has had enough experience. Additionally, the experimenter would inform the participant whenever he goes from one condition to another. Thus, we would expect the participant to be able to provide accurate reports. We would not expect the same level of accuracy if different conditions are mixed or if the participant is prevented from sampling each condition enough prior to judgment.

We could introduce ambiguity by changing the action–outcome contingency (probability of outcome given the action). Consider, for instance, a condition in which the response, "ring", would produce the ring 70% of the time, and withholding the response would produce the ring 50% of the time. In this condition, the probability of the bell ringing is not completely independent of the participants' action and, as such, participants have some degree of agency over the bell. Because this condition is ambiguous, we would not expect precise judgment even from neurologically intact participants and, therefore, we would not use this condition to test the capacity to form an accurate sense of agency. Instead, judgment of agency in such a condition would reflect the role of other factors such as individual bias, expectation, or recent experience.

An important feature of Condition 1 is expressed by the word "immediately". It is important that the bell rings immediately after the person says "ring". Because a similar experience of contiguity is not possible to implement in Condition 2 (it does not make much sense to talk about the exact moment of *not* performing a response), participants might experience a weaker sense of agency in Condition 2, or one that requires more time to develop, relative to Condition 1.

If we want to reduce the sense of agency in Condition 1, we could introduce a fixed or variable delay between the response "ring" and the ringing of the bell (Elsner & Hommel, 2004; Haggard, Clark, & Kalogeras, 2002).

Condition 4: The bell rings one second after the person says "ring". Although the contingencies are the same as Condition 1, the participant is expected to report a relatively weaker sense of agency.

Condition 5: In 50% of the trials, the bell rings immediately upon a response, and in the other 50% of the trials, the bell rings after a one-second delay. Participants are expected to report a higher sense of agency on no-delay trials and a lower sense of agency on delay trials.

The effect of delay (Conditions 4–5 vs. Condition 1), compared to the effect of contingency (Condition 3 vs. Condition 1), might be stronger in a task where participants report their subjective feeling of agency, though weaker in a task where participants attempt to provide an objective judgment of agency. If every time I say "ring," I hear the bell ring, albeit with a delay, then I have grounds for judging that I have agency over the bell, even though my feeling of agency might not be as strong as the case of immediate ringing. When forming an explicit judgment, in this case, I am relying on contingency, not contiguity. Once again, we could describe the partial sense of agency in terms of the different levels of the goal hierarchy: Introducing a variable delay (Condition 5) reduces agency at the relatively subordinate level, while preserving agency at the relatively superordinate level. A dramatic example is the aforementioned Condition 2, where the action and the outcome are negatively, though perfectly, correlated. We would expect the feeling of agency over the bell to be weaker in Condition 2 relative to Condition 1, due to the lack of control over the timing of the outcome. Let us consider two further conditions.

Condition 6: There are two bells in the room, each with its unique sound. Bell 1 rings if you say the word "cat", and Bell 2 rings if you say the word "dog". In both cases, the bell rings immediately after the word is spoken. In this condition, you can control both when a bell rings and which bell rings.

Condition 7: The setup is similar to that of Condition 6, and the two words still ring one of the two bells (i.e., you control when a bill rings), but now the words are not predictably associated with the bells. The two bells are equally probable (50%) and independent of your utterance. All we know, after learning the task, is that saying one of the words ("cat", "dog") causes either Bell 1 or Bell 2 to ring.

In Conditions 6–7, we have two actions and two possible outcomes. We could, of course, say that Condition 6 affords more control over the outcome, relative to Condition 7. If we assign two different groups of participants to the two conditions, and ask them to report the degree to which they feel in control of the bells, should we expect people in Condition 6 to report, on average, a stronger sense of agency? What if the participants do not know about the other condition? Furthermore, what if we (mis)inform people in Condition 6 that people in the other condition can control, not only *which* bell rings but the intensity and duration of the rings by varying the *intensity* and *duration* of their utterances? What if we inform people in Condition 7 that the other group has no control over the timing of the rings? Could such instructions affect the reports?

The problem is partly related to quantification and measurement (Michell, 1999; Tafreshi, Slaney, & Neufeld, 2016). When we ask people to report the extent to which they feel in control of an event, say, from 0 ("no control") to 9 ("full control"), we do not expect them to look into their experience of control, the way they can look at a thermometer, and read out a number based on verifiable units of measurement. Rather, we are asking them to assign a number to their overall experience of control, with reference to a series of other experiences. In such a task, participants choose some criteria for the upper and lower bounds (the "9" and the "0") of their report, based on their exposure to a number of trials, their exposure to different conditions, and perhaps based on whatever else they hear during the experiment. Without having those reference points, "full control" and "no control" would not have clear meaning.

A recent study by Wen and Haggard (2018) demonstrated how numerical reports of the sense of agency are sensitive to context. Participants in their study moved a computer mouse which could sometimes control a group of visual objects on the computer screen. In the "no-control" condition, the majority of objects were not under the participants' control, while in the "full-control" condition, the majority of objects were fully under the participants' control. The researchers were interested in the participants' report regarding one particular object (target), over which participants' control varied. When the connection between the mouse movements and target movement was partial and ambiguous (between 40 and 80%), participants' report was influenced by the overall context of control. That is, they tended to report a higher sense of agency over the target movement in the "no-control" condition, relative to the "full-control" condition (Wen & Haggard, 2018, p. 611). It is reasonable, therefore, to assume that explicit judgments of agency are based on criteria that can vary with context. Our experimental manipulations can influence both participants' judgments on particular instances, and their judgment criteria.

Instead of asking participants to assign numbers to their sense of agency, we might ask them to sample different conditions and then compare them with respect to their sense of control. We would be more directly asking participants to tell us whether our hypothesis is correct, which raises the question of what role the participants' judgment plays in hypothesis testing, in addition to the experimenter's own judgment of the task. Although this approach addresses some of the problems related to quantification, it requires a degree of distance from the task and reliance on memory that might change the nature of judgment. An alternative method involves asking people whether or not they feel in control, or feel they are the cause, of a given event. Even with a yes/no question, however, it is difficult to avoid the influence of the experimental conditions on the judgment criteria, and the fact that a participant, at the instance of a given report, has sampled a particular set of events.

In general, explicit judgments of agency in one context, including a comparison between a pair of conditions, might not be representative of similar judgments in a different context. Imagine, for example, that we are interested in comparing only two conditions and that we do, indeed, find a difference in an initial test. Could we assume that the observed difference between the two conditions will persist if we repeat the experiment and add one or two new conditions? What if the difference between the third condition and the first two conditions is so salient that participants would no longer be responsive to the subtle difference between the initial two

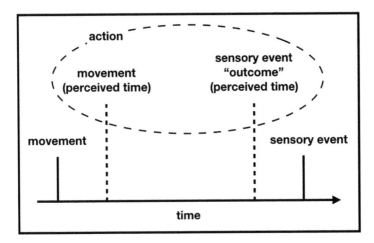

Fig. 7.4 When an action and a subsequent sensory event are perceived as causally related, their perceived time shifts toward each other, which indicates grouping the two as a single event. This phenomenon is referred to as "intentional binding"

conditions? What if the new conditions draw participants' attention to features of the task that were initially neglected and away from features that were initially attended to, which subsequently changes the participants' criteria for judging their agency?

To avoid the problems associated with explicit judgments of agency, we could turn to implicit measures. These include the phenomenon of intentional binding (Haggard et al., 2002; Hughes, Desantis, & Waszak, 2013; Moore & Obhi, 2012). As mentioned in the previous section, we could think about intentional binding as a derivative of the principle of temporal contiguity. When a movement and a sensory event are perceived as causally linked, their perceived time shifts toward each other (Fig. 7.4). In other words, the perceived time of onset for the action shifts forward, while the perceived time of onset for the sensory event shifts backward. This is a form of perceptual grouping—the movement and the sensory outcome are grouped into a single action–perception event (Hommel, 1996; Hommel, Müsseler, Aschersleben, & Prinz, 2001).

Haggard et al. (2002) compared the effects of fixed and randomized delays between the action and the sensory outcome (cf. Conditions 4–5 above). Intentional binding was stronger with fixed intervals, compared to randomized intervals. That is, repeated exposure to a fixed action–outcome delay enhances action–outcome grouping, relative to when different delay values are intermixed. Thus, the effect of action–outcome delay depends, not only on the length of delay but also on its consistency. A related study by Stetson, Cui, Montague, and Eagleman (2006) involved adapting to a fixed action–outcome delay interval. After having participants adapt to a particular interval, the outcomes were occasionally presented simultaneously with the action, in which case the outcome was (mis)perceived as occurring *before* the action.

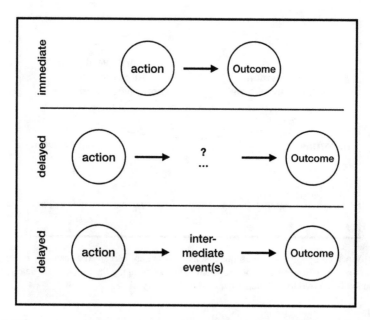

Fig. 7.5 When an outcome does not immediately follow an action, the delay could either be opaque to the actor or it could consist of intermediate events. In the latter case, the actor has access to an "explanation" of the delay, whereas in the former case the cause of the delay is unknown

A focus on the length of action–outcome delay might lead us to neglect the role of the content of the delay period. In most studies that manipulate action–outcome delay, the delay period is opaque from the perspective of the research participant. That is, the delay period does not consist of intermediate events, which might be perceived as the causal links between the action and the outcome. Intermediate events might be analogous to the intermediate domino pieces between the first piece and the last piece, providing some form of "explanation" for why there is a delay (Fig. 7.5). It might not be necessary for intermediate events to be directly observed by the agent, as long as they are known. For instance, if I know that after I open a can of cat food, it takes some time for the smell to reach my cat in the other room, then the delay in his arrival does not prevent me from sensing a causal role for myself. In this case, I understand that the delay is necessary because of the time it takes for the smell of food to reach my cat. Consequently, my action and my cat's arrival at the plate could still be grouped together.

Pursuing a similar line of thought, Caspar et al. (2016) filled the delay period between the participant's key-press actions and auditory outcomes. The intermediate event was the movement of a robot hand. One could imagine that the participant's action was causing the robot hand to move, which was in turn producing the tone. The authors found that when the robot movement was homologous to the participants' movement (index finger → index finger), it resulted in stronger action-tone intentional binding, compared to when the robot movement was not homologous to the participants' movement (index finger → middle finger). Thus, the presence of intermediate events can ameliorate the effect of action–outcome delay, especially when the sequence of events (action, intermediate events, and outcome) can be grouped.

Intentional binding can be found using several methods of time estimation (Moore & Obhi, 2012; Obhi, Swiderski, & Brubacher, 2012). A common method involves using a clock face and asking participants to report the location of the clock hand at the time of an action or a sensory event (Libet, Wright Jr, & Gleason, 1983). Another method involves asking participants to estimate the delay within a predetermined range (e.g., 0–2 s). For our purpose, we can set aside the difference between these methods. What matters to us is that intentional binding is based on time estimation and that it is taken as an implicit measure of the sense of agency. Relatively strong intentional binding, accordingly, is taken to indicate a relatively strong sense of agency over the event in question.

Two points with regard to the use of intentional binding as a measure of the sense of agency deserve our attention. First, although intentional binding consists of binding (perceptual grouping) an action and a sensory event, and although such a binding can occur due to the perceived causal relation between the two events (Kawabe, Roseboom, & Nishida, 2013), causal self-attribution is not the only means through which such grouping can take place. Events can be grouped due to perceptual similarity, continuity, and other such principles. The risk here is that of incorrectly interpreting perceptual grouping as perception of self-caused events. This possibility is present, for example, in studies that find binding of passive movements and sensory events. A passive movement (e.g., a passive key-press) is performed by a mechanical device or by an experimenter pushing one's finger on the response key. Certain manipulations such as drawing participants' attention to the relation between the key-press and a subsequent event can produce temporal binding, even with such passive movements (Dogge, Schaap, Custers, Wegner, & Aarts, 2012). We should be cautious when interpreting these results as variations in the sense of agency because grouping of sensory events can happen without self-attribution.

A second problem with intentional binding is that it might primarily reflect the sense of agency over subordinate (sensorimotor) events and, as such, is an inadequate representation of the sense of agency over superordinate events (Caspar, Cleeremans, & Haggard, 2018; Obhi & Hall, 2011; Strother, House, & Obhi, 2010). Intentional binding might, therefore, be best characterized as a measure of sensorimotor control, a subcategory of sense of agency. In Chap. 3, we considered the case of Jim who either told a joke to his friends or instructed someone else to tell his joke. In the latter case, Jim could still regard himself as the initiator of the joke-telling episode, the agent in the superordinate sense, although he does not have agency over the details of the joke telling. Assuming that the joke is followed by laughter (sensory outcome), and assuming that the joke teller has a sense of agency over the laughter and some degree of intentional binding, we would expect Jim to show a weaker, if any, intentional binding between the delivery of the punchline and the onset of the laughter, relative to a scenario in which he tells the joke himself (Caspar et al., 2018), even though he might feel agency, in the superordinate sense, over the episodes in both cases. What persists in Jim's sense of agency across the two conditions is not captured in a measure of intentional binding.

We have noted that the methods used in assessing sense of agency might themselves play a role in the results. For instance, it is possible that methods involving intentional binding, compared to methods involving explicit judgments of agency, might differently sensitize participants to other factors. A study by Ebert and Wegner (2010) confirms this point. The authors instructed participants to perform pull/push actions using a joystick. The actions were followed by animated visual outcomes, either consistent or inconsistent with the action (objects moving toward or away from the participant). Action–outcome delay varied across trials (100–700 ms). In Experiment 1, participants were instructed to perform both explicit judgment of agency *and* time estimation on each trial, which required them to pay attention to both the timing of events and the causal relations. By contrast, in Experiment 2, the two judgments were separated and performed in different blocks. Intentional binding was overall stronger in Experiment 1 than in Experiment 2, presumably because participants were paying attention to the causal relation between the events while estimating time intervals. Likewise, explicit judgments of agency were more influenced by the action–outcome delay in Experiment 1 than in Experiment 2, presumably because participants were paying attention to the timing of the events while reporting their sense of agency. The findings suggest that engaging in multiple tasks, and attention to different features of the tasks, renders participants more susceptible to manipulations (Memelink & Hommel, 2013).

I included these cautionary notes on the use of intentional binding because in the remainder of the chapter I will set aside the issue. Instead of questioning the validity of the use of intentional binding, we shall take the researchers at their word and regard their methods as including valid measures of the sense of agency. This will enable us to pay attention to other aspects of the research.

7.2 Levels of Control

It has been repeatedly acknowledged that sense of agency should not be treated as a unidimensional concept (Frith, 2005; Haggard & Chambon, 2012; Synofzik, Vosgerau, & Newen, 2008), although identifying different components does not, in principle, contradict theoretical coherence. In this section, I argue that the multidimensionality of the sense of agency is best understood with reference to the hierarchical organization of goals (Chap. 3). It would be useful to contrast my position with similar viewpoints that draw distinctions within the sense of agency without evoking goal hierarchies. For instance, we might read:

> There are two aspects of agency in action. At the lower level there is the perception that my act has caused some effect. For example, by pressing this button I have caused a sound to occur. At a more abstract level there is the perception that my intention to press the button has caused my act of pressing the button. (Frith, 2005, p. 763).

Frith's distinction seems to introduce an impassable divide between two senses of agency. It seems that, if such a distinction holds, we ought to be pursuing two lines of research, corresponding to the two aspects of agency (Chambon & Haggard, 2013). Is it possible to find a common logic that applies to both aspects, while still recognizing their difference?

There are two assumptions behind Frith's distinction. First, it assumes that thinking is essentially distinct from action. The first aspect of agency is about action and the relation between action and outcome; the second aspect is about intention and the relation between intention and action. This assumption can be disputed (Gallese & Lakoff, 2005; Melser, 2004). Thinking, which includes understanding real and imagined actions and their actual and possible outcomes, relies on our capacity for action. We might point out that thinking is devoid of the same distal effects that we observe in actions, but even actions typically require withholding a subset of possible sensory outcomes (Fig. 3.4). Pressing key A, for instance, might require not pressing keys B, C, etc. as much as it requires adequate timing and the right amount of force. In this sense, thinking is similar to acting because thinking about pressing key A requires, among other things, *not* pressing key A. Moreover, in our actions and thoughts, we can follow instructions and encounter unforeseen events (recall the discussion of thought experiments in Chap. 2). In the case of "thought insertion," a person's thinking can be misperceived as someone else's (Frith, 2005, p. 753). Similar to actions, we can feel, or fail to feel, a sense of agency over our thoughts. Therefore, the first assumption, regarding the separation between thoughts and actions, is difficult to defend.

Frith's (2005) second assumption is that the proximal and the distal outcomes are essentially different (cf. Pacherie, 2008). The key-press is always going to be a proximal event; the sound of the bell ringing is always going to be a distal outcome. Following Ey (1973), Frith describes the body as transparent, which is to say— despite its mediating role in producing distal outcomes—the body is usually not the focus of our attention (p. 764). Alternatively, what counts as proximal or distal may not be absolute, but depends on our frame of reference. Ringing a bell is relatively distal to the hand movement that causes the bell to ring, but the ringing of the bell is relatively proximal to the effect it has on the environment (causing irritation in others). The transparent status of the body can be lost after an injury, or after a prolonged hospitalization causing muscle atrophy, when the sensations and movements of the body lose their transparent status. In such a case, movements become distal relative to intentions. On the other hand, with sufficient practice, tools and even cooperative others can become transparent ("proximal") with regard to control, enabling us to extend our focus beyond them. Hence, the second assumption regarding a fixed proximal–distal dichotomy does not seem justified either. In short, the two premises suggested by Frith (2005) do not seem to provide a particularly safe starting point.

Instead of dividing the sense of agency into qualitatively distinct components (thought vs. action; proximal events vs. distal events), we could think of it in terms of the function of a hierarchically organized set of control systems (Chap. 3). Each level has an expected/desired and actual perceptions; each level may have a match or mismatch between the expected and the actual perceptions (Powers, 1998). Sense of control, at each level, arises from the match between the expected/desired and observed (Wolpert, 1997). Because the logic of control permeates the various levels of a goal hierarchy, participants can report *one* judgment with regard to their sense of agency, either based on an overall impression or based on the level of control that is most relevant for the task at hand. In the remainder of this chapter, I first review a selection of studies that highlight the role of goal hierarchies in our sense of agency. After that, I will apply the idea of levels of control to three subfields of research: sense of agency in shared tasks, the role of sensorimotor fluency in the sense of agency, and the effect of free choice.

First, we should consider experimental studies that reveal the importance of paying attention, not only to goals at a single level but also to goal hierarchies. These studies suggest that sense of agency can be analyzed in terms of the function of control at separate levels of the hierarchy. Kumar and Srinivasan (2014) examined participants' sense of control over one avatar in a collection of avatars. The avatars were described as a "group of wolves" chasing a sheep. Two independent factors included, first, whether or not the wolves caught the sheep and, second, how much sensorimotor control the participants had over their wolf. The authors found that when the sheep was caught (fulfillment of the relatively superordinate goal), participants were more likely to report a higher sense of control over their wolf, and their reports appeared insensitive to variations in actual sensorimotor control over the wolf (the fulfillment of relatively subordinate goals). On the other hand, when the wolves did not catch the sheep, participants reported a relatively weaker sense of control, and their reports were sensitive to variations in sensorimotor control.

In a similar study, Kumar and Srinivasan (2017) designed a computerized shooting task. Participants were instructed to aim at targets, using a crosshair, and shoot. The researchers varied, among other things, the level of noise added to the crosshair movement. Intentional binding (the perceived temporal proximity between the shot and the hit) was used as the measure of felt agency. Once again, when the target was hit, noise level did not impact sense of agency, whereas when the target was missed, high noise level was associated with reduced sense of agency. These findings demonstrate that sense of agency arises from a hierarchically organized process of action control, which affords senses of agency at various levels of the hierarchy.

Kumar and Srinivasan (2014, 2017) argued that the actors' overall sense of agency is determined, first and foremost, by the highest successful level of action control. This claim should be qualified in light of studies that manipulate not only success/failure at particular levels of control but also the presence/absence of goals at a particular level (Wen, Yamashita, & Asama, 2015b, 2016). The very presence of a difficult superordinate goal can reduce the sense of agency. In such situations, participants do not fall back on judging their agency based merely on the subordinate level (the sense of control over one's finger movements is reduced while trying to play a difficult piece on the violin). Nevertheless, Kumar and Srinivasan's (2014, 2017) general point is sound. Sense of agency arises from the function of a hierarchically organized process of control.

We have already discussed examples of research that neglects levels of control that are involved in a given task (Chap. 3). We reviewed Borhani, Beck, and Haggard's (2017) study, in which they divided their conditions based on (a) whether participants had control over the superordinate level (key-press/level of shock) and (b) whether they had control over performing the key-press (subordinate, sensorimotor level). Because they described the first factor as a type of abstract choice, seemingly divorced from action control, it appeared surprising to observe that both factors affected sense of agency and that their effects interacted. Similarly, Wen et al. (2015b) divided their conditions in terms of presence and absence of goals, concluding that the presence of goals can reduce participants' sense of agency. In these characterizations, the separation between, and independent effects of, "goals" and "sensorimotor control" is already tacitly presupposed by the researchers, when in reality, the two factors interact in giving rise to the overall sense of agency (Kumar & Srinivasan, 2014).

7.3 Shared Tasks

We are going to turn to studies on shared tasks, or performing part of a task, to further clarify the importance of paying attention to levels of control. The distinctions considered in Chap. 5 are going to help us interpret the following studies. To put it briefly, it is important to note whether co-actors are at the same level of a control hierarchy or whether one is subordinate to the other. With actors at the same level, it is important to note whether actor selection is subordinate or superordinate to other features of performance.

Sharing a task is not necessarily with another human co-actor; we could share tasks with automated machines. Moreover, we could share a task with an automated machine that follows our instructions, and we can follow instructions given by machines. An interesting example of human–machine task-sharing is a study by Berberian, Sarrazin, Le Blaye, and Haggard (2012). They used a flight simulation task, which involved keeping track of the flight trajectory, and detecting and avoiding obstacles. The experiment included four conditions, including a "fully automated" condition. The task of avoiding an obstacle involved the following steps:

1. Detection of obstacle (this step was always performed by the machine).
2. Deciding which direction to take in order to avoid the obstacle (this step performed by the participant in only one condition).
3. Implementation of the decision by turning a scroll wheel (this step was performed by the participants in two conditions).
4. Execution or setting off the decisions in steps 2 and 3 (this was performed by the participants in three conditions).
5. Seeing the outcome of their action (successful avoidance of the obstacle).
6. Finally, participants judged the time interval between execution and outcome (steps 4–5).

152 7 Sense of Agency

The authors found increasingly strong intentional binding as participants' control over the steps of the task increased. The more control people had over the procedure (less automation), the higher their sense of control over the outcome of the procedure. These findings were corroborated by the participants' explicit judgments of agency, demonstrating that sense of agency over sensorimotor events increases if those events are embedded within superordinate goals that are chosen by the actor.

We could extend Berberian et al.'s (2012) study and compare, on one hand, conditions in which the participant is given a superordinate goal by another agent/machine with, on the other hand, conditions in which the participant has previously chosen the goal. What if, we merely introduce a time delay (of 1 h) between the choices corresponding to steps 1–3 in Berberian et al.'s task (assuming, of course, that the task is not as urgent as avoiding obstacles during navigation), and executing the choices, corresponding to step 4 in Berberian et al.'s task. Such a design would closely resemble studies of how choosing how to pursue a goal, in advance, increases the likelihood of actually pursuing the goal (Gollwitzer, 1999). Exploring the intersection between these two research topics could reveal a possible trade-off between sense of agency and performance efficiency (Janczyk, Dambacher, Bieleke, & Gollwitzer, 2015). Compared to having to choose what to do, knowing what to do, via instructions or prior decisions, might reduce the sense of agency, while facilitating performance. I will return to this theme in Sect. 7.5.

Participants in Berberian et al.'s (2012) study had control over the task at the subordinate level, while their agency could also be extended to relatively higher levels of control. What if a person has selective control at the superordinate level? This question was addressed by Caspar et al. (2018), in a very different experimental design. Casper et al. assigned groups of three participants with the following roles: Victim (receiving electric shocks), Agent (administering shocks), and Commander (giving commands to Agent). The roles were changed throughout the experiment, such that every participant experienced all roles. Agent's key produced a tone and gave Victim a shock (choosing to give the shock was rewarded with money). The Agent was sometimes free to choose (acting as both Agent and Commander), and sometimes was forced to comply with the Commander's choice. Agents and Commanders were asked to report both their sense of responsibility (explicit sense of agency) associated with the shock and to estimate the interval between the Agent's action and the resulting tone (implicit sense of agency). For Agents, the sense of agency was stronger, according to both measures, when they were free to choose. For Commanders, the implicit measure consistently showed a weak sense of agency, although they reported a higher degree of responsibility when Agents had to follow their orders. This result reflects a dissociation between explicit and implicit measures in the case of Commanders who had control at the superordinate level. The authors concluded that when an action is shared among multiple people, the sense of control is reduced in all of them, compared with when the action is performed by one person.

Why did the explicit and implicit measures of agency diverge in the case of Commanders? Caspar et al. (2018) considered that the explicit report might reflect the tendency to provide the expected answer (social desirability effect). An alternative possibility is that intentional binding results from the kind of close sensorimotor monitoring that is not required of Commanders. Why should the Commander spend effort to keep track of the subordinate processes, while knowing that another person is taking care of that level of control? Recognizing the different levels of control opens the possibility for the Commander to feel responsible for the shock administered to the Victim, despite weak intentional binding between the Agent's action and outcome. The weak intentional binding might merely indicate that the Commander lets go of the subordinate level of control, precisely as a consequence of sharing the task with the Agent (Chap. 5).

We should compare the study by Caspar et al. (2018) with studies in which two actors have equal status in relation to the control hierarchy. For example, Strother et al. (2010) instructed pairs of participants to share a response button (cf. Fig. 5.10). During the experiment, two participants sat in front of a computer, each placing one index finger on one end of the same button (spacebar key). On each trial, one participant spontaneously began pressing the button, while the other participant merely allowed his/her finger to move passively with the button. Button-press actions were followed by tones, which were used to test intentional binding. As expected, explicit judgments showed that the participants who actually performed the response felt in control of the action. More surprisingly, intentional binding was observed, to the same degree, in both participants. In a follow-up study, Obhi and Hall (2011) added a condition in which participants had advance knowledge of who initiated the action. Again, intentional binding was observed for both participants. We should note, first, that the two participants had the same status within the control hierarchy. In contrast to Caspar et al.'s (2018) study, in which Commander's response was followed by Agent's response, in the "shared button-press" experiments (Obhi & Hall, 2011; Strother et al., 2010) one action—regardless of the actor—fulfilled the shared goal. By sharing the same response key, the selection of response (initiate vs. not-initiate) was made superordinate to the selection of actor (person 1 vs. person 2). Furthermore, to successfully complete the task, a passive participant had to monitor both his co-actor's action and the movement of his own passive finger. It might, in fact, take effort for the passive participants to *actively* withhold from moving once the co-actor has initiated an action (Pfister, Dignath, Hommel, & Kunde, 2013). These considerations help explain why intentional binding was indistinguishable across the "active" and "passive" participants.

We might be inclined to explain the intentional binding effect observed in the passive participant as an instance of sensorimotor empathy (Rizzolatti & Sinigaglia, 2016), or of collective intentionality (Obhi & Hall, 2011; Searle, 1995), in which case we would not be challenging the validity of intentional binding as a measure of the sense of agency. Alternatively, we could consider that perceived temporal proximity between a movement (one's own or another's) and a subsequent event can be caused by factors other than a sense of agency (cf. Dogge et al., 2012; Eagleman, 2008). Assuming the validity of intentional binding, it appears that the sense of agency can be comparable for participants who share the same level within a control hierarchy. Otherwise, sense of agency tends to decrease when we have selective control at some levels of the goal hierarchy, including when we fulfill goals set by co-actors or automated machines, and when we instruct others to fulfill our goals.

154

7 Sense of Agencysegment>

7.4 Fluency and Outcome Evaluation

A distinction that has become popular among experimental psychologists studying sense of agency is between processes *before* perceiving the outcome of an action and those *after* perceiving the outcome. In the act of throwing a dart, the distinction separates, on one hand, factors that influence the process of throwing and, on the other hand, the impact of seeing the dart land on the target. Researchers have described the first set of factors as sensorimotor *fluency* and the second set of factors as outcome evaluation (Chambon & Haggard, 2012, 2013; Sidarus et al., 2013; Sidarus & Haggard, 2016; Wenke, Fleming, & Haggard, 2010). I might feel confident, experiencing "motor fluency," while throwing a dart, and yet miss the target. Similarly, the throw might feel dysfluent and yet hit the target. Another way that the distinction has been characterized is in terms of *prospective* and *retrospective* sense of agency (Fig. 7.6). For a given action, we have:

- A prospective, future-oriented sense of agency (before encountering the outcome of the action), arising from the sensorimotor fluency of our action. This sense of agency is high if the *means* by which we pursue the outcome is fluent.
- A retrospective, past-oriented, sense of agency, which comes after encountering and presumably evaluating the outcome of the action. This sense of agency is high if the *end* pursued and anticipated by the action is met.

I agree that there is a distinction to be made here, although I disagree that the distinction is best characterized in terms of a difference between actions and outcomes (Hommel, 1996). It seems particularly unhelpful to divide events in time with reference to an outcome and anchor the meaning of the words, "retrospective" and "prospective," to the outcome, because what should be regarded as an outcome

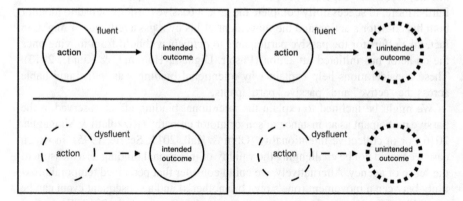

Fig. 7.6 Demonstrates a way of dissociating two components of the sense of agency. The first component has to do with the fluency with which the action proceeds (higher rows vs. lower rows), and the second is based on whether the actual outcome matches the intended outcome (left panel vs. right panel). Dissociating fluency from outcome evaluation, however, creates a theoretical gap that would not be necessary if we characterize the distinction in terms of the levels of control

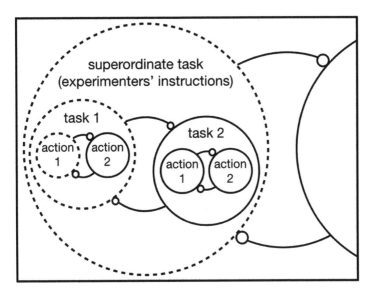

Fig. 7.7 The concept of fluency can apply to multiple levels of the control hierarchy because at each level of control, competing goals can interfere with the current goal. Likewise, the concept of outcome evaluation can apply to different levels of control because each level entails setting goals and evaluating perceived outcomes

is not fixed. There are action outcomes at each level of the control hierarchy. Throwing a dart, assuming it is not for the first time, involves recreating the sensorimotor conditions (subordinate, proximal event) associated with hitting the target (superordinate, distal event). The tight associations between relatively subordinate and superordinate levels of control do not appear to be obvious in laboratory tasks where the associations are arbitrary. Nonetheless, pressing a button involves control at the level of distal events (what the key-press is intended to accomplish in the environment) and at the level of sensorimotor enactment (how the key-press is intended to be performed: its timing, force, duration, etc.). Characterizing the distinction with reference to subordinate and superordinate goals would provide the most clear and comprehensive picture.

Nothing stops us from applying the concept of fluency to relatively superordinate levels of control (Fig. 7.7). When an actor feels sensorimotor fluency over the means by which an intended outcome is fulfilled, the actor is sensing a match between the intended outcome and the observed outcome at the subordinate (sensorimotor) level. In other words, fluency cannot be set in contrast to outcome evaluation because a form of outcome evaluation is involved in giving rise to the sense of sensorimotor fluency.

Similarly, retrospective and prospective agency ought to be defined, not in reference to a particular outcome but in reference to the moment the agent begins to act (Fig. 7.2). Rather than contrasting agency-over-means (fluency) with agency-over-ends (outcome), both of which could be described in terms of "I did…" or "I did

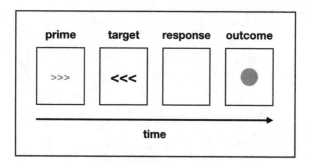

Fig. 7.8 Sequence of events during a trial of an experiment that could demonstrate the dissociable effects of fluency (driven by prime-target compatibility) and outcome evaluation (driven by response-outcome compatibility) (Chambon & Haggard, 2012; Wenke et al., 2010). In this example, imagine a two-choice task with left/right key-press responses mapped onto left/right-pointing arrows. Prior to seeing the target, participants are presented with a subliminal prime that could be compatible or incompatible with the target. Moreover, association between responses and outcomes could be manipulated using temporal proximity between the two, or using probability (e.g., left response associated with blue outcome) (Sidarus et al., 2013)

not…", we could contrast judgment of future actions ("I can") and judgment of past actions ("I did"). Given the currently dominant experimental methods, prospective sense of agency, in the sense that I use the term, does not fit within the scope of investigation.

What findings have been taken as support for the distinction between fluency and outcome evaluation? The findings come from experiments that combine outcome-related manipulations with the priming method (Chambon & Haggard, 2012; Moore, Wegner, & Haggard, 2009; Wenke et al., 2010) (Fig. 7.8). In one of these studies, Sidarus et al. (2013) used a two-choice task with left/right keys and left/right target arrows. Prior to seeing a target, participants were presented with brief and subliminal primes that were either compatible or incompatible with the targets. Prime-target compatibility was thought to affect sensorimotor fluency. The authors also manipulated outcome expectation by associating responses with specific outcomes (e.g., the right key was more likely to produce the color green than blue).

Sidarus et al. (2013) found an interaction of the two factors: sense of agency was relatively low when the primes and targets were incompatible *and* when the outcome was unexpected. This suggests, first, that fluency and outcome evaluation are, indeed, not independent factors (Borhani et al., 2017; Kumar & Srinivasan, 2014; Wen et al., 2015b; Wen, Yamashita, & Asama, 2017). Second, given that the reported sense of agency could be quantitatively equivalent across the "dysfluent" (lower-left quadrant in Fig. 7.6) and "unexpected outcome" (upper-right quadrant in Fig. 7.6) conditions, it is reasonable to assume participants' reports did not necessarily pinpoint the source of dysfluency. Although dysfluency at the subordinate and superordinate levels corresponds to different qualities in experience, they can be equivalent in our measures of the sense of agency.

We could usually achieve a goal through various means, which is to say some variation at the subordinate level can occur without change at the superordinate level. While throwing a dart, I might feel some sensorimotor dysfluency, particularly if the dart is unexpectedly light or heavy. Despite the motor dysfluency, I might still hit the bullseye. In that case, I might conclude that I did something right, despite my dysfluency. Indeed, something was correct, though unfamiliar, in my dysfluent throw, which I would attempt to re-create in my next throw (cf. Kumar & Srinivasan, 2014, 2017; Wen et al., 2017). If so, my attempt to repeat the dysfluent experience would render it fluent through repeated experience.

Just as sensorimotor dysfluency does not guarantee failure to achieve the desired outcome, sensorimotor fluency does not guarantee success. Actions can occasionally yield unexpected outcomes, due to unknown changes in the environment and intermediate events that connect our movements to our intended outcomes, in which case we discover that our sense of fluency is no longer a reliable indicator of the outcome. Again, further exploration and experience would be necessary to establish a new relationship between subordinate and superordinate events. When Sidarus et al. (2013, p. 1409) wrote that a decrease in sense of agency "could perhaps be a phenomenal marker of an instruction signal whose normal meaning outside the laboratory would be 'don't do that again'", they were grounding their speculation on experimental situations, where participants do not have a chance to explore and understand the sources of their dysfluency. As such, they neglect the possibility that, outside of the lab, a decrease in sense of agency might urge the organism to "try again!" contrary to their speculation (Anselme & Güntürkün, 2018; Ferster & Skinner, 1957). Indeed, as Wen and Haggard (2018) demonstrated, loss of control over an object can attract the actor's attention toward the object.

To summarize this section, rather than being qualitatively distinct sources of felt agency, fluency at the subordinate and superordinate levels of control is based on comparing intended and observed outcomes. The same logic applies to both, and the difference is the association with different levels of the control hierarchy. Moreover, by associating sensorimotor fluency with a prospective sense of agency, simply because it occurs prior to the actor's basic-level goal, we would exclude an important type of prospective agency, namely the feeling that is present prior to initiating an action ("I can"), and is based on the agent's history of interaction with the environment.

7.5   Free and Forced Choices

Barlas and Obhi (2013) compared intentional binding across three tasks that differed in the number of choices participants had (1, 3, or 7). Intentional binding was positively correlated with the number of choices. The first, though not the only, interpretation of these results is that more choices will increase our sense of agency. A second interpretation is based on the increase in the time it takes to select a response when participants are faced with more choices (Hick, 1952; Hyman,

1953). It takes more time to select a response from a set of 7 responses than to select from a set of 3. An increase in response selection time might extend the time window for action–outcome grouping. This hypothesis could be tested if we manipulate, in addition to the number of choices, other factors that can reduce response selection efficiency, including stimulus quality, and stimulus–response compatibility (Gozli, Huffman, & Pratt, 2016). A third interpretation is based on effort. It is more effortful to select a response if the number of choices increases, and if effort has been shown to be a factor influencing sense of agency. Minohara et al. (2016) varied the required force for a key-press response, and found that additional effort was associated with an increase in the sense of agency. Hence, time and effort are two confounding variables in studies that examine the effect of choice.

In a more recent study, Barlas, Hockley, and Obhi (2018) varied the type of response (free vs. forced) and response outcome (pleasant vs. unpleasant). Response outcomes varied randomly and independently of the response, which means the "free choice" was not over the outcome of the response, but merely over the sensorimotor/subordinate attributes of the response. Because response-outcome contingencies were unpredictable, participants did not gain the ability to control outcomes with experience. Barlas et al. (2018) found that response type made an impact on participants' feelings of agency. In particular, explicit judgments of feeling control over the outcome were strongest when participants freely chose a key *and* were presented with a pleasant outcome. With respect to the effect of outcome valence, the authors speculated that we might have a *retrospective* self-serving bias, attributing positive and negative outcomes, respectively, to ourselves and external sources. This retrospective account neglects the possible role of (superordinate) intention prior to perceiving the outcome.

The effect of outcome valence (Barlas et al., 2018) might indicate the participants' tendency to develop (ad hoc) event categories that are not recognized by the researchers (Dreisbach, 2012). Is it, for instance, possible that participants regarded "pleasant" and "unpleasant" outcomes, respectively, as "success" and "failure"? This would resemble the attitude we might adopt when gambling with a slot machine. A gambler does not play to get exposure to a set of pleasant and unpleasant outcomes; he plays with the intention of winning. In other words, the superordinate goal of his actions is to bring about a pleasant outcome, despite the unpredictability and low probability of such outcomes. A win would be considered self-caused because it matches the gambler's intention, whereas a loss would be considered bad luck. Similarly, is it possible that participants in an experiment tacitly adopt the superordinate intention associated with the pleasant outcome, despite the unpredictability of those outcomes? If so, then outcome valence would affect sense of agency because it is a better match for participants' intention. Importantly, this account is consistent with the observed interaction between the effects of outcome valence and response type (free vs. forced choice) (Barlas et al., 2018). Future studies could disentangle the role of valence and intention with the use of priming methods (priming a pleasant intention prior to action; Moore et al., 2009) and constructing tasks in which unpleasant events are necessary intermediate steps toward some pleasant goals.

7.6 Implications

Experimental research on sense of agency relies on artificially constructed situations where agency is ambiguous. When agency, or its absence, is not clearly felt, it can be pushed over the edge in either direction. This general approach is adopted and defended by many researchers. For instance, Watt and Quinn (2008, p. 353) stated that, "A good laboratory study is one that forces cognition to get it wrong". We learn about our psychological capacities, or about other systems, when we find ways to "trick" them. In the case of experimental psychology, however, tricks might be working in both directions (Gozli & Deng, 2018; Kingstone, Smilek, & Eastwood, 2008). When the question of agency and self-attribution arise in everyday life, we are usually not prevented from examining the situation, orienting our attention to various parts of the situation, repeating actions, introducing variations in our actions and observing the consequences (Gärdenfors et al., 2018). Without the freedom to examine the situation, our judgments can only be guesswork about the past events. When we examine performance in carefully constructed situations, designed to "trick" research participants, we are restricting ourselves to observing them under constrained conditions (recall our discussion of illusions in Sect. 2.4).

Given the hierarchically organized nature of goals and actions, judgment of agency can be directed toward various levels of the hierarchy. Despite knowing that the sense of agency can be analyzed in terms of multiple components, it *can* be treated as a unidimensional concept. When researchers instruct participants to report their sense of agency over an event, by assigning a number along a scale (1–9), they are treating the sense of agency as a unidimensional variable. Participants comply and adopt this assumption, in effect co-constructing with the researchers the meaning of the sense of agency (Valsiner, 2017). It is, indeed, an impressive skill that allows a research participant to provide answers to such vague questions. However, just because both sides agree on an assumption does not make it valid. It merely means that we can talk about the sense of agency *as if* it were unidimensional, just like as we can talk about a hierarchy of goals only in terms of a basic-level goal (Chap. 3).

Besides agreeing to provide tentative answers to vaguely posed questions, additional assumptions might guide the participants' responses, while being overlooked by the researchers. One of these might be the assumption of *variability in responses*. Imagine you are a participant in an experiment about the sense of agency. The experiment consists of a series of 200 trials. On each trial, you see a first event (E1), you perform an action, after which you see a second event (E2). At the end of each trial, you are required to report whether you feel that your action caused E2. Is it reasonable to assume that you should vary your responses from trial to trial? The experimenters might be varying certain aspects of the experimental condition, expecting to see variations in your responses. Even though you might very well be unaware of those manipulations, you would assume that your responses should vary on *some* basis, perhaps based on a general and vague impression that changes from trial to trial. Recall the ambiguity with which sense of agency is present in experimental conditions. You see E2 on a given trial, and you answer, "Yes," despite the ambiguity of your sense of agency over E2. The very next trial might be indistinguishable from the previous one. But, this time, you might answer, "No," partly to balance your response on the previous trial. Thus, a second source of variability might be the ambiguity of the experimental condition, combined with the researchers' assurance that "There is no right or wrong response".

A consideration derived from the assumption of variability in response has to do with some of the inconsistent results of the explicit and implicit measures of agency. Wen et al. (2015a) found that larger action–outcome delays did not reduce intentional binding (cf. Haggard et al., 2002), though they reduced explicit judgments of agency. We might, of course, claim that the two measures were sensitive to dissociable aspects of felt agency, but we could also consider that the explicit judgments were prone to influence by the assumption of response variability, particularly when action–outcome delay is a salient feature of the experiment and could be strategically associated with response variability. The main point here is to recognize that the participants' goal of reporting their sense of agency is embedded within the relatively superordinate goal of performing well in the experiment, which includes assumed additional goals, such as "vary responses across trials".

Framing research in terms of the levels of control has the additional benefit of guiding our replication attempts. Based on our review, we have seen that different levels of a control hierarchy can be, at least to some degree, dissociated and distributed across people. Our sense of agency might become weaker when we follow instructions or share a task with someone else (Borhani et al., 2017; Caspar et al., 2018), but the fact that we can give/follow instructions, or share tasks, reveals a tacit understanding of the levels of control. It would, therefore, be surprising to find failures to dissociate levels of control, particularly when they do not belong to the same task. It would be very surprising, indeed, if we find that recalling memories from their past could affect the strength of intentional binding in a sensorimotor task. This was found by Obhi et al. (2012), who had participants perform three separate blocks of a task that measured intentional binding. Prior to one of the blocks, participants were asked to recall a scenario in which they had control over other people; prior to another block, they were asked to recall a scenario in which others had control over them. The authors found stronger intentional binding after the participants recalled being "powerful," compared to when they recalled being "powerless." It is not my intention to cast doubt on these findings, but merely to point out that they are surprising. Given that the study was conducted with 15 participants (one of whom had to be excluded), and the importance of the results, I believe the study warrants a re-examination and perhaps a direct replication.

In framing the discussion in terms of levels of control, I have argued against certain qualitative distinctions, such as "intention- *vs.* action-based agency" or "fluency *vs.* outcome evaluation", that seem to introduce conceptual incoherence. We can accommodate various aspects of agency within the different levels of control (Powers, 1998; see also Chambon et al., 2011; Gozli & Dolcini, 2018). In so doing, we describe the various aspects of agency, and the sense of agency, in terms of a common logic. Moreover, the framework enables us to interpret a wide range of findings, from human–computer interaction (Berberian et al., 2012), shared tasks (Strother et al., 2010), social power relations (Caspar et al., 2018), free choice (Barlas et al., 2018), and sensorimotor fluency (Wenke et al., 2010). Importantly, we noted how dysfluency can occur at different levels of control, as well as indicating the loss of tight associations between subordinate and superordinate levels of control, in which case people might be urged to explore and re-gain the associations between the levels of control (Gozli & Gao, 2019), something that is not typically possible for participants in experimental research.

References

Anselme, P., & Güntürkün, O. (2018). How foraging works: Uncertainty magnifies food-seeking motivation. *Behavioral and Brain Sciences, 8,* 1–106.

Barlas, Z., Hockley, W. E., & Obhi, S. S. (2018). Effects of free choice and outcome valence on the sense of agency: Evidence from measures of intentional binding and feelings of control. *Experimental Brain Research, 236*(1), 129–139.

Barlas, Z., & Obhi, S. (2013). Freedom, choice, and the sense of agency. *Frontiers in Human Neuroscience, 7,* 514.

Berberian, B., Sarrazin, J. C., Le Blaye, P., & Haggard, P. (2012). Automation technology and sense of control: A window on human agency. *PLoS One, 7,* e34075.

Blakemore, S. J., Wolpert, D. M., & Frith, C. D. (2002). Abnormalities in the awareness of action. *Trends in Cognitive Sciences, 6*(6), 237–242.

Borhani, K., Beck, B., & Haggard, P. (2017). Choosing, doing, and controlling: Implicit sense of agency over somatosensory events. *Psychological Science, 28,* 882–893.

Caspar, E. A., Cleeremans, A., & Haggard, P. (2018). Only giving orders? An experimental study of the sense of agency when giving or receiving commands. *PLoS One, 13*(9), e0204027.

Caspar, E. A., Desantis, A., Dienes, Z., Cleeremans, A., & Haggard, P. (2016). The sense of agency as tracking control. *PLoS One, 11*(10), e0163892.

Chambon, V., Domenech, P., Pacherie, E., Koechlin, E., Baraduc, P., & Farrer, C. (2011). What are they up to? The role of sensory evidence and prior knowledge in action understanding. *PLoS One, 6*(2), e17133.

Chambon, V., & Haggard, P. (2012). Sense of control depends on fluency of action selection, not motor performance. *Cognition, 125*(3), 441–451.

Chambon, V., & Haggard, P. (2013). Premotor or ideomotor: How does the experience of action come about? In W. Prinz, M. Beisert, & A. Herwig (Eds.), *Action science: Foundations of an emerging discipline.* Cambridge, MA: MIT Press.

Dennett, D. C. (1984). Cognitive wheels: The frame problem in artificial intelligence. In C. Hookway (Ed.), *Minds, machines and evolution* (pp. 129–151). Cambridge, MA: Cambridge University Press.

Dogge, M., Schaap, M., Custers, R., Wegner, D. M., & Aarts, H. (2012). When moving without volition: Implied self-causation enhances binding strength between involuntary actions and effects. *Consciousness and Cognition, 21*(1), 501–506.

Dreisbach, G. (2012). Mechanisms of cognitive control: The functional role of task rules. *Current Directions in Psychological Science, 21*(4), 227–231.

Eagleman, D. M. (2008). Human time perception and its illusions. *Current Opinion in Neurobiology, 18*(2), 131–136.

Ebert, J. P., & Wegner, D. M. (2010). Time warp: Authorship shapes the perceived timing of actions and events. *Consciousness and Cognition, 19*(1), 481–489.

Eitam, B., Kennedy, P. M., & Higgins, T. E. (2013). Motivation from control. *Experimental Brain Research, 229*, 475–284.

Elsner, B., & Hommel, B. (2001). Effect anticipation and action control. *Journal of Experimental Psychology: Human Perception and Performance, 27*, 229–240.

Elsner, B., & Hommel, B. (2004). Contiguity and contingency in the acquisition of action effects. *Psychological Research, 68*, 138–154.

Ey, H. (1973). *Bodily hallucinations. Treatise on hallucinations: I-II/Traite des hallucinations: I-II.* Oxford, UK: Masson Et Cie.

Ferster, C. B., & Skinner, B. F. (1957). *Schedules of reinforcement.* East Norwalk, CT: Appleton-Century-Crofts.

Frith, C. (2005). The self in action: Lessons from delusions of control. *Consciousness and Cognition, 14*, 752–770.

Frith, C. D. (2014). Action, agency and responsibility. *Neuropsychologia, 55*, 137–142.

Gallagher, S., & Zahavi, D. (2007). *The phenomenological mind: An introduction to philosophy of mind and cognitive science.* Abingdon, UK: Routledge.

Gallese, V., & Lakoff, G. (2005). The brain's concepts: The role of the sensory-motor system in conceptual knowledge. *Cognitive Neuropsychology, 22*(3–4), 455–479.

Gärdenfors, P., Jost, J., & Warglien, M. (2018). From actions to effects: Three constraints on event mappings. *Frontiers in Psychology, 9*, 1391.

Gibson, J. J. (1986). *The ecological approach to visual perception.* Hillsdale, NJ: Lawrence Erlbaum Associates. (Originally published in 1979).

Gollwitzer, P. M. (1999). Implementation intentions: Strong effects of simple plans. *American Psychologist, 54*(7), 493–503.

Gozli, D. G., Aslam, H., & Pratt, J. (2016). Visuospatial cueing by self-caused features: Orienting of attention and action-outcome associative learning. *Psychonomic Bulletin & Review, 23*, 459–467.

Gozli, D. G., & Brown, L. E. (2011). Agency and control for the integration of a virtual tool into the peripersonal space. *Perception, 40*, 1309–1319.

Gozli, D. G., & Deng, W. (2018). Building blocks of psychology: On remaking the unkept promises of early schools. *Integrative Psychological and Behavioral Science, 52*, 1–24.

Gozli, D. G., & Dolcini, N. (2018). Reaching into the unknown: Actions, goal hierarchies, and explorative agency. *Frontiers in Psychology, 9*, 266.

Gozli, D. G., & Gao, C. J. (2019). Hope, exploration, and equilibrated action schemes. *Behavioral and Brain Sciences, 42*, E41.

Gozli, D. G., Huffman, G., & Pratt, J. (2016). Acting and anticipating: Impact of outcome-compatible distractor depends on response selection efficiency. *Journal of Experimental Psychology: Human Perception & Performance, 42*, 1601–1614.

Haggard, P., & Chambon, V. (2012). Sense of agency. *Current Biology, 22*, R390–R392.

Haggard, P., Clark, S., & Kalogeras, J. (2002). Voluntary action and conscious awareness. *Nature Neuroscience, 5*, 382.

Hick, W. E. (1952). On the rate of gain of information. *Quarterly Journal of Experimental Psychology, 4*(1), 11–26.

Hills, T. T., Todd, P. M., Lazer, D., Redish, A. D., Couzin, I. D., & Cognitive Search Research Group. (2015). Exploration versus exploitation in space, mind, and society. *Trends in Cognitive Sciences, 19*, 46–54.

Hommel, B. (1996). The cognitive representation of action: Automatic integration of perceived action effects. *Psychological Research, 59*, 176–186.

Hommel, B. (2017). Goal-directed actions. In M. Waldmann (Ed.), *Handbook of causal reasoning.* Oxford, UK: Oxford University Press.

Hommel, B., Müsseler, J., Aschersleben, G., & Prinz, W. (2001). The theory of event coding (TEC): A framework for perception and action planning. *Behavioral and Brain Sciences, 24*, 849–878.

Hughes, G., Desantis, A., & Waszak, F. (2013). Mechanisms of intentional binding and sensory attenuation: The role of temporal prediction, temporal control, identity prediction, and motor prediction. *Psychological Bulletin, 139*(1), 133–151.

Hume, D. (1739). *A treatise of human nature*. Retrieved from https://librivox.org/treatise-of-human-nature-vol-1-by-david-hume

Hyman, R. (1953). Stimulus information as a determinant of reaction time. *Journal of Experimental Psychology, 45*(3), 188–196.

Janczyk, M., Dambacher, M., Bieleke, M., & Gollwitzer, P. M. (2015). The benefit of no choice: Goal-directed plans enhance perceptual processing. *Psychological Research, 79*, 206–220.

Kant, I. (1781/1998). In P. Guyer & A. Wood (Eds.), *Critique of pure reason*. Cambridge, MA: Cambridge University Press.

Karsh, N., & Eitam, B. (2015). I control therefore I do: Judgments of agency influence action selection. *Cognition, 138*, 122–131.

Kawabe, T. (2013). Inferring sense of agency from the quantitative aspect of action outcome. *Consciousness and Cognition, 22*(2), 407–412.

Kawabe, T., Roseboom, W., & Nishida, S. Y. (2013). The sense of agency is action–effect causality perception based on cross-modal grouping. *Proceedings of the Royal Society B, 280*, 2013.0991.

Kingstone, A., Smilek, D., & Eastwood, J. D. (2008). Cognitive ethology: A new approach for studying human cognition. *British Journal of Psychology, 99*(3), 317–340.

Kumar, D., & Srinivasan, N. (2014). Naturalizing sense of agency with a hierarchical event-control approach. *PLoS One, 9*, e92431.

Kumar, D., & Srinivasan, N. (2017). Multi-scale control influences sense of agency: Investigating intentional binding using event-control approach. *Consciousness and Cognition, 49*, 1–14.

Libet, B., Wright, E. W., Jr., & Gleason, C. A. (1983). Preparation-or intention-to-act, in relation to pre-event potentials recorded at the vertex. *Electroencephalography and Clinical Neurophysiology, 56*(4), 367–372.

Melser, D. (2004). *The act of thinking*. Cambridge, MA: MIT Press.

Maier, S. F., & Seligman, M. E. (1976). Learned helplessness: Theory and evidence. *Journal of Experimental Psychology: General, 105*(1), 3–46.

Mammen, J. (2017). *A new logical foundation for psychology*. New York, NY: Springer.

Memelink, J., & Hommel, B. (2013). Intentional weighting: A basic principle in cognitive control. *Psychological Research, 77*, 249–259.

Michell, J. (1999). *Measurement in psychology: A critical history of a methodological concept*. Cambridge, MA: Cambridge University Press.

Minohara, R., Wen, W., Hamasaki, S., Maeda, T., Kato, M., Yamakawa, H., … Asama, H. (2016). Strength of intentional effort enhances the sense of agency. *Frontiers in Psychology, 7*, 1165.

Moore, J. W., & Obhi, S. S. (2012). Intentional binding and the sense of agency: A review. *Consciousness and Cognition, 21*, 546–561.

Moore, J. W., Wegner, D. M., & Haggard, P. (2009). Modulating the sense of agency with external cues. *Consciousness and Cognition, 18*, 1056–1064.

Obhi, S. S., & Hall, P. (2011). Sense of agency and intentional binding in joint action. *Experimental Brain Research, 211*, 655–662.

Obhi, S. S., Swiderski, K. M., & Brubacher, S. P. (2012). Induced power changes the sense of agency. *Consciousness and Cognition, 21*(3), 1547–1550.

Pacherie, E. (2008). The phenomenology of action: A conceptual framework. *Cognition, 107*, 179–217.

Pfister, R., Dignath, D., Hommel, B., & Kunde, W. (2013). It takes two to imitate: Anticipation and imitation in social interaction. *Psychological Science, 24*, 2117–2121.

Powers, W. T. (1998). *Making sense of behavior*. Montclair, NJ: Benchmark Publications.

Rizzolatti, G., & Sinigaglia, C. (2016). The mirror mechanism: A basic principle of brain function. *Nature Reviews Neuroscience, 17*(12), 757.

Searle, J. R. (1995). *The construction of social reality*. New York, NY: Simon & Schuster.

Sidarus, N., Chambon, V., & Haggard, P. (2013). Priming of actions increases sense of control over unexpected outcomes. *Consciousness and Cognition, 22*(4), 1403–1411.

Sidarus, N., & Haggard, P. (2016). Difficult action decisions reduce the sense of agency: A study using the Eriksen flanker task. *Acta Psychologica, 166*, 1–11.

Smedslund, J. (2016). Why psychology cannot be an empirical science. *Integrative Psychological and Behavioral Science, 50*(2), 185–195.

Stetson, C., Cui, X., Montague, P. R., & Eagleman, D. M. (2006). Motor-sensory recalibration leads to an illusory reversal of action and sensation. *Neuron, 51*(5), 651–659.

Strother, L., House, K. A., & Obhi, S. S. (2010). Subjective agency and awareness of shared actions. *Consciousness and Cognition, 19*(1), 12–20.

Synofzik, M., Vosgerau, G., & Newen, A. (2008). Beyond the comparator model: A multifactorial two-step account of agency. *Consciousness and Cognition, 17*(1), 219–239.

Tafreshi, D., Slaney, K. L., & Neufeld, S. D. (2016). Quantification in psychology: Critical analysis of an unreflective practice. *Journal of Theoretical and Philosophical Psychology, 36*(4), 233–249.

Valsiner, J. (2017). *From methodology to methods in human psychology.* New York, NY: Springer.

Watt, R., & Quinn, S. (2008). It depends what you do in the laboratory. *British Journal of Psychology, 99*(3), 351–354.

Wen, W., & Haggard, P. (2018). Control changes the way we look at the world. *Journal of Cognitive Neuroscience, 30*(4), 603–619.

Wen, W., Yamashita, A., & Asama, H. (2015a). The influence of action-outcome delay and arousal on sense of agency and the intentional binding effect. *Consciousness and Cognition, 36*, 87–95.

Wen, W., Yamashita, A., & Asama, H. (2015b). The influence of goals on sense of control. *Consciousness and Cognition, 37*, 83–90.

Wen, W., Yamashita, A., & Asama, H. (2016). Divided attention and processes underlying sense of agency. *Frontiers in Psychology, 7*, 35.

Wen, W., Yamashita, A., & Asama, H. (2017). The influence of performance on action-effect integration in sense of agency. *Consciousness and Cognition, 53*, 89–98.

Wenke, D., Fleming, S. M., & Haggard, P. (2010). Subliminal priming of actions influences sense of control over effects of action. *Cognition, 115*(1), 26–38.

Wolpert, D. M. (1997). Computational approaches to motor control. *Trends in Cognitive Sciences, 1*, 209–216.

Chapter 8
Varieties of Disengagement

Imagine a strict father who obsesses over the future of his children, insisting that the only way to secure a good future for them is through a good education. He will be happy when the children are doing school work, and everything else for him counts as distraction. He has a narrow conception of how the children should spend their time, and that consequently narrows down the way in which he thinks about their activities. Playing music, spending time with friends, playing sports, reading science fiction all count as the same type of activity ("not schoolwork"). They are all distractions, deviations from the main path. The strict father has falsely unified a range of activities that are contrary to what he believes should be the main focus of his children. He might have a theory about why and how these distractions occur, what they cause, and how to avoid them.

Something similar has happened in cognitive psychology (Callard, Smallwood, & Margulies, 2012). The central role of task performance, as the engine of data production, has led to recognition that research participants sometimes disengage from tasks. These disengagements have come under the umbrella of a single concept, mind wandering (MW), even though they might include a set of heterogeneous phenomena—daydreaming, fantasies, mental blanks, thoughts unrelated to the task at hand, self-generated thought, and stimulus-unrelated thought (Callard, Smallwood, Golchert, & Margulies, 2013). In recent years, MW has turned into a very popular topic of research (Smallwood & Schooler, 2015). The concept has common-sense appeal, not least because of its relevance to the domains of work and education. Once we hear about the concept, even when we are not given a clear definition, we quickly feel a vague sense of familiarity with it, perhaps readily agreeing that we have caught ourselves mind wandering. Our loose grasp of the concept of MW is counterbalanced by our familiarity with the fact that we do not always have control over our attention and thoughts. We hope that research on MW could help us understand this fact better and perhaps even overcome it.

We shall consider two approaches to defining MW—a negative (what it is *not*) and a positive (what it *is*) approach (cf. Christoff et al., 2018). The negative approach to MW considers it as deviation from task performance (Callard et al., 2012, 2013),

© Springer Nature Switzerland AG 2019
D. Gozli, *Experimental Psychology and Human Agency*,
https://doi.org/10.1007/978-3-030-20422-8_8

whereas a positive approach would construe MW in terms of task-independent features. Rather ironically, it is the negative approach that sustains an impression of MW as a unitary construct, while the positive approach gives way to fragmentation of the construct. I will review some of the research that aims to find the correlates of MW, including task difficulty, motivation, mood, and creativity. I will highlight places when the findings ought not to be taken as discovery of law-like regularities and places where research findings provide evidence against MW as a unitary concept.

8.1   Defining Mind Wandering

According to the negative approach, we ought to think about MW as stepping away from the task or a breakdown of cognitive control that enables task performance (McVay & Kane, 2009, 2010). We can know about MW in so far as we observe its detrimental effects on task performance, superficial processing of task-relevant stimulus, slower responses, worse memory, and so forth. In other words, it is the task that makes MW visible. The task also makes the communication between experimenter and participant unambiguous with regard to what counts as MW (particularly in studies in which participants are interrupted during task performance and are asked, "Were you mind wandering just now?"). This approach takes tasks to be the primary or default state, and it takes MW to be the secondary or derivative state. Accordingly, we would assess MW in situations with clearly identified tasks, where we can distinguish good performance from bad performance (Gozli, 2017), and where we can ask participants about "task-unrelated" or "stimulus-independent" thoughts. Without a task, identifying MW would not be straightforward. In trying to solve an open-ended or ill-defined problem, we might explore many mutually inconsistent lines of thought without calling any of them "task-unrelated."

Can we conceive of MW without a task? You might be sitting on the bus, or at a particularly dull dinner party, without a clear task. In such situations, it seems reasonable to assume that one's mind can wander, despite the absence of a clearly identified task (Christoff et al., 2018; Seli et al., 2018). Some researchers might still argue that, despite the presence of MW in the absence of task, we ought to think about MW with reference to its effects on tasks. On the bus, MW might cause one to miss one's stop; during the dull dinner, one might miss an important remark. Even though we might assume that MW can occur without a task, if we characterize it in terms of a failure of cognitive control, then we would accept that the MW becomes observable in its effects on task performance. Hence, the negative approach would encourage us to continue to characterize MW in terms of its relation to actual or potential tasks.

By thinking of MW in contradistinction to optimal task performance, the negative approach characterizes MW as a special kind of (anti)task. In Fig. 8.1, the left and right superordinate circles represent task and MW, respectively. In situations where the task is not clearly identified or particularly demanding, like the dull

Fig. 8.1 A schematic depiction of how "on-task" and "mind-wandering" states might differ from each other. In this example, the task is a two-alternative choice task, where at any given time the participant has to perform either "action 1" or "action 2", but not both. For the sake of simplicity, all task-unrelated goals are depicted as one superordinate goal, set up in an antagonistic relationship with the current task. A task-based approach emphasizes the activation of the task-unrelated goals and their potential effects on the current task. A style-based approach would emphasize the manner in which one might engage in a task

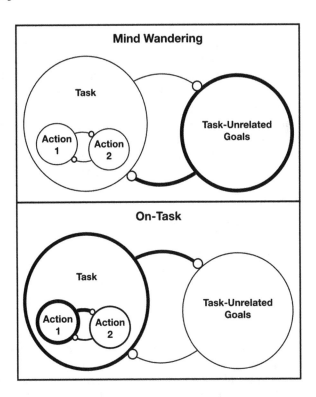

dinner party or the uneventful bus ride, one's mind can freely wander, unconstrained by competing task demands. In situations where there is a clear task, MW results in a decline of task performance (increased errors and response times). According to the negative approach to MW, removing the right-hand side superordinate circle from Fig. 8.1 will remove MW.

A second approach would characterize MW in terms of a style, rather than as a special type of (anti)task. MW might not necessarily involve disengaging from the current task, but causing a change in how the task is performed. You might have a conversation while mind wandering, without leaving the conversation. Your contributions to the conversation might become scattered, less relevant to what your conversation partner is saying, or perhaps your conversation would not follow a straight path. But you would still be in the conversation. The distinction is similar to that between walking through the woods in a straight path toward a clear destination and walking around without a clear direction. With regard to Fig. 8.1., while the negative approach identified MW with the right-hand side superordinate goal, the style-based approach identifies MW with the overall manner in which the goals relate to each other at multiple levels of the goal hierarchy. At the superordinate level, task-unrelated goals are relatively more active compared to the "on-task" state, which is associated with weakening task-related goals. MW is here conceived not in terms of disengaging from the task, but in terms of the weakening of a particular superordinate goal. Compared to the "on-task" state, in which the subordinate goals are set up in an antagonistic relation to each other (task requires performing either "action 1" or "action 2", but not both), the MW state is characterized by a decrease in the antagonistic relation between the subordinate goals, meaning that activating "action 1" would not necessarily involve inhibiting "action 2" (Goschke, 2013; Gozli & Dolcini, 2018; Hommel, 2015).

The style-based approach to MW does not presuppose a difference between goals related to the current task and goals unrelated to the task. Nothing is inherently special about the goals that happen to be task-unrelated at the current moment. Thoughts about the current task can later become "task-unrelated thoughts" when the person engages with a different task. Moreover, disengaging from a task should not automatically be equated with MW. In a task-switching paradigm, for instance, in which participants are required to regularly switch between Task 1 and Task 2, we would not regard switching from Task 1 to Task 2 as the participant's mind wandering away from Task 1, even though MW and task-switching might depend on the same underlying capacities (cf. Baird et al., 2012; Lu, Akinola, & Mason, 2017). The style-based approach does not even require the presence of clearly identifiable task-unrelated goals. Similar to explorative behavior (Chap. 3), MW might involve weakening of the current superordinate goal or the adoption of a more flexible relation to the goal. One might not begin mind wandering only after one takes note of a task-unrelated goal; rather, one might take note of a task-unrelated goal because, and *after*, one has already entered a flexible mode of task performance.

Identifying MW with a style leads to asking whether some tasks are more likely to encourage MW. Flexibility is a requirement in some tasks, such as when we are asked to switch between tasks repeatedly (Lu et al., 2017), when the stimuli we are presented with do not constitute a coherent whole (Smallwood, Baracaia, Lowe, & Obonsawin, 2003), when the stimuli are ambiguous (Murray, 1938), or when we are asked to list as many different ways of categorizing an object as we can (Chrysikou, 2006; Hommel, 2015). By requiring flexibility, these tasks might promote—if not demand—what we would otherwise call MW.

Because the style-based approach provides a positive account of MW, it is more vulnerable to criticism and fragmentation. You could offer counter-examples that do not fit my style-based description of MW. Being distracted by thoughts about an assignment during a lecture should presumably be categorized as MW, even when the thoughts are neither flexible nor explorative. What we called MW can include focused engagement, in thought, with what is currently absent (recall the example of waiting for a train, discussed in Chap. 2). Moreover, someone might wish to distinguish MW that is driven by a clearly identifiable competing goal, unrelated to the task at hand, and MW that is not driven by any clear goal. Taking such counter-examples seriously, we might have to let go of MW as a unitary concept. By contrast, the task-based approach can preserve the apparent unity of the concept of MW, which gives researchers a rhetorical advantage: it preserves the impression that all research under the title of MW is research on the same type of processes. I believe the dominance of the task-based and negative approach to MW has to be considered in light of this rhetorical advantage.

In the previous chapters, I pointed out that experimental psychology relies on tasks and that this reliance often stays in the background. Making this point explicit leads to the awareness that our research findings are conditional, dependent on the participants' adoption of task rules/goals. In the absence of tasks, particularly tasks that could be impaired due to covert disengagement or due to adopting a flexible mode of performance, it would be difficult to discuss MW. The rhetorical discourse about MW, what the researchers say about their research to students, journal editors, and funding agencies, in order to justify their research, does not usually include a reference to tasks used to examine MW. The discourse is framed in a way that is more in line with a positive approach to MW, while in practice, researchers adopt a task-based approach, operationalizing MW in antagonistic relation to specific tasks (Teo, 2018). As a matter of practical convenience, it is generally preferable to use tasks that not only enable the study of MW but also increase the likelihood of its occurrence. If the task is interesting to the participant, for example, the likelihood of disengaging from the task would be low (Silvia, 2008), and that would not be useful for a research project on MW. This is why research on MW relies on simple and repetitive tasks, which increase the likelihood of covert disengagement.

One type of task for the study of MW is the sustained attention to response task (SART) (Robertson, Manly, Andrade, Baddeley, & Yiend, 1997). Participants are instructed to perform a key-press response upon the onset of a stimulus ("go" trials). The task also requires withholding the response ("no-go" trials) for a subset of stimuli. For instance, in a task in which each stimulus is an Arabic numeral (1–9), participants might be asked to withhold responding whenever they see "3" and respond when they see any other digit. SART is a two-choice task (Fig. 8.2), in which selecting a correct choice requires sustained attention to the sequence of stimuli, which is why incorrect responses on no-go trials might indicate MW.

There is more than one possible reason for mistakenly responding on a no-go trial. Especially given that go trials are more frequent, the entire task could be approximated as a simple detection task: "Respond upon seeing *any* stimulus!". This approximation would be efficient, although it comes with the disadvantage of occasional mistakes. Hence, what might be taken as a sign of MW, the failure to withhold response on no-go trials, could be a sign of engaging with an alternative, efficient though occasionally incorrect, task rule. As an undergraduate student, I recall self-consciously adopting this strategy when participating in such an experiment. The strategy, while it could be regarded as a form of rule-violation (Pfister et al., 2019), is indistinguishable from correct performance on most trials. Importantly for our present purpose, it might also be taken as a sign of MW. It is possible that after adopting the task-approximation strategy, participants can more easily daydream or have task-unrelated thoughts (Forster & Lavie, 2009; Seli, Risko, & Smilek, 2016), but that subsequent disengagement from the task is not the same as the initial engagement with an approximate and easier version of the task.

Similarly, on some trials of SART, participants might form a strong expectation, prior to seeing the next stimulus, that the stimulus would signal a go response. Such a short-term variation in performance does not necessarily reflect MW, and researchers have developed methods of distinguishing MW from changes in performance strategy (Seli, Cheyne, & Smilek, 2012, 2013).

Fig. 8.2 A schematic view of SART that shows two possible reasons behind committing a mistake on a no-go trial

Seli, Cheyne, and Smilek (2013) and Seli, Jonker, Cheyne, and Smilek (2013) proposed an alternative to SART that does not include no-go trials. Participants respond to the beats of a metronome, attempting to keep their responses synchronous with the beats. The authors argued that deviations in RT (falling out of synchrony) can be used as a measure of MW. Removing the no-go trials, however, makes the task more predictable and monotonous than the standard SART, which can affect attention (Forster & Lavie, 2009; Seli, Risko, & Smilek, 2016; Zhao, Al-Aidroos, & Turk-Browne, 2013). By replacing SART with a metronome task, we would not merely change the method for examining failures of sustained attention. We might also change the frequency with which those failures occur, and quite possibly other features of the task-unrelated thoughts (Seli, Risko, & Smilek, 2016). Moreover, we might wish to distinguish, on one hand, between the failure to focus on the metronome task (due to task-unrelated thoughts), and on the other hand, and the failure to shield the metronome task from task-unrelated thoughts (i.e., failure to engage in a type of multi-tasking). I will revisit this idea later in this chapter.

If you recall our discussion in Chap. 5, it is not difficult to see how research on MW would benefit from the distinction between persistence and flexibility developed by researchers interested in cognitive control (Dreisbach & Fröber, 2019; Goschke, 2013; Hommel, 2015). This has to be done in light of a recognition for goal hierarchies (Gozli & Dolcini, 2018). At first glance, we might associate MW with flexible control, and associate optimal performance with persistence. But flexibility/persistence at which level of the control hierarchy? Figures 8.1 and 8.2 show that flexibility at the subordinate level of action selection is a part of being on task. Flexibility at the subordinate level enables switching between go and no-go responses and should not be equated with MW. Flexibility at the relatively superordinate level, at which task goals compete with task-unrelated goals, might be associated with MW. This is why we can distinguished errors that result from too much persistence at the subordinate level (what I described as task approximation, and what Seli et al. (2012) described as speed-accuracy trade-off), and those that result from too much flexibility at the superordinate level (what we would more readily describe as MW; Fig. 8.2) (Seli, Jonker, et al., 2013).

In addition to errors and response-time variability, MW has been examined in relation to eye movements. When we read a text, and are focused on what we are reading, the pattern of our eye movement is sensitive to the linguistic variables, such as word frequency and semantic fit. For instance, fixation duration tends to be shorter for highly frequent words, compared to infrequent words (Rayner & Duffy, 1986). This pattern is not observed when reading is accompanied by MW (Reichle, Reineberg, & Schooler, 2010). Not only do fixation durations become prolonged in general, the fixations become insensitive to features such as word frequency.

Despite their superficial differences, variations in eye movements, response times, and errors all point to a common performance characteristic. Namely, MW can be characterized as an insensitivity to the relevant task features. We intuitively recognize this, when we suspect that a conversation partner has covertly disengaged from listening, by inserting surprising information in our speech ("… and then I shook hands with the aliens …") and watching for their (lack of) response. We might be inclined to take this performance characteristic as the defining feature of MW. In the case of SART, the insensitivity to the stimuli, which occasionally signals a no-go trial, shows up in errors (Cheyne, Carriere, & Smilek, 2006); in the case of keeping a rhythm, the insensitivity to timing of stimuli shows up in higher response-time variability (Seli, Cheyne, & Smilek, 2013); in the case of reading, the insensitivity shows up in not discriminating between linguistic features of the text (Reichle et al., 2010). Another way of describing such insensitivity is "perceptual decoupling" (Schooler et al., 2011; Smallwood & Schooler, 2006). Let us consider further support in favor of perceptual decoupling as a defining characteristic of MW before considering its limitation.

Consistent with the perceptual-decoupling view, Weissman, Roberts, Visscher, and Woldorff (2006) found that increased response time, an implicit measure of MW, was associated with a decrease in visual evoked activity in occipital areas.

Other electrophysiological studies found a negative correlation between frequency of MW reports and sensory-evoked P3 for both targets and distractors (Barron, Riby, Greer, & Smallwood, 2011; Smallwood, Beach, Schooler, & Handy, 2008). Recall from Chap. 4 that a similar reduction in sensory-evoked P3 has been observed during rule-breaking (Pfister et al., 2016), where the strength of one goal (following the rule) is reduced because of a competing goal (breaking the rule). The point in drawing this comparison is that competing goals, which weaken the task-related goal and the associated stimulus-related processes, do not always reflect MW. Also consistent with the perceptual-decoupling view, Smilek, Carriere, and Cheyne (2010) found a positive correlation between eyeblink rate during the 5 s preceding a trial and the likelihood of reporting MW. Smilek et al. reasoned that due to their effect on reducing sensory visual input, an increase in eyeblink rate can be taken as a symptom of MW. Of course, rather than being causally related to each other, increased eyeblink rate and MW might result from common underlying processes of cognitive flexibility (Hommel, 2015; Jongkees & Colzato, 2016).

The shortcoming of the perceptual-decoupling view of MW is that it presupposes tasks that involve sustained attention to pre-specified features of external events. For perceptual decoupling to mean disengagement from a task, the task must specify the relevant features of the stimuli. I might present you with a shape-categorization task that requires observing a series of items and paying attention only to their shape, even though the items vary in size, color, texture, and whether or not they are accompanied by the sound of a bell. If you pay attention to colors, or the sound of the bell, while still keeping track of the shapes, are you perceptually less engaged with external stimuli? Even though we would recognize attention to irrelevant features as MW, we would also note that this instance of MW is associated with *more* engagement with the stimuli. In the well-known inattentional-blindness tasks, this would be the type of disengagement from task that increases the likelihood of finding the "gorilla" (Simons & Chabris, 1999; cf. Dreisbach, 2012). We should, therefore, qualify the perceptual-decoupling view: MW tends to involve perceptual decoupling from the *task-relevant* features of stimuli. Now, this circular description is much less useful because it requires and presupposes an understanding of the task (and optimal task performance) against which MW is identified.

Contrary to the perceptual-decoupling interpretation, MW can be associated with a more complex way of attending to stimuli, in the same manner that walking through the woods in several diverse paths is more complex than walking along a straight path. Similarly, a scattered conversation between two improvisational actors is more complex than a conversation that stays on a narrow course. In an improvised conversation, or during an explorative walk, each instance offers several different paths for further exploration. Similarly, in a metronome task, if I pay attention to the intensity of the sound of the metronome, and how far the metronome is from where I am sitting, rather than focusing on the rhythm, I am going from a superficial (single aspect) perception of the stimulus to a complex (multiple aspects) perception, although I would be covertly disengaging from the task and falling out of synchrony with the rhythm. In contrast to repetitive tasks that require sustained attention to particular features, are the so-called divergent-thinking tasks, which require a scattered search for many categories that can be applied to a given stimulus (Guilford, 1967). We might also include among these the projective tasks that involve free-associating with reference to an ambiguous image (Murray, 1938). These tasks blur the boundary between performance and MW (Singer, 1981, p. 51). In short, if we accept perceptual decoupling to be the defining characteristic of MW, we are presupposing a type of task that requires a stable and pre-specified perceptual engagement. This type of task, exemplified by SART, excludes those that involve searching for the relevant perceptual features, switching between stimulus features, rule-breaking, and exploration.

Related to the decoupling interpretation is the idea that MW involves attention away from external events and toward internal events (Smallwood & Schooler, 2006). Once again, this interpretation presupposes a type of task that requires attention to external stimuli, and does not require remembering events that are not currently present. Many tasks do not have these characteristics. When I am trying to commit a phone number to memory, or calculate the number of days left until a deadline, I am attending to stimuli that are no longer present externally, although I am not mind wandering. Playing a game of chess involves attention to both external stimuli and attention to plans, possible futures, tactics, and strategies that are not present on the board. Task engagement can, in many cases, narrow down attention to external stimuli because only a subset of what is perceptually available is relevant to the current action plan (Bilalić, McLeod, & Gobet, 2008; Eitam, Shoval, & Yeshurun, 2015; Eitam, Yeshurun, & Hassan, 2013). Unless we limit ourselves to a particular type of task, the external–internal dichotomy does not map onto the distinction between being on-task and MW (Chun, Golomb, & Turk-Browne, 2011).

Is the search for the defining feature(s) of MW in vain? Seli, Kane, et al. (2018) pointed out that although definitions of MW are varied across different studies, we could adopt a family-resemblances view of the concept (Mervis & Rosch, 1975; Wittgenstein, 1953). There are four features, the authors argued, that are typically present in the family of phenomena we identify as MW. MW is usually (1) unrelated to the task at hand, (2) initiated without the person's intention, (3) independent of what is perceptually present, and (4) aimless and unguided. The features ought not to be used to draw a boundary around the category and include/exclude instances that are true/false members of the category. Treating the first feature as necessary would exclude occasions where there is no clearly identifiable task. The second feature would exclude intentionally initiated daydreaming (Singer, 1981). The third feature would exclude perceptual exploration that is unguided by a clear task (Gozli & Dolcini, 2018; Hill et al., 2015). Finally, the fourth feature would exclude persistent and intrusive thoughts, which are task-unrelated but are usually focused around a theme (Baer, 2002).

Although the family-resemblances proposal does not draw a boundary around the concept, it does imply the existence of *prototypical* family members. Accepting Seli, Kane, et al.'s (2018) family-resemblances view, we would take the prototypical instances of MW to be those states of mind that are task-unrelated, unintentionally initiated, independent of the present stimuli, and aimless. The problem with this identification of a prototypical instance of MW is that it consists of four *lacks*:

lacking relevance to the task, lacking intentional initiation, lacking relevance to stimuli, and lacking guidance by goals. Hence, the family-resemblances view is an offspring of the task-based and negative approach for MW (Callard et al., 2012, 2013). Although the family-resemblances approach might ultimately succeed, the prototypical family member might have to include positive features (Christoff et al., 2018).

The search for positive features of MW has led to the idea that it might be associated with activity in the so-called default mode network (DMN) of the brain (Christoff, Gordon, Smallwood, Smith, & Schooler, 2009; Mason et al., 2007; Weissman et al., 2006). If we cannot uniquely relate MW to patterns of behavior, then we might be able to uniquely associate it with patterns of neural activity. We should keep in mind that the cognitive-neuroscientific research starts with the psychological categories and distinctions that are already presupposed by the researchers (Robinson, 2016). For example, Mason et al. (2007) assumed that MW would be associated with performance in easier and more predictable tasks because they more readily enable covert disengagement. They trained participants on a task for 4 days, and on the fifth day, they conducted the experiments either with the practiced task or with a novel task. Higher DMN activity was found with the practiced task, relative to the novel task. Moreover, although DMN activity was positively correlated with MW self-reports, it was not correlated with scores on a daydreaming scale. Identifying a type of neural activity, such as the higher activity level in DMN, as the defining feature of MW would not be helpful if such a commitment required excluding subcategories of MW (daydreaming). Another study by Christoff et al. (2009) found that MW was associated not only with DMN activity but also with activity in the network known to underlie executive functions (optimal task performance). Thus, the antagonistic relation between task and MW, which researchers might take as a starting point, has not gained support in the neuroimaging literature.

Given that MW has not been uniquely tied to a behavioral or neural measure, observable from a third-person perspective, reliance on self-reports continues to be necessary. Self-report data on MW is collected using questionnaires presented after performing a task (Cheyne et al., 2006), or by probes presented during performance (Kane et al., 2007). While performing the SART, participants may be occasionally interrupted with the probe, "Were your thoughts on task or off task just now?", or more directly, "Was your mind wandering just now?". Yana Weinstein (2018) recently reviewed 105 published articles that had included the probe method, and found 69 variations on the method. Probes differ with respect to the words used, the number of available options for response, and which option is presented first. In some studies, the choice is binary (on-task vs. off-task), while other studies provided more options (on-task, task-related distraction, task-unrelated distraction, mind blank). When the term "mind wandering" is used, experimenters and participants might come to an agreement about the meaning of MW, and the agreed-upon meaning might differ across studies. For example, Antrobus, Singer, Goldstein, and Fortgang (1970) instructed participants that feeling hungry during the experiment did not count as MW, though thinking about what to eat after the experiment did.

The particular features of instructions, the agreed-upon working definition of MW shared by the researchers and their participants, as well as the features of the probe, might affect the frequency of MW reports. Weinstein, De Lima, and van der Zee (2018) found that emphasizing on-task state ("Were you on task just now?"), as opposed to MW ("Was your mind wandering just now?"), in the probe question, was associated with 10% decrease in MW reports. Seli, Carriere, Levene, and Smilek (2013) found an increase in MW reports when there was a longer delay between probes, although they interpreted this change as a change in decision criteria, and not MW frequency per se. Robison, Miller, and Unsworth (2019) found no association between MW reports and the frequency of probe presentation, but they found a decrease in MW reports when the instructions and the probes highlighted the role of intention (distinguishing between intentional and unintentional MW).

How could emphasizing the role of intention influence MW reports? Did it enhance engagement with the task, reducing the rate of MW, or did it change participants' judgment criteria with regard to how to identify instances of MW? Recall from our discussion of research on the sense of agency (Chap. 7) that it is often the ambiguity of the judgment in question ("Do you feel in control of event X?", "Were your thoughts on task or off task?") that renders participants' judgment especially susceptible to situational manipulations. The observation that factors, which presumably ought not to affect MW reports, do affect these reports is an indication of the ambiguity of what is being judged.

Given that MW is now a theoretical construct, associated with a host of assumptions and empirical findings, researchers' thinking about the construct might diverge from the participants' ways of thinking, as the latter bring their own understanding of words into the experimental setting (Teo, 2018). For this reason, it might be worth formulating probe questions using words that are less theoretically loaded, such as "task-related" and "task-unrelated". Understandably, this would not satisfy researchers who wish to identify MW as a subset of task-unrelated thoughts, distinguishing the thought, "I am feeling hungry" (not MW), from "I will have a sandwich at the nearby cafeteria after the experiment is finished" (MW) (Antrobus et al., 1970). This highlights the importance of a clear understanding regarding the target of investigation, which would be communicable both to research participants and to the wider research community. To achieve such an understanding, it is worth clarifying the meaning of the construct, and its associated features, prior to conducting experiments. We will now turn to one such attempt.

In an attempt to understand the meaning and attribute of *daydreaming*—presumably a subcategory of MW—James Morley (1998) conducted a qualitative study involving extensive interviews with five participants. The interviews were analyzed using a descriptive phenomenological method (Giorgi, 1997): identifying common themes and invariant features in the descriptions of the participants. Although the study focused on daydreaming, I believe the findings would be both interesting and useful for researchers on MW. Morley concluded that a daydream tends to be the *enactment of a restrained desire*. What enables a daydream includes a desire that cannot be fulfilled in the current situation, and the undemanding nature of the current situation that allows for our attention to wander off. This approach more directly confronts the very possibility of daydreaming and its necessary implications. Daydreaming implies a *mind* (Engelsted, 2017). In contrast to direct sensorimotor engagement with the world (e.g., sentience or goal-directed movement), mind enables one to imagine, pretend, or covertly enact situations that are not yet experienced, which is why the mind has been likened to a theater stage (Engelsted, 2017; Morley, 1998; Singer, 1981).

Morley described three distinct subjective points of view that could be involved in a daydream: (a) the subject as director and spectator of the daydream, (b) the subject as participant in the daydream, and (c) the subject who is left behind in the actual reality. The three positions can vary in salience. A vivid daydream, in which the daydreamer is fully immersed, (a) and (c) are in the margins of experience, while (b) comes to the foreground. Moreover, in a vivid daydream, (b) gains emotional valence through a willing suspension of disbelief, while (c) loses some of its emotional valence. Finally, salience in (a) is associated with a feeling of control, feeling like the god of an imagined world.

While daydreaming, people can achieve a more reflective and self-aware relation to their own desire, by enacting scenarios in which the desire is conceived in concrete terms (Morley, 1998). Of course, the possibility of reflection and self-awareness does not guarantee that we always reach these states in relation to our daydreams. Nevertheless, even when it lacks reflective self-awareness, a daydream is already a move toward explicating an implicit and unreflective mood. As such, it offers an opportunity for further explication and reflective awareness.

Morley's findings are consistent with some of the intuitive decisions made by experimental researchers. Recall the distinction between feeling hungry (not MW) and thinking of what one would like to eat for lunch (MW), during an experimental task. The distinction agrees with Morley's analyses. The restrained desire itself is not a daydream. To become a daydream, the desire and its imagined fulfillment must be staged. In addition, Morley's findings fit well with the perceptual-decoupling assumption (Smallwood & Schooler, 2006). To engage in an elaborate staging of a desire, one has to disengage from what is perceptually present (Barsalou, 2008), especially when what is perceptually present has nothing to do with one's restrained desire. Thus, we recognize the probability of perceptual decoupling without seeing it as a necessary feature of daydreaming.

By providing a direct description of daydreaming, Morley's (1998) findings leaves room for variation regarding positive and negative affect. Daydreaming does not have to be associated with either positive or negative mood. If daydreamers believe that the object of their desire is unavailable, then they will likely experience a negative feeling after the daydream. If they believe that the object of desire might be attainable, then they might experience a positive feeling. Hence, in light of Morley's analyses, we do not need two distinct types of daydreaming that correspond to positive and negative affect. Similarly, one can argue that reflective and unreflective daydreaming correspond, not to two distinct types of phenomena, but to variations in relative dominance of the three points of view involved in any daydream. A reflective daydream can be characterized by the relative dominance of the "spectator" point of view, whereas an unreflective daydream can be characterized by the relative dominance of the "participant" point of view. Again, we do not immediately have to assume two distinct types of daydreaming that correspond to reflective and unreflective states when we can attribute the differences to features of a multidimensional concept.

With reference to Morley's analysis, we might identify daydreaming as a type of MW, while also identifying types of MW that do not constitute daydreaming (perhaps those that do not involve restrained desire, or those that do not involve perceptual decoupling). For instance, Wang et al. (2018) identified two statistically dissociable individual traits that could be described as MW. These two traits were described as "habitual positive-thinking" and "habitual distractibility". Similarly, Kane et al. (2017) identified two types of MW, associated with inside-the-lab tasks and outside-the-lab activities. The first category was correlated with trait Neuroticism, whereas the second was correlated with trait Openness. These findings suggest that various subcategories of MW correspond to categories of goals and concerns, which could in turn be primed in the context of different tasks and relationships. Identifying positive attributes of MW and its subcategories raises the question: What are the common features of MW? And, in what ways is the construct useful? It is possible that MW, in the way it is currently discussed by cognitive-experimental psychologists, does not correspond to a coherent category.

Is MW more frequent when our actions are subordinate to the goals of other people (Kane et al., 2017)? This possibility is open to empirical investigation, using experiments in which participants are assigned different roles in a shared task (Caspar, Cleeremans, & Haggard, 2018, reviewed in Chap. 7). While remembering that all participants in such tasks have roles that are subordinate to the role of the researchers, the relations among participants can change. Is MW more frequent in participants who are given relatively subordinate roles, compared to participants who are given relatively superordinate roles? If that is the case, then we ought to interpret experimental research on MW in light of the relative subordinate roles of the research participants. Rather than reflecting phenomena "out there", discovered by experimental psychologists, MW might reflect phenomena that are constructed, brought about, and amplified by experimenters, through the roles they offer to their research participants.

In sum, we might wish to explicate and organize the phenomena of MW with respect to a set of attributes (e.g., desire, restraint, hope, and points of view), similar to Morley's (1998) analysis of daydreaming. Such a conceptual clarification, however, would largely come prior to experimental investigation (Smedslund, 1997, 2016). Alternatively, MW might consist of a set of phenomena that are not related to each other in any useful or interesting way. At present, what unites different instances of MW is a task-based and negative approach, which vaguely defines MW as some type of covert disengagement from experimental tasks. It is this opposition, more than anything else, that maintains both the unity and the elusive nature of MW. In the following sections, I will sidestep the question of definition and consider empirical studies on the causes and consequences of MW, the role of intention, and the relation between MW and creativity.

8.2   Causes and Consequences

Assuming that MW refers to a coherent category of phenomena, with identifiable characteristics, causes, and consequences, we might search for laws or law-like regularities that govern the occurrence and attributes of MW. As pointed out by Smallwood and Schooler (2015), experiments do not have direct control over the occurrence of MW, although they could set up conditions that might increase its probability. If the task is relatively simple, frequency of MW is thought to increase (Forster & Lavie, 2009; Seli, Risko, & Smilek, 2016). Motivation is another factor. Seli, Schacter, Risko, and Smilek (2017) compared MW reports across two conditions. In the "low-motivation" condition, participants received the standard instructions about how to perform the task. In the "high-motivation" condition, participants were informed that a high level of accuracy would allow them to leave the experiment earlier. MW reports were fewer in the high-motivation condition. We could think about motivation in terms of the relative dominance/salience of goals. With high level of motivation, the task-related goal hierarchy dominates, which in turn reduces the tendency to disengage from the task and entertain competing goals.

Organization and coherence of the task is another factor that might contribute to the rate of MW. Smallwood et al. (2003) found reduced frequency of MW reports when people were asked to read a list of words that belonged to the same category ("categorical condition"), compared to when the words did not belong to the same category ("random condition"). In general, the factors that increase the rate of MW might be those that encourage cognitive flexibility, discourage the strict imposition of a goal hierarchy, and do not require sustained and focused attention (Chermahini & Hommel, 2010; Christoff et al., 2018; Kounios et al., 2006, 2008; Zmigrod, Colzato, & Hommel, 2015).

We might wish to characterize cognitive flexibility, disengagement from the task goals, or engagement with task-unrelated goals, as breakdowns of executive function, especially when they have undesirable consequences (McVay & Kane, 2009, 2010). The correlations between MW and working-memory capacity should be considered in this context (McVay & Kane, 2009; Wiemers & Redick, 2019). The term "breakdown" is open to two different interpretations. First, it is possible that the presence of multiple goals (e.g., daydreaming during task performance) is itself the breakdown. Accordingly, the breakdown occurs when the participant's mind begins to wander during task performance. Perhaps participants first disengage from the task because of their low WM capacity, after which they become susceptible to MW.

Alternatively, it is possible that the breakdown arises *after* multiple goals have occupied working memory, and that the breakdown is the inability to simultaneously pursue multiple goals. According to the second interpretation, individuals with high working-memory capacity may mind wander during the task, but their ability to pursue and switch between multiple goals enables them to mind wander without a cost on their performance. Thus, low working-memory capacity might not make the onset of MW more probable, but instead increase the negative consequence of MW on performance. Performance might suffer due to participants' inability to organize subtasks into a coherent whole (Smallwood et al., 2003). In fact, tasks that are used for estimating working-memory capacity include a task-switching component, requiring participants to keep track of multiple subtasks, each corresponding to a different subordinate goal (Redick et al., 2012; Wiemers & Redick, 2019). This suggests that the measures of working-memory capacity might reflect, in part, participants' ability to be flexible in relation to subordinate goals while at the same time persisting on a superordinate goal. According to both interpretations, individual differences in cognitive control cause differences in MW tendency, although the two interpretations characterize the causal connection differently.

In addition to task features and individual differences in cognitive control, we can think about "tools" that enable or facilitate MW. In a review of his own daydreaming episodes, Jerome L. Singer (1981) described the use of pen and paper for daydreams that had elaborate details (e.g., a series of baseball games). What if the daydreamer encounters the notes from a previous daydream? Will he be more likely to initiate another episode of daydreaming? Will the daydream be easier to sustain because of the notes, and will it be more vivid? With the ubiquitous role of technology in our lives, it is worth considering in what ways a smartphone might be a tool for MW. Students who do not study near their smartphones might have daydreams that differ in both quantity and quality from students who study next to their smartphones.

Rosen, Carrier, and Cheever (2013), who observed students studying for an exam, found that students spent, on average, 65% of their 15-min study session on social media. Would it be reasonable to describe such distractions as MW, given that while on social media, the students were not pursuing any clear goal? If daydreaming is the enactment of a desire, it stands to reason that certain tools might facilitate it. Social networking sites might provide the tools for daydreaming about one's social status, social comparison, and relationships. We might also be able to control MW with the help of technologies designed to regulate our attention. Consistent with this idea, Mrazek, Smallwood, and Schooler (2012) found a decrease in explicit and implicit measures of MW after only 8 min of mindfulness training.

As noted above, we might begin searching for laws or law-like regularities, without a clear definition of MW. We might ask, for instance, "Is MW related to positive or negative mood?", "What do people think about during MW?" Pursuing such questions empirically might result in taking contingent observations as general regularities (Smedslund, 2016), or it might discourage us when we do not find consistent results. What people think about during MW might vary widely, ranging from positive to negative, self-related to other-related, past-related to future-related (Stawarczyk, 2018). That is not to say that every possible content is equally prevalent, but the prevalence of a finding should not be mistaken as a necessary or universal attribute of MW. It might be possible, for instance, that MW is more frequently associated with negative affect in aggregate data (Killingsworth & Gilbert, 2010; Ruby, Smallwood, Engen, & Singer, 2013), but that such a prevalence results from contents of thought that are historically and culturally contingent.

The relation between content and affective valence of MW was demonstrated by Ruby, Smallwood, Sackur, and Singer (2013), who found that thinking about oneself and the future are more strongly associated with positive affect, whereas thinking about others and the past are more strongly associated with negative affect. One could imagine further divisions among past-related positive thoughts and past-related negative thoughts. Again, prevalence does not indicate necessity. It appears that no universal answer can be given to the questions regarding the content and affective valence of MW. Similar remarks can be made about the costs and benefits of MW (Mooneyham & Schooler, 2013; Stawarczyk, 2018). Thinking about the future, planning and preparing for possible events, creative exploration, searching for new meaning, envisioning one's activity within different contexts, taking mental breaks from boredom might all be regarded as benefits, although none are necessary features of MW (Christoff et al., 2018; Seli, Kane, et al., 2018).

8.3   Reflectiveness and Intention

Instead of asking participants whether or not they were mind wandering, we could give them three choices: "Were you on-task, mind wandering intentionally, or mind wandering unintentionally?" Is the distinction between the second and the third choice significant? Seli, Risko, Smilek, and Schacter (2016) made a persuasive case for distinguishing between them as distinct types of MW. Out of the two, they found that only unintentional MW could be linked to obsessive-compulsive disorder and attention-deficit hyperactivity disorder (Seli, Risko, Purdon, & Smilek, 2017; Seli, Smallwood, Cheyne, & Smilek, 2015). Furthermore, evidence suggests that task difficulty and motivation might selectively reduce intentional MW, which favors a dissociation between intentional and unintentional MW.

Intention can be considered both with respect to initiating MW and with respect to the continuation and guidance of MW. When MW is not initiated deliberately, the person might later adopt a reflective relation to the episode (Morley, 1998). During daydreaming, for instance, we might suddenly notice that we have control over the content of our daydream and begin to exert more control. We might wish to return to a daydream later, in order to add further detail to it (Singer, 1981). The question of intention appears less straightforward when it comes to experimental tasks because (a) participants might be working with a vague definition of MW and (b) they might infer MW, or the attributes of MW, based on their performance.

In our discussion of the sense of agency (Chap. 7), we saw how performance (success vs. failure) can affect the degree to which participants report being in control of events. When the ostensive goal of the task is achieved, people are more likely to report being in control (Kumar & Srinivasan, 2014), and when the task goal is difficult to achieve, people are less likely to report being in control (Wen, Yamashita, & Asama, 2015). With regard to MW reports, task difficulty might selectively increase the frequency of unintentional MW, while decreasing the frequency of intentional MW (Seli, Risko, & Smilek, 2016). Regardless of the replicability of these findings (Seli, Konishi, Risko, & Smilek, 2018), we could consider the possibility that an instance of MW is more likely to be felt as intentional with an easy task (in which the task goal is easily achieved), than in a difficult task (in which the task goal is difficult to achieve). The relationship between task goals, required effort, and felt agency has been demonstrated (Demanet, Muhle-Karbe, Lynn, Blotenberg, & Brass, 2013; Minohara et al., 2016), and these insights can be applied in MW research. After all, the consequence of MW is different when we move from an easy task to a difficult task, just as the meaning of MW changes when we move from a low-motivation to a high-motivation situation: what was a harmless daydream before is now a troublesome intrusion. Do these changes in task characteristics change the nature of MW, or do they change our judgment of MW? Connecting the two domains of felt agency and MW would be useful, as it can lead to a more mindful and cautious view of intentional MW.

8.4   Relation to Creativity

Creativity is another construct that is operationalized differently in different studies. Two broad classes of problems that are thought to require creativity are those that require "convergent" thinking and those that require "divergent" thinking (Guilford, 1967). Tests of convergent thinking include the remote association test, anagram tests, or any other test that requires drawing connections among ostensibly disparate elements to find one correct solution. The solution to these problems can sometimes occur to us all at once, in a moment of insight.

Tests of divergent thinking, on the other hand, include the alternative uses task, unusual uses task, alternative categories task, or any other test that requires free-associating with reference to a given item ("name as many ways of using a brick as you can"). Unlike convergent-thinking problems, divergent-thinking problems do not involve searching for one correct solution. Strength in divergent thinking has been associated with the tendency to daydream and openness to new ideas (Singer, 1981, pp. 66–67; see also Kane et al., 2017).

The divergence–convergence distinction can be mapped onto two phases of problem-solving: an initial explorative phase and a later testing phase. The two have been linked to different oscillation frequencies in brain activity (Li, Tseng, Tsai, Huang, & Lin, 2016), as well as different affective states (Bocanegra, 2017, 2018). If MW is characterized in terms of a tendency to disengage from one's current task, then the relation between MW and creativity seems neither obvious nor necessary. On the other hand, if MW is more specifically characterized in terms of divergent and explorative thinking, then linking it to creativity would appear tautological. In the latter case, we could ask further questions related to MW and creativity, such as their task dependence or generalizability, whether MW can be associated with both divergent and convergent thinking, and the role of perceptual decoupling.

A positive correlation between the tendency to mind wander and the number of proposed solutions was reported by Ruby, Smallwood, Sackur, and Singer (2013).

The authors noted, however, that the solutions proposed by the frequent mind wanderers were less efficient than the solutions offered by the infrequent mind wanderers. The authors argued that the tendency to mind wander might encourage perceiving a situation in multiple ways, not all of which are useful. These findings favor a relationship between MW and divergent thinking.

With regard to a possible transfer across tasks, Chrysikou (2006) argued that the exercise of seeing the same object as belonging to many different categories is a style of thinking that can be practiced with effects on later task performance. In Chrysikou's study, practicing a divergent-thinking categorization task had a benefit on a subsequent insight test. The benefit was observed regardless of whether the items in the practice task appeared in the test, which suggested that the search for new categories, as a general skill, was transferred to performance in another task. Consistent with Chrysikou's findings, Kounios et al. (2006, 2008) argued that sudden insight solutions arise from a state of diffuse attention and attenuated sensory processing, which we might also describe as perceptual decoupling. The ability to reach this state might be enhanced through training (Chrysikou, 2006) or through neural stimulations that can weaken the strength of a superordinate goal (Reedijk, Bolders, & Hommel, 2013; Zmigrod et al., 2015).

The cognitive flexibility involved in both MW and divergent thinking might be triggered by the requirement to switch between tasks (Dreisbach & Fröber, 2019) and break rules (Pfister, Wirth, Schwarz, Steinhauser, & Kunde, 2016; Wirth, Foerster, Herbort, Kunde, & Pfister, 2018). I do not know of any study on the effect of task-switching and rule-breaking on subsequent MW, although such studies can be motivated on the basis of existing literature (Christoff et al., 2018; Hommel, 2015; Smallwood et al., 2003). In task-switching, the relevant feature of stimuli changes from trial to trial. In some trials, a red square has to be seen as square, whereas in other trials it has to be seen as red. While investigating transferrable effects of task-switching, Lu et al. (2017) found evidence that performance in task-switching can improve divergent thinking in a subsequent task. Crucially, the effect was found with forced task-switching and not when switching was voluntary. We could speculate about the benefit of forced task-switching over voluntary task-switching in terms of the benefit of overcoming the tendency to persist on a subordinate goal.

Finally, there is evidence for the benefit of MW in divergent thinking. A study by Baird et al. (2012) tested participants twice on a set of divergent-thinking tasks. Participants were divided into four conditions, based on what they did between test and re-test. They either (1) immediately went to re-test, (2) had a rest period, (3) performed a relatively difficult working memory ("1-back") task, or (4) performed a relatively easy ("0-back") task. Additionally, the problems on the re-test were either repetitions from the first test or they were new. The authors found improvement in divergent thinking for repeated problems in the "easy task" condition. Given the evidence for increased MW during easy tasks, the findings suggest a benefit for MW as an intermediate step in tasks that require divergent thinking. The cognitive flexibility involved in MW might, therefore, promote the search for new categories and ways of thinking about problems.

The link between MW and creativity might surprise us if we forget how close our definition of MW already is to our definition of divergent thinking. The overlap might not be perfect, of course, as creativity and MW both consist of a set of heterogeneous phenomena. However, to the extent that divergent thinking is already inherent in our concept of MW, empirical findings that connect the two serve more as demonstration and test-of-procedure, rather than as discovery of new links between conceptually independent phenomena (Gergen, 2018; Smedslund, 2002).

8.5 Implications

The very possibility of MW entails that two or more competing goals can be active at the same time. The goal of completing an experiment, for instance, can be concurrent with the goal of minimizing effort. Thus, when faced with a difficult task, participants might covertly adopt an approximation of the task rules that (a) allows them to be efficient and (b) results in occasional errors. Although such a change in strategy might more readily give rise to MW, due to its efficiency, the change in strategy should itself be distinguished from MW. MW further indicates that tasks can be treated in more or less flexible ways. Participants might switch between the original form of the task and their own approximation of the task, while occasionally daydreaming or reflecting on their boredom. We might think about MW in terms of the focus (succeeding vs. failing to maintain focus on task) or in terms of multi-tasking (succeeding or failing to maintain multiple tasks at once).

Task characteristics can limit the way we think about MW. Relating MW to perceptual decoupling is an example of how the methods we use determine the nature of what we investigate. If the task for studying MW requires sustained attention to perceptual events, then disengagement from the tasks would necessarily involve a decrease in attention to those perceptual events. As an extreme counter-example, consider the following task. Participants are sitting in front of a movie screen, on which a movie about dolphins is being shown. While their eyes are directed at the screen, they are instructed to completely ignore the movie and, instead, to imagine playing a game of golf. They are instructed to imagine the golf game in as much detail as possible. Successful performance in this task requires perceptual decoupling from the dolphin movie. We might even consider attention to the dolphins as MW in this context.

In Sect. 8.2, I briefly discussed the idea of tools for mind wandering. In the above example, where participants are imagining a game of golf, we could describe the movie as a distraction. We could also describe the movie as a tool for mind wandering. This tool could be used differently by different participants. One person might unreflectively become immersed in the movie, forgetting about the task. Another participant might deliberately imagine playing golf under water with a group of dolphins, in an attempt to combine the movie with the task requirement. MW tools might include familiar objects and artifacts, such as a smartphone or a song. An opaque piece of art or an unfamiliar piece of music can become entangled with our ongoing thoughts and feelings, taking us in directions we would not have gone without them. Characterizing MW in terms of perceptual decoupling, or in terms of attention to "internal" and private events, neglects instances where MW is enabled, triggered, and guided by perception of external events.

MW research has highlighted the distinction between, on one hand, the intention to engage or remain in a task and, on the other hand, the intention to perform a specific action within the task. In a stimulus–response task, the intention to fulfill task requirements ("continue to press left/right keys in response to blue/green items") can be distinguished from the intentions embedded within the task ("press the left key now in response to the blue item"), but both intentions are so foreign to participants' own concerns that the participants' MW—regardless of its varied frequency, intensity, and content—does not usually change task performance in any qualitative way. To clarify this point, let us compare stimulus–response tasks with a slightly more complex scenario.

Imagine that I decide to play a game of chess against Peter in order to impress Sally. Win-against-Peter is not the same goal as win-to-impress-Sally. We could describe the latter as a "distraction" or as an object of MW. We could also think of it as a source of influence or a concurrent goal. If I am simply immersed in the game, driven by win-against-Peter, I might adopt a boring and cautious style of play that leads to victory, but is not very interesting. If I am "distracted" by the goal of impressing Sally, I might play a daring tactical combination that wins *and* is impressive. The cognitive flexibility entailed by MW can, therefore, result in disengagement from an activity (reduced effect of the first goal), switching to a different activity (increased effect of the second goal), or modifying the first goal to accommodate the second goal. The third outcome is possible in tasks that are open to modification. Experimental tasks, with pre-specified and usually non-negotiable goals, cannot be modified in this way.

Regardless of the limits imposed by experimental methods, research on MW continues to be interesting and attractive. This is in part due to the elusive character of the concept of MW. Why do our minds wander? Do we feel happy or sad because of MW? What do we think about during MW? Is MW one type of phenomenon or many types? Despite the diversity of phenomena that are described as MW, the term is useful in preserving the unity and elusiveness of what is under investigation, guaranteeing the rhetorical success of MW research. As long as MW is conceived in negative and task-based terms, its apparent unity can be preserved.

I used "disengagement" as an alternative term to MW because it is a less ambiguous word and does not have the mysterious connotations of MW. Whereas MW implies unity, disengagement does not. To say that a participant disengaged from a task clearly leaves open the reasons for and the consequences of the disengagement. The disengagement could have many possible causes and consequences, and we are not compelled to ask why (in general) people disengage from tasks and what happens (again, in general) when they do. Similarly, we are not compelled to ask whether people feel happy or sad when they disengage from an activity. We might target specific tasks and specific types of disengagement, which would lead to claims that apply only to those tasks and those types of disengagement. Similarly, daydreaming is in many ways preferable to mind wandering, as a target of investigation, because daydreaming better lends itself to concrete analysis and can be more easily distinguished from other phenomena.

By contrast, MW is both unitary and ambiguous. It maintains the impression of unity, and the promise that we are dealing with a common set of underlying principles, causes, and consequences. As such, "Are people happy when they mind wander?" does not appear to be a misguided and futile question. Regardless of repeated empirical disconfirmations, the term "mind wandering" (with its negative, task-based operationalizations) continues to justify the corresponding field of research into this elusive construct.

References

Antrobus, J. S., Singer, J. L., Goldstein, S., & Fortgang, M. (1970). Mind wandering and cognitive structure. *Transactions of the New York Academy of Sciences, 32*, 242–252.

Baer, L. (2002). *The imp of the mind: Exploring the silent epidemic of obsessive bad thoughts.* New York, NY: Penguin.

Baird, B., Smallwood, J., Mrazek, M. D., Kam, J. W., Franklin, M. S., & Schooler, J. W. (2012). Inspired by distraction: Mind wandering facilitates creative incubation. *Psychological Science, 23*, 1117–1122.

Barron, E., Riby, L. M., Greer, J., & Smallwood, J. (2011). Absorbed in thought: The effect of mind wandering on the processing of relevant and irrelevant events. *Psychological Science, 22*, 596–601.

Barsalou, L. W. (2008). Grounded cognition. *Annual Review of Psychology, 59*, 617–645.

Bilalić, M., McLeod, P., & Gobet, F. (2008). Why good thoughts block better ones: The mechanism of the pernicious Einstellung (set) effect. *Cognition, 108*(3), 652–661.

Bocanegra, B. R. (2017). Troubling anomalies and exciting conjectures: A bipolar model of scientific discovery. *Emotion Review, 9*, 155–162.

Bocanegra, B. R. (2018). How emotion-cognition interactions drive affective bipolarity. *Archives of Psychology, 2*(5), 1–17.

Callard, F., Smallwood, J., Golchert, J., & Margulies, D. S. (2013). The era of the wandering mind? Twenty-first century research on self-generated mental activity. *Frontiers in Psychology, 4*, 891.

Callard, F., Smallwood, J., & Margulies, D. S. (2012). Default positions: How neuroscience's historical legacy has hampered investigation of the resting mind. *Frontiers in Psychology, 3*, 321.

Caspar, E. A., Cleeremans, A., & Haggard, P. (2018). Only giving orders? An experimental study of the sense of agency when giving or receiving commands. *PLoS One, 13*(9), e0204027.

Chermahini, S. A., & Hommel, B. (2010). The (b)link between creativity and dopamine: Spontaneous eye blink rates predict and dissociate divergent and convergent thinking. *Cognition, 115*, 458–465.

Cheyne, J. A., Carriere, J. S., & Smilek, D. (2006). Absent-mindedness: Lapses of conscious awareness and everyday cognitive failures. *Consciousness and Cognition, 15*(3), 578–592.

Christoff, K., Gordon, A. M., Smallwood, J., Smith, R., & Schooler, J. W. (2009). Experience sampling during fMRI reveals default network and executive system contributions to mind wandering. *Proceedings of the National Academy of Sciences, 106*, 8719–8724.

Christoff, K., Mills, C., Andrews-Hanna, J. R., Irving, Z. C., Thompson, E., Fox, K. C., & Kam, J. W. (2018). Mind-wandering as a scientific concept: Cutting through the definitional haze. *Trends in Cognitive Sciences, 22*(11), 957–959.

Chrysikou, E. G. (2006). When shoes become hammers: Goal-derived categorization training enhances problem solving performance. *Journal of Experimental Psychology: Learning, Memory, and Cognition, 32*, 935–942.

Chun, M. M., Golomb, J. D., & Turk-Browne, N. B. (2011). A taxonomy of external and internal attention. *Annual Review of Psychology, 62*, 73–101.

Demanet, J., Muhle-Karbe, P. S., Lynn, M. T., Blotenberg, I., & Brass, M. (2013). Power to the will: How exerting physical effort boosts the sense of agency. *Cognition, 129*(3), 574–578.

Dreisbach, G. (2012). Mechanisms of cognitive control: The functional role of task rules. *Current Directions in Psychological Science, 21*, 227–231.

Dreisbach, G., & Fröber, K. (2019). On how to be flexible (or not): Modulation of the stability-flexibility balance. *Current Directions in Psychological Science, 28*, 3.

Eitam, B., Shoval, R., & Yeshurun, Y. (2015). Seeing without knowing: Task relevance dissociates between visual awareness and recognition. *Annals of the New York Academy of Sciences, 1339*, 125–137.

Eitam, B., Yeshurun, Y., & Hassan, K. (2013). Blinded by irrelevance: Pure irrelevance induced "blindness". *Journal of Experimental Psychology: Human Perception and Performance, 39*, 611–615.

Engelsted, N. (2017). *Catching up with Aristotle: A journey in quest of general psychology.* New York, NY: Springer.

Forster, S., & Lavie, N. (2009). Harnessing the wandering mind: The role of perceptual load. *Cognition, 111*(3), 345–355.

Gergen, K. J. (2018) The limits of language as the limits of psychological explanation. *Theory & Psychology, 28*(6), 697–711.

Giorgi, A. (1997). The theory, practice, and evaluation of the phenomenological method as a qualitative research procedure. *Journal of Phenomenological Psychology, 28*(2), 235–260.

Goschke, T. (2013). Volition in action: Intentions, control dilemmas and the dynamic regulation of intentional control. In W. Prinz, A. Beisert, & A. Herwig (Eds.), *Action science: Foundations of an emerging discipline* (pp. 409–434). Cambridge, MA: MIT Press.

Gozli, D. G. (2017). Behaviour versus performance: The veiled commitment of experimental psychology. *Theory & Psychology, 27*(6), 741–758.

Gozli, D. G., & Dolcini, N. (2018). Reaching into the unknown: Actions, goal hierarchies, and explorative agency. *Frontiers in Psychology, 9*, 266.

Guilford, J. P. (1967). *The nature of human intelligence.* New York, NY: McGraw-Hill.

Hills, T. T., Todd, P. M., Lazer, D., Redish, A. D., Couzin, I. D., & Cognitive Search Research Group. (2015). Exploration versus exploitation in space, mind, and society. *Trends in Cognitive Sciences, 19*, 46–54.

Hommel, B. (2015). Between persistence and flexibility: The Yin and Yang of action control. In A. J. Elliot (Ed.), *Advances in motivation science* (Vol. 2, pp. 33–67). New York, NY: Elsevier.

Jongkees, B. J., & Colzato, L. S. (2016). Spontaneous eye blink rate as predictor of dopamine-related cognitive function—A review. *Neuroscience & Biobehavioral Reviews, 71*, 58–82.

Kane, M. J., Brown, L. H., McVay, J. C., Silvia, P. J., Myin-Germeys, I., & Kwapil, T. R. (2007). For whom the mind wanders, and when: An experience-sampling study of working memory and executive control in daily life. *Psychological Science, 18*(7), 614–621.

Kane, M. J., Gross, G. M., Chun, C. A., Smeekens, B. A., Meier, M. E., Silvia, P. J., & Kwapil, T. R. (2017). For whom the mind wanders, and when, varies across laboratory and daily-life settings. *Psychological Science, 28*(9), 1271–1289.

Killingsworth, M. A., & Gilbert, D. T. (2010). A wandering mind is an unhappy mind. *Science, 330*, 932–932.

Kounios, J., Fleck, J. I., Green, D. L., Payne, L., Stevenson, J. L., Bowden, E. M., & Jung-Beeman, M. (2008). The origins of insight in resting-state brain activity. *Neuropsychologia, 46*, 281–291.

Kounios, J., Frymiare, J. L., Bowden, E. M., Fleck, J. I., Subramaniam, K., Parrish, T. B., & Jung-Beeman, M. (2006). The prepared mind: Neural activity prior to problem presentation predicts subsequent solution by sudden insight. *Psychological Science, 17*, 882–890.

Kumar, D., & Srinivasan, N. (2014). Naturalizing sense of agency with a hierarchical event-control approach. *PLoS One, 9*, e92431.

Li, Y. H., Tseng, C. Y., Tsai, A. C. H., Huang, A. C. W., & Lin, W. L. (2016). Different brain wave patterns and cortical control abilities in relation to different creative potentials. *Creativity Research Journal, 28*, 89–98.

Lu, J. G., Akinola, M., & Mason, M. F. (2017). "Switching On" creativity: Task switching can increase creativity by reducing cognitive fixation. *Organizational Behavior and Human Decision Processes, 139*, 63–75.

Mason, M. F., Norton, M. I., Van Horn, J. D., Wegner, D. M., Grafton, S. T., & Macrae, C. N. (2007). Wandering minds: The default network and stimulus-independent thought. *Science, 315*(5810), 393–395.

McVay, J. C., & Kane, M. J. (2009). Conducting the train of thought: Working memory capacity, goal neglect, and mind wandering in an executive-control task. *Journal of Experimental Psychology: Learning, Memory, and Cognition, 35*, 196–204.

McVay, J. C., & Kane, M. J. (2010). Does mind wandering reflect executive function or executive failure? Comment on Smallwood and Schooler (2006) and Watkins (2008). *Psychological Bulletin, 136*, 188–197.

Mervis, C. B., & Rosch, E. (1975). Family resemblance: Studies in the internal structure of categories. *Cognitive Psychology, 7*, 573–605.

Minohara, R., Wen, W., Hamasaki, S., Maeda, T., Kato, M., Yamakawa, H., … Asama, H. (2016). Strength of intentional effort enhances the sense of agency. *Frontiers in Psychology, 7*, 1165.

Mooneyham, B. W., & Schooler, J. W. (2013). The costs and benefits of mind-wandering: A review. *Canadian Journal of Experimental Psychology, 67*, 11–18.

Morley, J. (1998). The private theater: A phenomenological investigation of daydreaming. *Journal of Phenomenological Psychology, 29*, 116–134.

Mrazek, M. D., Smallwood, J., & Schooler, J. W. (2012). Mindfulness and mind-wandering: Finding convergence through opposing constructs. *Emotion, 12*, 442–448.

Murray, H. A. (1938). *Explorations in personality: A clinical and experimental study of fifty men of college age*. Oxford, UK: Oxford University Press.

Pfister, R., Wirth, R., Schwarz, K. A., Foerster, A., Steinhauser, M., & Kunde, W. (2016). The electrophysiological signature of deliberate rule violations. *Psychophysiology, 53*, 1870–1877.

Pfister, R., Wirth, R., Schwarz, K., Steinhauser, M., & Kunde, W. (2016). Burdens of nonconformity: Motor execution reveals cognitive conflict during deliberate rule violations. *Cognition, 147*, 93–99.

Pfister, R., Wirth, R., Weller, L., Foerster, A., & Schwarz, K. A. (2019). Taking shortcuts: Cognitive conflict during motivated rule-breaking. *Journal of Economic Psychology, 71*, 138.

Rayner, K., & Duffy, S. A. (1986). Lexical complexity and fixation times in reading: Effects of word frequency, verb complexity, and lexical ambiguity. *Memory & Cognition, 14*(3), 191–201.

Redick, T. S., Broadway, J. M., Meier, M. E., Kuriakose, P. S., Unsworth, N., Kane, M. J., & Engle, R. W. (2012). Measuring working memory capacity with automated complex span tasks. *European Journal of Psychological Assessment, 28*, 164–171.

Reedijk, S. A., Bolders, A., & Hommel, B. (2013). The impact of binaural beats on creativity. *Frontiers in Human Neuroscience, 7*, 786.

Reichle, E. D., Reineberg, A. E., & Schooler, J. W. (2010). Eye movements during mindless reading. *Psychological Science, 21*(9), 1300–1310.

Robertson, I. H., Manly, T., Andrade, J., Baddeley, B. T., & Yiend, J. (1997). 'Oops!': Performance correlates of everyday attentional failures in traumatic brain injured and normal subjects. *Neuropsychologia, 35*(6), 747–758.

Robinson, D. N. (2016). Explanation and the "brain sciences". *Theory & Psychology, 26*(3), 324–332.

Robison, M. K., Miller, A. L., & Unsworth, N. (2019). Examining the effects of probe frequency, response options, and framing within the thought-probe method. *Behavior Research Methods, 51*, 398–408.

Rosen, L. D., Carrier, L. M., & Cheever, N. A. (2013). Facebook and texting made me do it: Media-induced task-switching while studying. *Computers in Human Behavior, 29*, 948–958.

Ruby, F. J., Smallwood, J., Engen, H., & Singer, T. (2013). How self-generated thought shapes mood—The relation between mind-wandering and mood depends on the socio-temporal content of thoughts. *PLoS One, 8*, e77554.

Ruby, F. J., Smallwood, J., Sackur, J., & Singer, T. (2013). Is self-generated thought a means of social problem solving? *Frontiers in Psychology, 4*, 962.

Schooler, J. W., Smallwood, J., Christoff, K., Handy, T. C., Reichle, E. D., & Sayette, M. A. (2011). Meta-awareness, perceptual decoupling and the wandering mind. *Trends in Cognitive Sciences, 15*, 319–326.

Seli, P., Carriere, J. S., Levene, M., & Smilek, D. (2013). How few and far between? Examining the effects of probe rate on self-reported mind wandering. *Frontiers in Psychology, 4*, 430.

Seli, P., Cheyne, J. A., & Smilek, D. (2012). Attention failures versus misplaced diligence: Separating attention lapses from speed–accuracy trade-offs. *Consciousness and Cognition, 21*(1), 277–291.

Seli, P., Cheyne, J. A., & Smilek, D. (2013). Wandering minds and wavering rhythms: Linking mind wandering and behavioral variability. *Journal of Experimental Psychology: Human Perception and Performance, 39*, 1–5.

Seli, P., Jonker, T. R., Cheyne, J. A., & Smilek, D. (2013). Enhancing SART validity by statistically controlling speed-accuracy trade-offs. *Frontiers in Psychology, 4*, 265.

Seli, P., Kane, M. J., Smallwood, J., Schacter, D. L., Maillet, D., Schooler, J. W., & Smilek, D. (2018). Mind-wandering as a natural kind: A family-resemblances view. *Trends in Cognitive Sciences, 22*, 479–490.

Seli, P., Konishi, M., Risko, E. F., & Smilek, D. (2018). The role of task difficulty in theoretical accounts of mind wandering. *Consciousness and Cognition, 65*, 255–262.

Seli, P., Risko, E. F., Purdon, C., & Smilek, D. (2017). Intrusive thoughts: Linking spontaneous mind wandering and OCD symptomatology. *Psychological Research, 81*(2), 392–398.

Seli, P., Risko, E. F., & Smilek, D. (2016). On the necessity of distinguishing between unintentional and intentional mind wandering. *Psychological Science, 27*(5), 685–691.

Seli, P., Risko, E. F., Smilek, D., & Schacter, D. L. (2016). Mind-wandering with and without intention. *Trends in Cognitive Sciences, 20*, 605–617.

Seli, P., Schacter, D. L., Risko, E. F., & Smilek, D. (2017). Increasing participant motivation reduces rates of intentional and unintentional mind wandering. *Psychological Research.* https://doi.org/10.1007/s00426-017-0914-2

Seli, P., Smallwood, J., Cheyne, J. A., & Smilek, D. (2015). On the relation of mind wandering and ADHD symptomatology. *Psychonomic Bulletin & Review, 22*(3), 629–636.

Silvia, P. J. (2008). Interest—The curious emotion. *Current Directions in Psychological Science, 17*(1), 57–60.

Simons, D. J., & Chabris, C. F. (1999). Gorillas in our midst: Sustained inattentional blindness for dynamic events. *Perception, 28*(9), 1059–1074.

Singer, J. L. (1981). *Daydreaming and fantasy.* Oxford, UK: Oxford University Press.

Smallwood, J. M., Baracaia, S. F., Lowe, M., & Obonsawin, M. (2003). Task unrelated thought whilst encoding information. *Consciousness and Cognition, 12*, 452–484.

Smallwood, J., Beach, E., Schooler, J. W., & Handy, T. C. (2008). Going AWOL in the brain: Mind wandering reduces cortical analysis of external events. *Journal of Cognitive Neuroscience, 20*, 458–469.

Smallwood, J., & Schooler, J. W. (2006). The restless mind. *Psychological Bulletin, 132*, 946–958.

Smallwood, J., & Schooler, J. W. (2015). The science of mind wandering: Empirically navigating the stream of consciousness. *Annual Review of Psychology, 66*, 487–518.

Smedslund, J. (1997). *The structure of psychological common sense.* Mahwah, NJ: Lawrence Erlbaum.

Smedslund, J. (2002). From hypothesis-testing psychology to procedure-testing psychologic. *Review of General Psychology, 6*(1), 51–72.

Smedslund, J. (2016). Why psychology cannot be an empirical science. *Integrative Psychological and Behavioral Science, 50*(2), 185–195.

Smilek, D., Carriere, J. S., & Cheyne, J. A. (2010). Out of mind, out of sight: Eye blinking as indicator and embodiment of mind wandering. *Psychological Science, 21*, 786–789.

Stawarczyk, D. (2018). Phenomenological properties of mind-wandering and daydreaming: A historical overview and functional correlates. In K. C. R. Fox & K. Christoff (Eds.), *The Oxford handbook of spontaneous thought: Mind-wandering, creativity, and dreaming* (pp. 193–214). Oxford, UK: Oxford University Press.

Teo, T. (2018). *Outline of theoretical psychology: Critical investigations.* New York, NY: Palgrave.

Wang, H. T., Poerio, G., Murphy, C., Bzdok, D., Jefferies, E., & Smallwood, J. (2018). Dimensions of experience: Exploring the heterogeneity of the wandering mind. *Psychological Science, 29*, 56–71.

Weinstein, Y. (2018). Mind-wandering, how do I measure thee with probes? Let me count the ways. *Behavior Research Methods, 50*, 642–661.

Weinstein, Y., De Lima, H. J., & van der Zee, T. (2018). Are you mind-wandering, or is your mind on task? The effect of probe framing on mind-wandering reports. *Psychonomic Bulletin & Review, 25*(2), 754–760.

Weissman, D. H., Roberts, K. C., Visscher, K. M., & Woldorff, M. G. (2006). The neural bases of momentary lapses in attention. *Nature Neuroscience, 9*, 971–978.

Wen, W., Yamashita, A., & Asama, H. (2015). The influence of goals on sense of control. *Consciousness and Cognition, 37*, 83–90.

Wiemers, E. A., & Redick, T. S. (2019). The influence of thought probes on performance: Does the mind wander more if you ask it? *Psychonomic Bulletin & Review, 26*, 367–373.

Wirth, R., Foerster, A., Herbort, O., Kunde, W., & Pfister, R. (2018). This is how to be a rule breaker. *Advances in Cognitive Psychology, 14*(1), 21–37.

Wittgenstein, L. (1953). *Philosophical investigations.* New York, NY: Macmillan.

Zhao, J., Al-Aidroos, N., & Turk-Browne, N. B. (2013). Attention is spontaneously biased toward regularities. *Psychological Science, 24*(5), 667–677.

Zmigrod, S., Colzato, L. S., & Hommel, B. (2015). Stimulating creativity: Modulation of convergent and divergent thinking by transcranial direct current stimulation (tDCS). *Creativity Research Journal, 27*(4), 353–360.

Chapter 9
A Reflective Science

Throughout the preceding chapters, my aim was to add a layer of discussion to existing psychological research. The discussion is not intended to dismiss experimental psychology. It does not suggest ceasing to conduct all experiments. Nor does it offer an indiscriminate critique, to which all experimental psychology is equally subjected. The discussion is one that enables reflection and critical engagement. The critique can show the limits and ambiguity of research findings and, at the same time, reveal the relevance (or lack of relevance) of the findings within a wider context of human concerns.

In a psychological experiment, we usually compare multiple conditions with respect to some dependent variables. We do this while manipulating, or keeping track of, a set of independent variables, within a context that includes other controlled variables. With this general outline in mind, let us review our methods of critique. First, we can identify places where an intended manipulation is confounded with an unintended change. When we compare, for instance, participants' sense of agency across two conditions, we usually assume that their criteria for evaluating their agency do not change across those conditions. If our independent variables can change the participants' criteria for evaluating their sense of agency, then a straightforward interpretation of the findings becomes impossible.

Second, we can identify places where the findings, in retrospect, undermine the assumption of controlled variables. For instance, if two groups show different patterns of performance on a simple stimulus–response task (e.g., key-press in response to a flash of light), we cannot assume that we have successfully isolated the difference between the two groups with our task, or that the two groups differ only in their visual-motor processes and in no other respect (their understanding of the task, interest, or motivation). Accordingly, when we claim that religious or political affiliations are reflected in different patterns of sensorimotor response, based on the results of experimental tasks (e.g., Colzato, Hommel, & Shapiro, 2010), we undermine the assumption that participants across the different groups went through the same controlled conditions. Higher-level psychological processes are made up, in part, of the same lower-level processes we aim to isolate in experiments. Therefore,

© Springer Nature Switzerland AG 2019
D. Gozli, *Experimental Psychology and Human Agency*,
https://doi.org/10.1007/978-3-030-20422-8_9

if two groups of participants differ with regard to the capacities we aimed to isolate in our experiment, then they probably also differ with regard to the events that surround the experiment—their understanding of the task, their interpretation of the instructions, their impression of the researcher, their interest, their emphasis on attributes of the experimental task, or their motivation to perform well in the task.

The first style of critique identifies unintended consequences of experimental manipulations, while the second identifies theoretical restrictions imposed by the researchers' ways of thinking about phenomena. The two styles of critique fall under a more general critical method that identifies the active role of subjects—researchers and participants—involved in research. This critical method has wide range of applications in experimental psychology. One such application is the identification of particular task features in the production of research findings. When examining sense of agency, for example, researchers design tasks in which agency is ambiguous; when examining mind wandering, researchers design tasks that can induce boredom and disengagement; when investigating free-choice response selection, researchers construct tasks in which participants are required to maintain an impression of spontaneity and balance over a series of choices. When participants perform a task, they adopt one particular mode among many possible modes of engagement with the situation. By leaving out the characteristics of experimental design in the description, a study would construct the impression that the findings are independent of the experiment.

Our description of situations can vary in the degree to which it is anchored by the perspective and activity of subjects. Subjects have preferences, pursue goals, and evaluate objects and events. In experimental psychology, active roles ought to be recognized on both sides of the researcher–participant relation. Concern with the scientific status of psychology might lead us to exclude references to the active role of subjects, choosing statements of the form "X causes Y", instead of the more modest claims "When people are asked to perform task T, then X causes Y". We identify places where the controlled conditions of an experiment are constitutive of the findings, meaning that the findings depend on the very conditions that are set up to "discover" them. When we pay attention to what is actually present in the context of experimental research, we might recognize ambiguity in research findings and their openness to multiple interpretation. A reflective science is mindful of the ways in which the findings and interpretations depend on active, goal-directed subjects, whose activities are constitutive of their scientific observations, and whose seemingly value-neutral statements of facts are embedded and guided by their goals and preferences.

One necessary requirement (goal) in many experimental studies is to keep research participants uninformed about the researchers' manipulations and predictions. Participants should not know about possible sources of bias as they respond to ambiguous questions (e.g., "Did you feel in control of the ringing of the bell?" and "Which one of these two images do you prefer?"). Unreflective perception does not allow participants to dissociate the percepts from the basis of their response (e.g., Zajonc, 2001). By informing participants about our hypothesis, we would be directing their attention to the sources of bias, which could in turn enable them to reflectively dissociate their responses from the sources of bias (Frith, 2014). Working with informed and reflective participants—perhaps on tasks that they care about—would extend the study of naïve-uninterested participants into a study of knowing-interested participants (Blackman, 2014). This would be useful if our aim is to identify not only variations in performance and states of mind but also how those variations are open to reflection and change, such that we could move (reflectively) away from undesirable states and toward desirable ones.

At first glance, it might seem that only research participants are given an unreflective role. In an important sense, however, the researchers' role mirrors that of the participants. Perhaps as a matter of coincidence, or perhaps by virtue of the belief in their meta-scientific assumptions (e.g., a mechanistic view of nature), the study of unreflective and uninterested research participants begins to produce unreflective and uninterested researchers. An unreflective researcher is concerned only with the short-term consequences of one's research career, even though the goals that are most readily identified in our description, the basic-level goals (Rosch, 1978) are embedded within relatively less visible, long-term, superordinate goals. An unreflective researcher neglects the association between our actions and the hierarchy of goals they represent. It is, of course, possible to pursue basic-level goals without reflective awareness of their superordinate goals. It is similarly possible to fall victim to the cultural trends that set those goals for us, becoming mindless agents of those goals.

To avoid potential ambiguities of behavior, experimental psychology operates within normatively and descriptively fixed contexts (Chaps. 4 and 5). These contexts establish pre-specified goals for their participants, as well as pre-specified ways of pursuing those goals, which enable researchers to readily categorize the behavior of research participants. Similar to how participants are prepared to respond to stimuli, by virtue of engaging with tasks, experimental psychologists are prepared to categorize their observations. Hence, we end up with labels, such as "creative solutions", "mind wandering", or "brazen liars", and so forth, according to criteria that exist prior to data collection. The simple goals of an experimental task, and how they should be fulfilled, are not usually open to negotiation.

There is a difference between treating participants as means to an end (means to hypothesis-testing) and treating them as ends in themselves. The latter attitude treats research participants as—at least potentially—reflective and autonomous, interested in self-understanding. But what can we expect from psychologists who have turned themselves into tools of research productivity? Why would we expect them to treat others as self-governing, if they have not adopted such an attitude toward themselves? A change in attitude, if it is going to occur, would have to apply to both sides.

While working on this book, I discussed the ideas in conversations with several experimental psychologists. What struck me was how my colleagues would change the topic of conversation. More often than not, the topic would switch to the instrumental value of their research career and the practical obstacles to a critical approach. A junior colleague said that, ultimately, he would like to have a job to support his family, rather than worrying about the validity of his research. A more senior colleague told me that he does not worry about big-picture questions. Instead, he follows a simple system (read: a simple *task*). He conducts his experiments, ensures he has enough publications for the next round of grant applications, and then submits the next grant proposal. A third colleague said, "At this point, I have realized that I cannot be fulfilled with my research [given its lack of relevance to everyday life], so I tend to focus on being a good person, a good friend, and a good family member, rather than focusing on a good research". The change of focus did not stop him from publishing nearly 20 articles in the following year. Indeed, not worrying about the merits of one's research might be of practical value. Analogous to the detrimental effect of "mind wandering" on research participants' task performance, our reflections on the superordinate goals of our research might have a detrimental effect on our research productivity, which is why repressing the reflective layer of discussion has become a prevalent response.

A fourth colleague urged me to remember that academic freedom, including the freedom to pursue trivial questions, is a sign that our scientific inquiries are not currently subject to ideological-political restrictions. He argued that we ought to be grateful for such freedom, even though it enables unreflective research. I certainly do not wish to advocate a top-down set of rules that restrict scientific research, although I am skeptical about the claim that we are currently operating in the absence of any selective pressure (Smaldino & McElreath, 2016). The forces that reward scientific productivity play a role in disincentivizing reflective science.

Finally, a fifth colleague, after listening to a talk I gave, asked me to reassure him that he can continue conducting his experiments. It might seem puzzling to find researchers relying on others to reflect upon and evaluate their research. But such an outcome is to be expected if reflective approaches to science are disincentivized long enough. I share these anecdotes to point out the obstacle against a reflective approach to experimental psychology that go beyond mere argumentation. Having invested time and effort in a tradition of research can lead us to mindlessly perpetuate the tradition and repress critique, especially if perpetuating the tradition is rewarding for one's career.

The current situation in experimental psychology might seem bleak, but it also offers abundant potential for theoretical work. If you find yourself sympathetic to the general style and spirit of this book, I encourage you to try your own hand at writing in this reflective-theoretical genre. The topics and studies I covered in the preceding chapters are just a starting point. They are far from reflecting the entire scope of experimental psychology. Perhaps more than anything else, they reflect my interest in the topic of human agency. Nonetheless, I hope that my method is sufficiently transparent to facilitate similar work by others.

Rather than taking every single question into the lab, you could take a look at the ocean of experimental work already done on many different psychological topics. You could try to see how various lines of research fit together, and whether they fulfill the promises they make at the outset. With an eye on the broader context of human concerns, you could find the place and relevance of a particular line of research. In addition to laboratory work, you could draw on various other scholarly resources, including common-sense psychology (Smedslund, 1997), general-theoretical psychology (Bergner, 2010; Engelsted, 2017; Mammen, 2017), philosophical analysis (Hibberd, 2014), social sciences (Elster, 2015), methodology (Valsiner, 2017), and phenomenological analysis (Giorgi, 2009). Given the popularity of laboratory work in contemporary academic psychology, such theoretical explorations offer a vast area of untapped potential, waiting for motivated and talented scholars. If you do embark on such a journey, I would love to hear from you.

References

Bergner, R. (2010). What is descriptive psychology? An introduction. In K. Davis, F. Lubuguin, & W. Schwartz (Eds.), *Advances in descriptive psychology* (Vol. 9, pp. 325–360). Ann Arbor, MI: Descriptive Psychology Press.

Blackman, L. (2014). Affect and automaticy: Towards an analytics of experimentation. *Subjectivity, 7*(4), 362–384.

Colzato, L. S., Hommel, B., & Shapiro, K. (2010). Religion and the attentional blink: Depth of faith predicts depth of the blink. *Frontiers in Psychology, 1*, 147.

Elster, J. (2015). *Explaining social behavior: More nuts and bolts for the social sciences.* Cambridge, UK: Cambridge University Press.

Engelsted, N. (2017). *Catching up with Aristotle: A journey in quest of general psychology.* New York, NY: Springer.

Frith, C. D. (2014). Action, agency and responsibility. *Neuropsychologia, 55*, 137–142.

Giorgi, A. (2009). *The descriptive phenomenological method in psychology: A modified Husserlian approach.* Pittsburgh, PA: Duquesne University Press.

Hibberd, F. J. (2014). The metaphysical basis of a process psychology. *Journal of Theoretical and Philosophical Psychology, 34*(3), 161–186.

Mammen, J. (2017). *A new logical foundation for psychology.* New York, NY: Springer.

Rosch, E. (1978). Principles of categorization. In E. Margolis & S. Laurence (Eds.), *Concepts: Core readings* (pp. 189–206). Cambridge, MA: MIT Press.

Smaldino, P. E., & McElreath, R. (2016). The natural selection of bad science. *Royal Society Open Science, 3*(9), 160384.

Smedslund, J. (1997). *The structure of psychological common sense.* Mahwah, NJ: Lawrence Erlbaum.

Valsiner, J. (2017). *From methodology to methods in human psychology.* New York, NY: Springer.

Zajonc, R. B. (2001). Mere exposure: A gateway to the subliminal. *Current Directions in Psychological Science, 10*(6), 224–228.

Index

© Springer Nature Switzerland AG 2019
D. Gozli, *Experimental Psychology and Human Agency*,
https://doi.org/10.1007/978-3-030-20422-8